THE FIFTEEN BIGGEST
LIES
ABOUT THE ECONOMY

And Everything Else the Right
Doesn't Want You to Know about
Taxes, Jobs, and Corporate America

JOSHUA HOLLAND

WILEY
John Wiley & Sons, Inc.

Published by John Wiley & Sons, Inc., Hoboken, New Jersey
Published simultaneously in Canada

Cartoon credits: page 20 © Tom Tomorrow; page 59 © Lloyd Dangle; page 158 © Matt Bors.

For general information about our other products and services, please contact our Customer Care Department within the United States at (800) 762-2974, outside the United States at (317) 572-3993 or fax (317) 572-4002.

Wiley also publishes its books in a variety of electronic formats. Some content that appears in print may not be available in electronic books. For more information about Wiley products, visit our web site at www.wiley.com.

Library of Congress Cataloging-in-Publication Data:

Holland, Joshua.
    The fifteen biggest lies about the economy : and everything else the right doesn't want you to know about taxes, jobs, and corporate America / Joshua Holland.
        p   cm.
    Includes bibliographical references and index.
    ISBN 978-0-470-64392-1 (pbk.); ISBN 978-0-470-64392-1 (ebk);
ISBN 978-0-470-91280-5 (ebk); ISBN 978-0-470-91282-9 (ebk)
        1. United States—Economic policy—2009– 2. United States—Economic conditions—2099– 3. Rights and left (Political science)—United States. 4. Conservatism—United States—History—21st century. I. Title.
    HC106.84.H65 2010
    330.973—dc22

                                                                2010028343

Printed in the United States of America

10 9 8 7 6 5 4 3 2 1

Contents

Acknowledgments

Without all of the support my family has given me over the years, I wouldn't be able to do a job I love. I'm deeply appreciative. I owe a special debt of gratitude to my father, John Holland, who read the following chapters and offered me spot-on feedback. Without his help, I doubt that this book would have been possible.

I'm also grateful to Don Hazen, my boss at AlterNet, for giving me the chance to work on this project, to Eric Nelson at Wiley for making it happen, and to Wiley's Rachel Meyers, whose "copyediting" turned out to be much more than that.

Thanks also to Tom Tomorrow, Lloyd Dangle, and Matt Bors, for their razor-sharp editorial cartoons, and to Larry Beinhart for the perfect excerpt to accompany chapter 5.

INTRODUCTION

How our conventional wisdom fails us

Hope and change were in the air on that cold January day when Barack Obama was sworn in as the nation's first African American president. But there was also a darker shadow looming. Our economy lay in ruins, and the American people were mad as hell.

They had every reason to be. Unemployment was approaching 8 percent and rising. They'd seen their retirement funds dry up and their home values tank. They'd funded an enormous bailout of the banking industry, only to see Wall Street's movers and shakers earn fat bonuses just as they had in better times. The wisdom of the pundits, the experts, and the prognosticators—the high priests of the global economy—turned out to be woefully wrong. The nation's elites had been exposed as disastrously incompetent managers, yet their own positions of comfortable privilege had, by and large, remained secure.

Everyone agreed that things were bad, but who was to blame? What exactly had happened to our sense of economic security?

Since that day, many Americans, from across the political spectrum, have gone from hopping mad to *spitting mad*. Progressives not only became disenchanted with the GOP's obstructionism, but also blamed the administration for dropping the ball. Many felt that the hopey-changey promises that candidate Obama had made on the stump had been abandoned. Some said that the administration hadn't really fought the good fight it had promised or hadn't fought it well.

But the really juicy anger was on the Right—the kind of dramatic, often over-the-top anger the media love, complete with misspelled signs suggesting that the new president was a "socialist" who hadn't been born in this country. The "Tea Parties" had arrived, and they captured the imagination of the chattering class during 2009 and 2010. The pundits debated whether they represented a spontaneous uprising of "ordinary," apolitical people awoken from their slumber by the coming of the econopocalypse and the bailouts given to Wall Street and Detroit. Were they salt-of-the-earth moderates inflamed by fear of runaway government spending, or were they a bunch of wing-nuts who had no coherent ideological beliefs but were simply responding to some good old-fashioned racist dog whistles?

What was striking about these debates is that they often began with the premise that whatever else the Tea Partiers might be, their economic concerns were valid. Yet it was apparent that although their economic pain and anxiety were all too real, their analysis of what caused it was nothing short of insane. It was a "movement" whose members lived in a parallel universe, embracing wild conspiracy theories about how ACORN and MoveOn.org had brought down the global economy to advance their "radical" agendas. They saw creeping socialism in the most benign government programs. It was a movement whose views reflected the simmering paranoia of its intellectual muse, Fox News host Glenn Beck.

More important, it was a movement that had only a tenuous grasp on the role that government plays in our society. In 2009, an enraged constituent at a town hall meeting in South Carolina yelled at Republican representative Bob Inglis to "keep your government hands off my Medicare!" Another woman reportedly sent a letter to the White House stating in no uncertain terms, "I don't want government-run health care, I don't want socialized medicine and don't touch my Medicare."[1] According to *Slate*'s Timothy Noah, such calls were common during that long, hot summer.[2]

In 2010, National Public Radio did a fawning profile of "Liberty Belle," aka Keli Carender, one of the founders of the Tea Party movement. When asked why her congressman's support for health-care reform had so enraged her, she summed up the Tea Party rhetoric pretty well. "I tried to boil down in essence what makes me so angry about it," Carender told NPR. "And it was this idea that he and other people decide what the needs are in society. They get to decide. But in order to fund those things, they have to take from some people in order to give to the other people." What NPR didn't tell its audience is that Carender, an actress, had done six shows for a Seattle theater company that had received a Washington State arts grant, and had worked on a research project funded by the National Science Foundation before that.[3]

A few weeks later, the *Washington Post* interviewed Mike Vanderboegh, "a 57-year-old former militiaman from Alabama, who took to his blog urging people who opposed the historic health-care reform legislation—he called it 'Nancy Pelosi's Intolerable Act'—to throw bricks through the windows of Democratic offices nationwide." He told a *Post* reporter, "The federal government now demands all Americans to pay and play in this system, and if we refuse, we will be fined, and if we refuse to pay the fine, they will come to arrest us, and if we resist arrest . . . then we will be killed." The *Post* also noted that Vanderboegh is disabled and receives a $1,300 check from the tyrannical U.S. government each month.[4]

These activists firmly believe that they're "speaking truth to power" in a way that those dirty hippies in the 1960s never had. But the reality is that much of the organizing behind the Tea Party movement—the ideas, the seed money, the infrastructure that brings their events together—comes from two corporate-funded GOP front-groups. These were the people behind the people railing against the perfidy of "the elites."

The first, FreedomWorks, founded by former Republican vice presidential nominee Jack Kemp and former House Republican leader Dick Armey, is generally credited with launching the movement. FreedomWorks is no newcomer to the art of "astro-turfing"; in 2005, *Newsweek* reported that the Bush White House coordinated a series of staged "town hall events" with the group to tout the president's Social Security scheme. The "ordinary Americans" asking the questions at those town halls? They were conservative activists bused in by FreedomWorks to serve as living, breathing props.[5]

The second group, the "Tea Party Express," was previously operated as a political action committee (PAC) run by veteran operatives tied to the Republican PR firm Russo Marsh and Rogers. According-ing to *Politico*, the group used "campaign-style advance work and event planning, slick ads cut by Russo Marsh, impressive crowds and a savvy media operation" to make the PAC "among the prolific fundraising vehicles under the tea party banner." That, in turn, has "meant a brisk business for Russo March . . . and a sister firm called King Media Group." The two firms had received $1.9 million of the $4.1 million in payments made by the PAC through the spring of 2010.[6]

These anecdotes capture part of another story. It's a story that's important to understand as we grapple with some very new economic realities. It's a story about how the conservative movement manipulated our economic discourse to obscure the ways in which they've rigged the "free market" so that they tend to come out on top. It explains why so few noticed as a new Gilded Age emerged under a haze of lies, half-truths, and distortions.

This book will dissect some of those lies, and we'll start with a simple question: how could a sizable number of "ordinary" Americans, enraged at Wall Street more, perhaps, than at any other time in history, possibly be led to believe that new banking regulations are a threat to their own self-interest?

Using a Big Lie to Torpedo Financial Reform

In the spring of 2010, after a bitter yearlong debate over health-care legislation, congressional Democrats set their sights on financial reform. Most analysts agreed that new rules of the road were needed for the Wall Street high-flyers who had almost brought the global economy to a screeching halt in 2008.

Chris Dodd, the Democrat from Connecticut who chaired the Senate Finance Committee, offered up a package of rather mild reforms that most progressive analysts immediately criticized for not going far enough to rein in the banks. The bill would have created a new financial consumer protection agency, allowed the feds to dissolve insolvent banks in an orderly way, and created a new body that would oversee risky behavior on Wall Street.

As you might imagine, it didn't sit well with the financial industry. The American Bankers Association—the leading industry group—released a statement calling the proposals "unwarranted, detrimental regulatory structures" and adding, "we are strongly opposed to the draft regulatory reform proposal that . . . Christopher Dodd has advanced."[7]

Dodd's bill came amid almost unprecedented public hostility toward Wall Street, so opposing the measure as some radical socialist endeavor—the usual rhetorical strategy—was unlikely to get much traction. But an unknown advocacy group calling itself (ironically) the Committee for Truth in Politics took a different tack. The group, organized by a former North Carolina Republican Party operative, started running a series of ads suggesting that Dodd's reforms were, paradoxically, a *gift* to the banking industry—a rich, undeserved bailout that only Wall Street executives could love.[8] The reality, as FDIC chair Sheila Bair put it, was that the bill made bailouts "impossible," as "it should." She explained that lawmakers had "worked really hard to squeeze bailout language out of this bill. . . . In a true liquidity crisis, the [government] can provide systemwide support in terms of . . . lending and debt guarantees—but even then, a default would trigger resolution or bankruptcy."[9]

In technical terms, this particular lie might be called a classic example of "chutzpah." But it wasn't being uttered only by shady right-wing front-groups. Minnesota representative Michele Bachmann, one of the most reactionary members of Congress and a darling of the Tea Partiers, had called an earlier version of the bill a "permanent bailout" for Wall Street. Soon after that, Senate Minority Leader Mitch McConnell (R-TN) made the rounds of the Sunday talk shows to spread the meme. All were playing off a script developed by Frank Luntz, the GOP's super-pollster, who prepared a memo in early 2010 suggesting that opponents of the bill paint it as "punishing tax-payers" while rewarding the very "big banks and credit card companies" that were at that very moment furiously trying to kill the bill.[10]

It's likely that nobody would even have *thought* of characterizing new regulations as a giveaway to the banks if not for the success the conservative movement (backed by corporate America's deep pockets) has had in framing the economic issues of our day. When the ads went up, *Mother Jones*'s Kevin Drum commented,

> And that, boys and girls, is how the game is played. Just portray a bill meant to rein in banks as a bill meant to bail out banks. . . . Maybe suggest that instead of protecting consumers, it will remove consumer protections. Or that instead of regulating derivatives, it will set them free. Simple. Why bother making up complicated lies when simple ones will do just fine?[11]

Turning reality on its head is nothing new for Frank Luntz, a key figure in the conservative message machine. He's probably best known for penning an influential 2002 memo to then president George W. Bush suggesting that conservatives undermine the scientific consensus on global warming. He also played a pivotal role in popularizing the term "death tax," which is much easier than explaining why ordinary Americans should oppose a modest inheritance tax on a few thousand of the richest families in the country.

In other words, the mendacity of the Committee for Truth in Politics was standard fare. And when you pause for a moment to examine this kind of spin, a few themes emerge. Every progressive policy is decried as a "job killer" or an act of wild-eyed social engineering. Almost without exception, those policies are painted as "radical." Conversely, every measure that affects the wealthiest Americans is spun as an assault on the working class. Minimum wage increases, environmental protections, and even paid sick days "kill jobs," and anything that impacts huge multinationals' bottom lines is spun as an issue of vital concern to "small business owners."

The message is clear—the United States may be a hyper-individualistic country, but when it comes to our economic policies, somehow we're all in it together. Bill Gates's interests always dovetail neatly with those of Joe and Jane Six-Pack.

What We've Lost

All of that populist anger was a result of the growing economic insecurity most American families face today. And in order to understand how we got there, you need to step back a few decades, to a period of seismic economic changes that took place in the 1970s and the 1980s—changes that would profoundly transform the U.S. economy, rendering it almost unrecognizable from the one in which our grandparents raised their kids.

For three decades following World War II, a "liberal consensus" prevailed within America's ruling class. Our workers' productivity exploded, and the rewards were broadly shared. Labor unions were part of the fabric of American life—membership for private-sector wage-earners (other than construction workers) peaked at 39.2 percent in 1955[12]—and the wealthiest Americans paid up to 92 percent of their incomes in taxes. That tax structure prevented the lopsided accumulation of wealth by a small handful of families that had marked the robber-baron era and contributed to the loose speculation that resulted in the Great Depression. Highways were built to transport products to market, U.S. factories produced much of the goods the world consumed, and electricity and telephone service were extended to the most backward corners of the United States.

It was a bold experiment in liberal democracy, and it created the first economy built around a large middle class. The result was a virtuous cycle in which Americans could afford the products they produced, and each generation was expected to fare a little bit better than the one that came before it. It was far from a perfect society—think institutionalized racism and sexism, kids learning to duck and cover to survive a Soviet H-bomb, and, in the latter years, America's disastrous involvement in Vietnam and her ghettos in flames. But despite the social tensions of that era, the economy worked for a broad swath of the population. For (at least white) Americans, a public education and hard work at a factory job could lead to a decent middle-class life and the ability to send the kids to college so that they'd have a shot at the executive suite.

The Gilded Age had finally come to an end. In 1928, just before the Great Depression, the top 10 percent of the population controlled 49.3 percent of the nation's income, leaving nine out of ten Americans to share the other half. By 1953, the bottom nine-tenths shared 67.7 percent of the economic pie. It was an economic sea change.[13] But by 2006, the gains U.S. workers had made during the previous seventy years had been *entirely reversed*, with the top 10 percent of the population grabbing 49.7 percent of the income— slightly higher than at the peak of the robber-baron era.[14]

Between 1973 and 2006, the U.S. economy tripled in size.[15] In 1973, the income of the bottom 90 percent averaged $32,135 dollars per year (adjusted to 2007 dollars). But despite that trebling of the economy, by 2006 the bottom 90 percent had taken a cut, pulling down an average income of $31,528.[16] Even with thirty-three years of healthy growth in the economy, the vast majority of Americans earned a bit *less* than they had in 1973.

During that same period, the average incomes of those in the top 10 percent *doubled*, from $138,738 to $276,140. Folks in the top 1 percent saw their incomes rise by 221 percent, and a small number of prominent families occupying the top tenth of a percent of the economic pile saw their incomes increase by a whopping *441 percent.*[17]

It's important to understand how everything changed so dramatically.

Class War and the Great Risk Shift

Economist Doug Henwood offered a succinct description of the kind of seismic changes that occurred in that era. "You have to start this history in the 1970s, with a period of great inflation," he explained. "The U.S had lost the Vietnam War, there were wild-cat strikes, the third world was in broad rebellion. From the point of view of the American elite . . . it looked like things were spinning out of control. So there was this great rightward move in politics" that culminated in the "Reagan Revolution" (and the advent of "Thatcherism" in the UK).[18]

The backlash, Henwood explained, was brutal, as the new conservative movement launched "a very successful class-war from above—big crack-down on labor, union-busting, paring back the welfare state. And at the same time Wall Street was making its contribution to things. Shareholders, who had been kind of sleeping for the previous several decades, awoke and started demanding much higher profits, and much leaner and meaner ways of running corporate America." What followed was a fifteen-year bull market for stocks, "based on a correct assumption that the class war had turned, that the elites were back in control, that the period of rebellion in the third world was over and corporate profits [would begin] rising."[19]

Union busting became popular in corporate America. Membership declined from almost 4 in 10 private-sector workers in the mid-1950s, to 7.2 percent—less than 1 in 12—in 2009.[20] At the same time, the rapid growth that had marked the early decades of the postwar era, fueled by huge gains in worker productivity in the manufacturing sector, was coming to an end.[21]

That's an important piece of context. Since the middle of the last century, investors' returns on *real* production in the advanced economies—manufacturing—have steadily declined. In the booming years after World War II, the United States did very well making goods for the entire planet. But as Europe and Japan rose from the ashes, and later, as production in countries such as Taiwan, South Korea, and, of course, China increased, the industrial world simply started to make more crap than there were consumers to purchase it.

Economist Robert Brenner described what followed as a "long downturn" in the world's richest countries. The seven leading industrial economies had grown by a steady rate of 5 percent or more annually from the end of World War II through the 1960s, but in the 1970s that rate fell to 3.6 percent, and it's averaged around 3 percent since 1980.[22]

Investors started to seek higher returns elsewhere: in developing countries. The era of globalization was ushered in, and under the guise of "free trade" (itself a lie, as we'll see in chapter 15), corporations in richer countries began to offshore manufacturing (and later, services) to locales with cheaper labor, weaker environmental standards, and less regulation.

The result: manufacturing, which represented almost 30 percent of the U.S. economy at its peak in 1953, fell sharply, to just 12 percent by 2005.[23] The good, solid jobs on which a hard-working American without a college education could support his or her family were becoming a thing of the past. But that was okay, we were assured by the politicians and the pundits, because we were building a "new economy," an information economy that would more than make up for the loss. What really happened is that many of those solid jobs were replaced by service jobs that paid less, came with fewer benefits, and offered far less security.

During the 1980s, Ronald Reagan also began a relentless assault on the top marginal tax rates that continues to this day. The inevitable result was that huge fortunes were amassed by those at the top. In 1985, the combined net worth of the four hundred richest people (and families) in the United States was $238 billion, adjusted for inflation[24]; by 2007, just before the Great Recession, it had grown sixfold, to $1.57 *trillion*.[25]

Corporate profits started to climb. In 2006, the *New York Times* reported, "wages and salaries now make up the lowest share of the nation's gross domestic product since the government began recording the data in 1947, while corporate profits have climbed to their highest share since the 1960s."[26] And while the big corporations were becoming ever more profitable, the taxes they paid were plummeting—from one in four federal tax dollars in the 1950s to one in ten in the 2000s. Much of the shortfall was made up on the backs of working people, with Social Security taxes, excise taxes, and fees.[27]

At the same time, the New Deal's promise of a *minimally* dignified existence was being eroded, as corporate America and the government shrugged off much of the burden for providing workers with health care, educating their kids, and assuring them a decent retirement. It's what political scientist Jacob Hacker termed "The Great Risk Shift."

In 1989, the number of workers with 401(k) plans—subject to the ups and downs of the stock market—exceeded those with fixed-benefit pensions for the first time. Even megacorporations got into the act. In 1998, nine out of ten Fortune 100 companies still offered employees a pension; that number had been cut in half by 2008.[28] The share of workers with employer-provided health insurance fell by 14 percent between 1979 and 2006, while insurers got stingier with their benefits.[29] And after adjusting for inflation, the average cost of tuition, board, and books at a four-year public university *doubled* in the thirty years between 1975 and 2004.[30] Those tuition hikes were a necessary response to the long-term decline in states' support for public colleges.

A One-Sided War

All of this occurred before the Great Recession that began in 2008. American families then lost approximately $13 trillion in wealth during the crash—in home values and stocks and bonds—stoking the kind of anger we've seen from pissed off progressives and from the Tea Partiers who dominated the news in the summer of 2009.

But although a lot of people threw around some angry rhetoric—and even invoked the specter of armed revolution—the reality is that when the economy nosedived, we basically took it. We didn't riot; we took the bailouts, tolerated our stagnant wages, and accepted that Washington wasn't about to give struggling families any real relief.

Yet the meltdown was global in nature, and it's worth noting that citizens of other wealthy countries weren't so complacent. As the *Telegraph*, a British tabloid, reported, "A depression triggered in America is being played out in Europe with increasing violence, and other forms of social unrest are spreading. In Iceland, a government has fallen. Workers have marched in Zaragoza, as Spanish unemployment heads towards 20%. There have been riots and bloodshed in Greece, protests in Latvia, Lithuania, Hungary and Bulgaria. The police have suppressed public discontent in Russia."[31] Another British paper, the *Guardian*, reported scenes of "Burned-out cars, masked youths, smashed shop windows and more than a million striking workers" in France. French officials went so far as to delay the release of unemployment data, "apparently for fear of inflaming the protests."[32]

You might wonder why Americans are so docile compared to others in the face of such a brutal economic onslaught by a small and entitled elite. Any number of theories have been offered to explain the apparent disconnect. Thomas Frank argued eloquently in his book *What's the Matter with Kansas?* that wedge social issues—"God, guns and gays"—which the American Right nurtures with such care, obscure the fundamental differences between rich and poor, the powerful and the disenfranchised. Class consciousness, common to other liberal democracies, has been trumped by social anxieties, according to Frank.

I would offer two additional explanations. First, the 90 percent of Americans who haven't seen a raise in thirty-five years compensated for their stagnant incomes and kept on consuming—continued to buy TVs and go out to dinner. How did they do it? They started by bringing women into the workforce in huge numbers, transforming the "typical" single-breadwinner family into a two-earner household. Between 1955 and 2002, the percentage of married women who had jobs outside the home almost doubled.[33] Workers' salaries stayed pretty much the same, but the "typical" family now had two paychecks instead of one.

After that, we started to finance our lifestyles through debt—mounds of it. Consumer debt blossomed; trade deficits (which are ultimately financed by debt) exploded, and the government started to run big budget deficits, year in and year out. In the period after World War II, while wages were still rising along with the overall economy, Americans socked away 7 to 12 percent of the nation's income in savings annually (the data only go back as far as 1959). But in the 1980s, that began to decline—the savings rate fell from around 10 percent in the 1960s and the 1970s to about 7 percent in the 1980s, and by 2005, it stood at less than 1 percent (it's rebounded somewhat since the crash—to 3.3 percent at the beginning of 2010).[34]

The second reason Americans seem complacent in the face of this tectonic shift in their economic fortunes is more controversial: the "New Conservative Movement" built a highly influential message machine that's helped obscure not only the economic history of the last four decades, but the very notion of class itself.

The Lies That Corporate America Tells Us

Let's return to the early 1970s, when a rattled economic elite became determined to regain control of the U.S. economy. How do you go about achieving that in a democracy?

One way, of course, is to depose the government and replace it with one that's more to your liking. In the 1930s, a group of businessmen contemplated just that—a military takeover of Washington, D.C., to stop Franklin Delano Roosevelt's dreaded New Deal from being enacted. The plot fell apart when the decorated general the group had tapped to lead the coup turned in the conspirators.[35]

A more subtle approach is to convince a majority of voters that your interests are, in fact, their own. Yet there's a big problem with this: if you belong to a rarified group, then the notion of aligned interests doesn't reflect objective reality. And in the early 1970s, the media and academia provided a neutral arbiter of that reality (of sorts).

We've all grown accustomed to conservatives' conspiracy theories about the corporate media having a far-left bias and college professors indoctrinating American youths into Maoism. In the early 1970s, a group of very wealthy conservatives started to invest in what you might call "intellectual infrastructure" ostensibly designed to counter the liberal bias they saw all around them. They funded dozens of corporate-backed think tanks, endowed academic chairs, and created their own dedicated and distinctly *conservative* media outlets.

Families with names such as Olin, Coors, Scaife, Bradley, and Koch may not be familiar to most Americans, but their efforts have had a profound impact on our economic discourse. Having amassed huge fortunes in business, these dynasties used their foundations to fund the movement that would culminate in the election of Ronald Reagan in 1980 and eventually bring about the coronation of George W. Bush in 2000.

In 1973, brewer Joseph Coors kicked in $250,000 for seed money to start the now highly influential Heritage Foundation (with the help of the Olin, Scaife, Bradley, and DeVos foundations). In 1977, Charles Koch, an oil billionaire, started the libertarian Cato Institute. Richard Mellon Scaife, a wealthy right-wing philanthropist who would later fund the shady "Arkansas Project" that almost brought down Bill Clinton's presidency, bought the *Pittsburgh Tribune-Review* in 1970. The American Enterprise Institute, which was founded as the American Enterprise Association in the 1930s and remained relatively obscure through the 1960s, was transformed into an ideological powerhouse when it added a research faculty in 1972. The Hoover Institution, founded by Herbert himself in 1928, saw a huge increase in funding in the 1960s and would be transformed during the 1980s into the Washington advocacy organization that it is today.

In 1982, billionaire and right-wing messianic leader Sun Myung Moon started the *Washington Times* as an antidote to the "liberal" *Washington Post*. The paper, which promoted competition in the free market over all other human virtues, would be subsidized by "the Moonies" to a tune of $1.7 billion during the next twenty years.[36] In 2000, United Press International, a venerable but declining newswire, was bought up by Moon's media conglomerate, World News Communications.

With generous financing from that same group of conservative foundations, the Federalist Society was founded in 1982 by former attorney general Ed Meese, controversial Supreme Court nominee Robert Bork, and Ted Olsen—who years later would win the infamous *Bush v. Gore* case before the Supreme Court in 2000 and then go on to serve as Bush's solicitor general. The Federalist Society continues to have a major impact on our legal community.

In 2005, one of the most influential right-wing funders, the John M. Olin Foundation, actually declared its "mission accomplished" and closed up shop. The *New York Times* reported that after "three decades financing the intellectual rise of the right," the foundation's services were no longer needed. The *Times* reported that the loss of Olin wasn't terribly troubling for the movement, because whereas "a generation ago just three or four major foundations operated on the Right, today's conservatism has no shortage of institutions, donors or brio."[37] And that's not even mentioning Rupert Murdoch's vast, and vastly dishonest, media empire.

The rise of the conservative "noise machine" has been discussed at length in a number of other works, and conservatives dismiss it as a conspiracy theory of sorts. In truth, it's anything but—it's simply a matter of people with ample resources engaging in some savvy politics in an age of highly effective mass communication. There's nothing new about that; what's changed is that the world of advertising and marketing has become increasingly sophisticated, and the Right has played the instrument of modern public relations like a maestro.

Taken as a whole, it's difficult to overstate how profound an impact these ideological armies have had on our economic debates. Writing in the *Washington Post*, Kathleen Hall and Joseph Capella, two scholars with the Annenberg School of Communication, discussed the findings of a study in which they coded and analyzed the content broadcast across conservative media networks. They found a tendency to "enwrap [their audience] in a world in which facts supportive of Democratic claims are discredited and those consistent with conservative ones championed." The scholars warned, "When one systematically misperceives the positions of those of a supposedly different ideology, one may decide to oppose legislation or vote against a candidate with whom, on some issues of importance, one actually agrees."[38]

A larger issue is that the corporate Right's messaging doesn't remain confined to the conservative media. The end of the Cold War brought about a sense of economic triumphalism, which infected the conventional wisdom that ultimately shapes the news stories we read—U.S.-style capitalism had slain the socialist beast, proving to many that "government is best when it governs least."

A wave of mergers also concentrated our media in the hands of a few highly influential corporations. In 2009, there was a rare (public) example of one such corporation nakedly exerting editorial control over the decisions of one of its news "assets." During a meeting between the top management of General Electric, which owned NBC-Universal with its various news networks, and Rupert Murdoch's News Corporation, GE executives agreed to force MSNBC's firebrand host Keith Olbermann to cease fire in his long-standing feud with Fox News's Bill O'Reilly.

As journalist Glenn Greenwald noted at the time, "The most striking aspect of this episode is that GE isn't even bothering any longer to deny the fact that they exert control over MSNBC's journalism."[39]

Most notably, the deal wasn't engineered because of a perception that it was hurting either Olbermann or O'Reilly's show, or even that it was hurting MSNBC. To the contrary, as Olbermann himself has acknowledged, his battles with O'Reilly have substantially boosted his ratings. The agreement of the corporate CEOs to cease criticizing each other was motivated by the belief that such criticism was hurting the unrelated corporate interests of GE and News Corp.[40]

Five months previously, MSNBC host Joe Scarborough had been criticized for touting GE's stock on his show, *Morning Joe*, without disclosing that the company owned the network that employed him. "I never invest in the stock market because I think—I've always thought—that it's just—it's a crap shoot," he said. "[But] GE goes down to five, six, or seven, and I'm thinking, 'My god. I'm gonna invest for the first time, and I'm gonna send my kids to college through this.'"[41]

A week after that, Scarborough invited Nancy Snyderman, a regular medical correspondent for NBC's networks, onto the show to discuss the health-care reform bill then moving through Congress. Snyderman, who was presented to the audience as an impartial medical expert, had lost the ABC News job she'd previously held for seventeen years due to a conflict of interest. The *Nashville Examiner* reported that "she was briefly suspended for being paid to promote J & J's product Tylenol. She later spent four years with Johnson & Johnson as Vice President of Consumer Education."[42]

In another ABC segment, Snyderman weighed in on congressional hearings about autism without disclosing that a Johnson & Johnson subsidiary was the target of litigation alleging that one of its vaccines may help cause the condition. It was a "blatant conflict of interest," in the words of National Autism Association vice president Ann Brasher.[43]

Snyderman is hardly unique. A months-long investigation in 2010 by the *Nation*'s Sebastian Jones revealed what he called a far-reaching "media-lobbying complex"—dozens of corporate hired guns who appear on network broadcasts without disclosing their ties to the firms they work for. Jones wrote of "the covert corporate influence peddling on cable news," citing appearances such as that of former Homeland Security chief Tom Ridge, who went on MSNBC—which conservatives insist is the liberal anti-dote to Fox News—to urge the Obama administration to launch an ambitious energy program.

> The first step [toward a green economy], Ridge explained, was to "create nuclear power plants." Combined with some waste coal and natural gas extraction, you would have an "innovation setter" that would "create jobs, create exports."
> As Ridge counseled the administration to "put that pack-age together," he sure seemed like an objective commentator. But what viewers weren't told was that since 2005, Ridge has pocketed $530,659 in executive compensation for serv-ing on the board of Exelon, the nation's largest nuclear power company. As of March 2009, he also held an estimated $248,299 in Exelon stock, according to SEC filings.

Jones found that during just the previous three years, "at least seventy-five registered lobbyists, public relations representatives and corporate officials—people paid by companies and trade groups to manage their public image and promote their financial and political interests"—had appeared on the major news channels. "Many have been regulars on more than one of the cable networks, turning in dozens—and in some cases hundreds—of appearances," he wrote.[44]

There's a final piece of this puzzle that's less insidious than what Jones unearthed but probably has a bigger impact on our discourse: the standard-issue "he-said/she-said" reporting that's so instinctive to neutral, "unbiased" journalists. Reporters are expected to get "both sides" of every story, even if one of those sides is making factually dishonest arguments. And there are an untold number of consultants, corporate flacks, lobbyists, and right-wing think-tankers who are always good for a quick quote for a reporter working on deadline.

The economic perception that emerges from all of this simply doesn't depict the economy in which most Americans live and work. Before the crash of 2008, most Americans saw news of a relatively robust economy, with solid growth and rising stock prices. But their own incomes had essentially stagnated for a generation. I've long thought that the disconnect may help explain why Americans suffer from depression at higher rates than do the citizens of most other advanced countries—if you think the economy's solid, everyone else is prospering, and yet you still just can't get ahead, isn't it natural to conclude that it must be the result of some fundamental flaw in yourself?

Maybe you do have flaws—sure, you do—but it's important to understand how the economy in which one is trying to thrive helps shape one's fortunes. In the chapters that follow, we'll look at some of the Right's most cherished rhetoric and try to burn off some of the fog that shrouds our economic discourse.

1

CONSERVATIVES DON'T WANT GOOD GOVERNMENT

Don't believe that limited government means anything would be better for you, personally

I love the idea of people being able to own something. . . . People from all walks of life, all income levels are willing to take risks to start their own company. . . . And I like the idea of people being able to say, I'm in charge of my own health care. . . . I particularly like the idea of a Social Security system that recognizes the importance and value of ownership.
—*George Bush, on his "Ownership Society" agenda, December 16, 2004*

Consider for a moment how much conservative rhetoric about the economy is based on airy, nonspecific claims of defending our "freedom" and "liberty."

After the Democrats passed their health-care reform bill in 2010, Tony Blankley, the former aide to Newt Gingrich and a prominent conservative commentator, wrote about efforts to repeal the decidedly *centrist* law—a plan similar to the scheme Mitt Romney, a perennial Republican presidential candidate, had enacted as governor of Massachusetts. Blankley melodramatically claimed, "Upon this battle depends the survival of a nonsocialist America."

Upon it depends our own American way of life and the long continuity of our institutions and our history. . . .

If they can stand up to the coming propaganda, America may be free, and the life of the wider free world may move forward into broad, sunlit uplands.

But if the voters succumb . . . then free America—including all that we have known and cared for—will sink into the abyss of a new Dark Age.[1]

That kind of hyperbole is pretty comical, but it's nothing new. Journalist Steve Benen noted that in 1961, when John F. Kennedy introduced the Medicare bill, Ronald Reagan "warned that if Medicare became law, there was a real possibility that the federal government would control where Americans go and what they do for a living." Reagan told the nation, "If you don't [stop Medicare] . . . one of these days you and I are going to spend our sunset years telling our children and our children's children what it once was like in America when men were free."[2]

Dig a little deeper, and it becomes clear that "freedom" for the Right offers most of us anything but. It's the freedom for companies to screw their workers, pollute, and otherwise operate free of any meaningful regulations to protect the public interest. It's about the wealthiest among us being free from the burden of paying a fair share of the taxes that help finance a smoothly functioning society.

The flip side, of course, is that programs that assure working Americans a decent existence are painted as a form of tyranny approaching fascism. The reality is that they impinge only on our God-given right to live without a secure social safety net. It's the freedom to go bankrupt if you can't afford to treat an illness; the liberty to spend your golden years eating cat food if you couldn't sock away enough for a decent retirement.

It's worth restating a central rule of the U.S. political economy: people are attracted to the idea of "limited government" in the abstract—and certainly don't want the government intruding in their homes—but they really, *really* like living in a society with adequately funded public services. They like what government does in the specific, even if they have an inherent suspicion of the idea of "big government" (the phrase itself was coined to counter liberal attacks on "big business").

One need look no further for evidence of that assertion than a March 2010 poll of hard-core Tea Party activists conducted by Bloomberg News. It found that 90 percent of the Tea Partiers think "the U.S. is verging more toward socialism than capitalism, the federal government is trying to control too many aspects of private life and more decisions should be made at the state level," but, at the same time, fully seven out of ten of the libertarian activists wanted "a federal government that fosters job creation," and half of them thought that "the government should do something about executive bonuses" on Wall Street.[3]

At heart, that's the reason the Right can't honestly argue for its preferred policies. They can win votes by shouting about "government tyranny," and they can make inroads by decrying the perfidy of "socialism " but when they try to mess with a program like Social Security or cut the budgets that put cops on the beat and firemen into shiny red trucks and provide health care to poor children and the elderly, they get clobbered.

The Right's Roadmap for Economic Disaster

In early 2010, the American people got some rare insight into what conservatives' vision of "economic freedom" really means, in specific terms, when Representative Paul Ryan (R-WI) released a remarkable document that quickly became a political hot potato in Washington, D.C.

The author of the "Roadmap for America's Future," which the Democrats were eager to label as the GOP's plan, is no ordinary member of the House. Just forty years old, Ryan is considered the GOP's policy maven and the party's most serious economic expert. The *Milwaukee Journal-Sentinel*'s Craig Gilbert wrote that Ryan has a "geeky head for numbers and detail" and is "one of his party's most touted young politicians, a GOP point man on the economy, and a darling of the conservative movement." Cesar Conda, who served as an adviser to Dick Cheney and supervised Ryan when he was a lowly Hill staffer, told the *Sentinel* that Ryan is "the most influential elected Republican on economic issues."[4]

Ryan was considered a lock to chair the House Budget Committee if the Republican Party were to retake Congress. So his Roadmap can fairly be characterized as a kind of "shadow budget" like those released by the minority in the British Parliament—Ryan is essentially the GOP's Shadow Finance Minister.

Many Republicans, however—all but those farthest to the Right—sought to distance themselves from Ryan's proposals. House Minority Leader John Boehner (R-OH) told reporters, "It's his," and added, "I know the Democrats are trying to say that it's the Republican leadership. But they know that's not the case." Yet when he was asked which parts of the Roadmap he didn't favor, Boehner responded, "Off the top of my head, I couldn't tell you."[5]

The reason many Republicans were cautious about embracing Ryan's Roadmap—and Democrats eager to tout its supposed virtues— is that it was not only the embodiment of modern conservative thinking about the roles of private enterprise and government but, as Pete Wehner, a senior fellow at the conservative Ethics and Public Policy Center, put it, the plan represents an "intellectually honest document," and, as such, "has real numbers and it puts forward real proposals."[6]

That's problematic for conservatives—a much harder sell than some ideologically spun notion of preserving our "freedom." In a nutshell, the proposal would further the economic trends that have prevailed since the Reagan Revolution. It slashes and burns most of the bedrock social security programs on which Americans have come to rely, shifting ever-greater quantities of risk onto the backs of the middle class; it would offer deep tax cuts to businesses and the country's wealthiest individuals and eliminate taxes on investment gains altogether.

According to an analysis of the plan by the nonpartisan Tax Policy Center, "The Roadmap's tax provisions would be highly regressive compared with the current tax system." If the Road-map were enacted, the bottom 80 percent of the economic ladder would see their after-tax incomes remain about the same, those in the top 1 percent of the economic heap would see theirs shoot up by 26 percent, and the incomes of those in the top tenth of the top 1 percent would increase by 36 percent. The result? According to the Tax Policy Center's figures, "The share of total taxes paid by the bottom 80 percent would rise from 35 percent to 42 percent, while the share paid by the top 1 percent would fall by nearly half from 25 percent to 13.5 percent."[7] As we'll see in chapter 5, that would only be a continuation of decades-long trends in the U.S. tax system.

Ryan's proposal would replace the surety of Social Security with privatized accounts held by Wall Street brokerage firms (these firms, in turn, would gain a fat new stream of fees and have lobbied for the scheme for years). The idea is that by harnessing the "magic of compound interest," working people would be able to put away enough acorns for a comfortable retirement.

The Cato Institute, the Heritage Foundation, and others have touted the 7 percent annual returns the S&P 500 delivered on average since the mid-1920s. Yet that number is itself misleading. According to an analysis of historical stock market gains conducted by Steven Johnson, the director of the SimCivic organization, two-thirds of those long-term "returns" were from dividends being reinvested in additional purchases of stock. The actual rate of capital growth over that time averaged only 2.3 percent per year, comparable to the 1.8 percent returns on the Treasury bills sitting in the Social Security Trust Fund.[8]

The stock market is significantly riskier than T-bills, and more risk does bring a higher rate of return, which is fine for some investors but a bad idea for a guaranteed retirement program. Americans forcefully rejected a similar proposal during George W. Bush's term in office, and it was a good thing that they did—U.S. families lost $7 *trillion* in stock wealth during the recession that followed.[9] Those nearing retirement age face frightening prospects as it stands, with the value of their homes and IRAs in the tank, but they would have been truly screwed if not for the modest but guaranteed income afforded by Social Security.

Yet the 0.5 percent difference doesn't tell the whole story. If Social Security were privatized, its insurance provisions would be eliminated (sorry, no more aid to needy widows and orphans or the severely disabled). If adopted, the conservative Roadmap would also eliminate Medicare, Medicaid, and the S-chip program that offers free health care to children living in poverty. It would eliminate the tax deductions that employers receive for providing their workers with health insurance.

In their stead, Ryan's Roadmap would create a system of vouchers for those kicked off our existing public health programs. They would theoretically allow people to purchase private insurance policies. At first. But the value of the vouchers would be indexed to inflation, and health-care costs are rising *much faster* than that. From 1998 to 2008, insurance premiums increased by 131 percent, while inflation during that same period amounted to only a little less than 30 percent.[10]

According to the Center on Budget and Policy Priorities, Ryan's Roadmap "calls for radical policy changes that would result in a massive transfer of resources from the broad majority of Americans to the nation's wealthiest individuals."[11] But here's the rub: Ryan and those who advocate his economic approach justify these "radical" transfers of wealth as a hard solution to a pressing problem—the so-called entitlement crisis (more on that in chapter 4) and the supposedly crushing deficits it's causing. Yet the Center on Budget and Policy Priorities found that under Ryan's scheme, "The [national] debt would continue to grow in relation to the size of the economy for at least 40 more years—reaching over 175 percent of GDP by 2050."[12]

Small wonder that conservatives stick to lofty rhetoric about "liberty" and "economic freedom"—they certainly can't honestly sell policies like these to the American public on their merits.

A Murderer's Morality

On its face, the Roadmap is not exactly consistent with the principle of "compassionate conservatism" espoused by George W. Bush. Yet for conservatives like Ryan, it represents the *very height of morality*. In order to square that circle, one has to understand the deep and lasting influence that a schlocky fiction writer named Ayn Rand has had on the conservative movement. Her best known books, *Atlas Shrugged* and *The Fountainhead*, offer moral and intellectual justification for the most regressive policies—those that cause ordinary working families the deepest economic pain.

"The reason I got involved in public service, by and large, if I had to credit one thinker, one person, it would be Ayn Rand," said Paul Ryan at a D.C. event honoring the author.[13] On another occasion, he proclaimed, "Rand makes the best case for the morality of democratic capitalism."[14]

In the Randian worldview, the world is made up of a few virile, virtuous "producers" and the many "parasites" who feed off their labors. It's the producers who create wealth and make a better world, and they do so by pursuing their own dreams of success. In Rand's books, though, moochers and petty, visionless bureaucrats persistently bite at the ankles of her capitalist "supermen," which has the effect—unintended, but pernicious nonetheless—of harming all of society. Therefore, freeing the wealthy from their obligations— freeing the elite from their social contract with the rest of us—is in fact *the apex* of morality.

It's a philosophy that should be familiar to anyone who has heard a stump speech by a conservative true believer, listened to some right-wing talk radio on the drive home, or watched an hour of Fox News. But journalist Mark Ames dug a bit deeper into the inspirations for Rand's "moral vision," and the conclusion he drew was that a broad swath of the conservative movement is actually adhering to the philosophy of a sociopath.

Ames wrote, "The best way to get to the bottom of Ayn Rand's beliefs is to take a look at how she developed [John Galt,] the superhero of her novel *Atlas Shrugged*."

> Back in the late 1920s, as Ayn Rand was working out her philosophy, she became enthralled by a real-life American serial killer, William Edward Hickman, whose gruesome, sadistic dismemberment of a 12-year-old girl named Marion Parker in 1927 shocked the nation. Rand filled her early notebooks with worshipful praise of Hickman. . . .
>
> What did Rand admire so much about Hickman? His sociopathic qualities: "Other people do not exist for him, and he does not see why they should," she wrote, gushing that Hickman had "no regard whatsoever for all that society holds sacred, and with a consciousness all his own. He has the true, innate psychology of a Superman. He can never realize and feel 'other people.'"
>
> This echoes almost word for word Rand's later description of her character Howard Roark, the hero of her novel *The Fountainhead*: "He was born without the ability to consider others."[15]

Ames thinks that the United States is the only country "where right-wing elites can openly share their distaste for the working poor" and attributes that in part to Rand's popularity (according to a 2007 Zogby poll, more than 8 percent of Americans say they've read the book; a 1991 poll by the Library of Congress found that *Atlas Shrugged* was the second most influential book in the United States, after the Bible).[16]

Ames's conclusion is important for understanding today's political economy. "Whenever you hear politicians or Tea Partiers dividing up the world between 'producers' and 'collectivism,'" he wrote, "just know that those ideas and words more likely than not are derived from the deranged mind of a serial-killer groupie. . . . And when you see them taking their razor blades to the last remaining programs protecting the middle class from total abject destitution—Social Security, Medicare and Medicaid—and bragging about how they are slashing these programs for 'moral' reasons, just remember Ayn's morality and who inspired her."[17]

Translated into the real world of politics and policy, the Randian Dream looks something like Arizona governor Jan Brewer's response to her state's fiscal crisis. In early 2010, Brewer signed a budget that eliminated the Children's Health Insurance Program, denying health care to forty-seven thousand low-income children in Arizona. She also proposed a hike in the state sales tax—the most regressive tax, whose burden falls disproportionately on working people. Finally, at the time of this writing Brewer was hedging on whether she'd support a series of deep tax cuts for the "supermen" who run Arizona businesses.[18]

Way to stick it to those collectivist moochers!

The Seductive Lure of the Ownership Society

These policies are generally pushed with fear tactics. As we'll see in chapter 4, the Corporate Right has done a remarkable job convincing the American people that our social safety net is driving us to fiscal ruin (in reality, it's the rapidly escalating cost of health care that's actually the budget killer, despite the fact that those costs have grown more slowly in the public sector than in the private one).

Yet there is also a positive message: "ownership." The rhetoric was at the heart of George W. Bush's economic policies—he called his vision the "ownership society." It was an incredibly seductive frame. Every working person dreams of sharing in the nation's wealth, of owning a home and controlling his or her future. That dream is the hook on which the conservatives' "ownership society" hung—it was a visceral appeal to our naked self-interest.

The premise was that just as we value and care for our homes, we would also attend to our own health care and retirement if only we, rather than those nasty bureaucrats in Washington, "owned" them. And in exchange for losing the security offered by government-run social programs—to sweeten the deal, if you will—we'd get tax cuts!

The narrative is in line with a distinctly right-wing form of economic populism. In a way, it turns the very notion on its head; while liberal populism promises underserved groups that "We will stand with you against the heartless and powerful," the central theme of the "ownership society" was that we're all big capitalists just waiting to blossom—even the lowliest among us. If only we could get the yoke of taxes, asbestos litigation, and regulations off our backs, we would all be in a position to worry about losing a piece of our multimillion-dollar estate to the "death tax." Forget about a semblance of economic justice; it's about giving you, the individual, the tools you need to beat your neighbor.

The Bushies employed that kind of rhetoric to push radical "reforms" of cradle-to-grave issues as diverse as the move from universal public education to school vouchers, transitioning from Medicare to Health Savings Accounts, and privatizing Social Security—the Ryan Roadmap in a nutshell.

Ownership: A Conservative Spin on a Progressive Concept

It's worth noting that the idea of giving average Americans' greater "ownership"—empowering them to save and invest—is one that originated on the Left and was subverted by movement conservatives. Twice during Clinton's second term, he proposed establishing "USA Accounts"—private IRAs that the government would subsidize with fully refundable tax credits for the poor and working classes. But they would augment, rather than replace, Social Security. Hillary Clinton made a similar proposal during the 2008 presidential primary campaign.

"Universal Savings Accounts," Bill Clinton argued, "do just what the name says, they make savings universal. . . . And by rewarding responsibility, USA Accounts would help set [working people] on the road to further savings." Note how similar that is to the rhetoric George W. Bush would use to promote his scheme to partially privatize Social Security years later.

The Clintons' plans weren't new ideas on the Left. Michael Sherraden, a professor at Washington University in St. Louis, first proposed these kinds of universal asset-building accounts in his seminal 1992 book *Assets and the Poor: A New American Welfare Policy*. Since then, the idea of spreading ownership around has been reiterated again and again by progressives. Ray Boshara, the director of the Asset Building Program at the New America Foundation, had an even bolder approach than the Clinton plan; he'd give every baby born in the United States $6,000 dollars in what he called an "American Stakeholder Account," which could be used only for asset-building expenses such as buying a first home, starting a new business, or paying for college. Anything left over would go toward retirement, supplementing Social Security.[19]

Others have suggested using microcredits and community-based development accounts for small businesses and various programs to help the working poor buy first homes. Some have even proposed selling off public low-income housing to residents for next to nothing so that they might have a real stake in improving their communities.

Those are but a few of the dozens of initiatives out there that might create a *progressive* ownership society. These liberal proposals address the kernel of truth behind the Right's rhetoric: asset ownership *is* a darn good thing. The difference is this: everything progressives have proposed would function *in addition* to our bedrock social safety programs. They'd make working people's lives better. The conservative "ownership society programs," now known as the Ryan Roadmap, are intended to replace the last vestiges of the New Deal—they simply shift more risk onto the backs of ordinary working families.

A CLOSER LOOK

Is Big Business Passing Itself Off as "Small Business"?

In 2009, Americans' trust in the business community took a nosedive. Fewer than 40 percent of those polled expressed any faith in corporate America,[1] and only one in twenty had a "great deal of confidence" in large corporations.[2] But a Gallup poll taken in early 2010 found that more than 90 percent of the population still held a favorable view of *small* business."[3]

Now, conservatives can read polls and have long spun the most egregious corporatist policies as extending a helping hand to "small business." Don't think about Enron, they say. Look at how these tax cuts are helping the mom-and-pop grocery down the road. A perfect example of this meme came during the debate over George W. Bush's budget-busting tax cuts.

The reality was pretty simple. Reporting on a study conducted by the Congressional Budget Office in 2007, the *New York Times* wrote that Bush's "cuts were much deeper, and affected far more money, for families in the highest income categories." Households in the top 1 percent, with a fat average income of $1.25 million, saw their tax rates drop from 24.2 percent in 2000 to 19.6 percent in 2004. This cut their tax bills by an average of $58,000.[4] An analysis by the Tax Center found that the bottom 20 percent of the population pocketed only around 1 percent of the value of Bush's cuts.[5]

In 2003, however, Republicans were trotting out the spin that most of those cuts were going to "small business owners": the proverbial lifeblood of Small Town, U.S.A. Then Republican national chair Ed Gillespie launched the meme with a speech that December, saying that "80% of the tax relief for upper income filers goes to small businesses."[6]

Fact-check.org, the nonpartisan campaign watchdog, looked at the claim, which was cooked up by GOP staffers on the House

Economic Committee, and concluded that "It's untrue—and a classic example of a statistical distortion gone amok":

> [The] report concluded that 79% of the highest-income Americans have some business income. Then the report made a huge leap, claiming "These small business owners would receive 79 percent of the . . . tax savings" from cutting the top tax rate. But wait a second—very few of those "small business owners" are really running dry-cleaning stores. A Republican committee staff member confirmed to Fact-Check.org that their report is counting anybody who made even one dollar of profit from a hobby business as a "small business owner" if they reported that income on Schedule C of their federal income-tax returns.[7]

Although this was widely commented on at the time, few pointed out an interesting fact about U.S. "small businesses." Namely, that in the United States, the federal government classifies a lot of what most people would consider medium-size or even pretty *large* companies as small businesses.

Most developed nations offer programs to assist small firms, as defined by either a maximum number of employees or annual revenues. The European Union defines a small business as one with 50 or fewer workers; in Australia it's 15 or fewer. The United States sets the maximum number of employees by individual industry, and in many sectors, companies with up to 500 or 1,000 or even *1,500 employees* are considered "small businesses." A fiber-optic cable company with 1,000 workers, an aircraft manufacturer with 1,500 employees, even an oil refiner with 1,500 people toiling away—all of these are classified as small businesses in the United States.[8] In the European Union, having 250 workers is the upper limit for a *medium-size enterprise*.[9]

It's worth noting that people probably have a favorable view of small business based on the widespread belief that small, rather than large companies, create most of our net job growth. But Steve

Pearlstein of the *Washington Post* called that "one of the most enduring lies in American politics."

> In terms of new job creation, the data show that most of it happens in a small number of very fast-growing companies that are no longer what most of us would consider small. . . .
>
> [And] the dirty little secret is that a lot of small-business job growth has also been driven by the decision of big businesses to outsource many tasks that they used to do in-house. In an economic sense, jobs haven't been so much "destroyed" and "created" as they have been shifted from one company to another.[10]

The thing to keep in mind is that true small business owners' interests are the same as those of anyone else who is trying to carve out a decent middle-class existence: they struggle to cover health-care costs, send the kids to school, and put away a little nest egg for retirement, just as other families do.

Remember that the next time you hear some right-winger talking about the impact of a certain policy on small business owners. They're definitely *not* talking about that little barber shop down on Main Street.

2

IT'S NOT YOUR FAULT THERE AREN'T ENOUGH GOOD JOBS

Don't believe America is still the land of opportunity

> We cannot make the next two years merely a battle between Democrats and Republicans. We must make the next two years a debate about what makes America great and whether we are still a land of opportunity for everyone willing to dream big and work hard or whether we have accepted a slow decline into European-style paternalism.
>
> —*Rep. Mike Pence (R-IN), House Republican Conference chair, after the election of Barack Obama*

I've never actually owned a set of bootstraps, but conservatives are awfully fond of them.

It's difficult to argue that a wealthy country such as the United States should have a threadbare social safety net—arguably the weakest of any advanced economy—simply because the well heeled want to keep their tax bills low. So conservatives instead claim that when government steps in to make working people's lives a bit easier, it only ends up hurting them by nurturing a "culture of dependency" (a narrative that we'll examine in greater detail later). They say food stamps, minimum wages, and programs for the poor sap one's will to go out there, work hard, and make something of oneself. It's the proverbial "nanny state," and for the Right, avoiding its harms generally trumps other concerns, often including common sense.

In 2010, with millions out of work, Senator Jim Bunning (R-TN) blocked a bipartisan bill to extend unemployment benefits. The *Washington Post* reported that in defense of his colleague, Senator Jon Kyl (R-AZ) "told the Senate he questioned why anyone would see unemployment benefits as helpful to the economy, or to the job market." Kyl remarked, "If anything, continuing to pay people unemployment compensation is a disincentive for them to seek new work."[1] It's actually a tenable argument in countries that offer decent unemployment benefits. But in the United States, a married worker with kids will get half of his or her wages replaced on unemployment, one of the lowest rates in the developed world. Nobody's living the high life.[2]

But that doesn't trump right-wing columnist Jonah Goldberg in providing the most jaw-dropping example of letting ideology trump human empathy. In the wake of the earthquake that decimated Haiti, leaving 300,000 of that poor country's inhabitants dead and millions more displaced, Goldberg argued that what Haiti really needed was not immediate assistance and lots of it, but some "tough love." He blamed the foreign aid that Haitians had received before the quake for creating "a poverty culture" and concluded, "It's hardly news that poverty makes people vulnerable to the full arsenal of Mother Nature's fury."[3]

In 2007, when Congress passed a bill that would have expanded a highly popular program that offers health insurance to poor kids—with an *overwhelming* bipartisan majority—then president George W. Bush vetoed the measure. He admitted that he had no problem at all with the program itself but argued on purely ideological grounds that "the policies of the government ought to be to help people find private insurance, not federal coverage. And that's where the philosophical divide comes in."[4]

Now, the idea that "dependency" is what makes people poor might make some sense if we were all born with the same opportunities to get ahead. Tragically, however, that American dream is dead, or, at the very least, it lies broken and bleeding on the side of the road. In today's economy, the single greatest predictor of how much an American child will earn in the future is how much his or her parents take home. Working Americans have essentially bought into a unique social contract: they forgo much of the economic security that citizens of other wealthy countries take for granted in exchange for a more "dynamic," meritorious economy that supposedly offers them plenty of opportunities to succeed. Of course, this is never explicitly stated, and most of us don't know about the deal, but it's reinforced all the time in our economic discourse.

The belief that our chances of moving up the economic ladder are limited only by our innate abilities and our appetite for hard work is almost universal in the United States. Around 3 percent of Americans are actually millionaires[5] (or were before the crash of 2008), but in 2003, almost one in three Americans told Gallup that they expected to be millionaires at some point in their lives.[6] A 2006 poll found that more than half of those surveyed believed "Almost anyone can get rich if they put their mind to it."[7]

Contrary to that popular notion, the United States is not a meritocracy, and Americans are getting the worst of both worlds—not only is a significant portion of the middle class hanging on by the narrowest of threads, not only do fewer working people have secure retirements to look forward to, not only are nearly one in seven Americans uninsured,[8] but working people also enjoy fewer opportunities to pull themselves up by their bootstraps than do the citizens of other advanced countries.

What Happened to the American Dream?

When you define the "American dream" as the ability of working-class families to afford decent middle-class lives—to put their kids through school and have access to quality health care and a secure retirement—most people will tell you it simply doesn't exist anymore.

That was how it was routinely defined prior to the economic collapse of 2008. But a 2009 Met Life study of the "American dream" painted a different picture. It found that "Americans were struggling with increased financial obligations" that "had profound implications for the American dream." Specifically, most people's definition of the dream had shifted from the two-car garage and the comfortable home "to an almost singular focus on financial security."[9]

Yet in stark contrast to those findings, when you define the dream according to the opportunities people *believe* they have, you get a radically different picture. According to a study of public opinion in twenty-five wealthy countries, Americans are almost twice as likely as those working in other advanced economies to believe that "people get rewarded for intelligence and skill." At the same time, fewer than one in five say that coming from a wealthy family is "essential" or "very important" to getting ahead— significantly lower than the twenty-five-country average.[10]

It's impossible to overstate the impact these beliefs have on our policy debates. Americans are less than half as likely as people in other wealthy nations to believe that it's "the responsibility of government to reduce differences in income."[11]

Yet in reality, the United States' much-ballyhooed upward mobility is a myth, and it appears to be getting farther from reality with each new generation. Contrary to the popular characterization of Americans, several studies released in recent years suggest that they enjoy significantly *less* upward mobility than do the citizens of a number of other industrialized nations. German workers have 1.5 times the upward movement of Americans, Canada's economy is nearly 2.5 times as mobile, and Denmark's is 3 times as mobile. Norway, Finland, Sweden, and France (France!) are all more upwardly mobile societies than the United States. Of the countries included in the studies, the United States ranked near the bottom; only in the United Kingdom was it tougher to shake off a low social status that one had been born with.[12]

Movin' On Up?: Our Upwardly Mobile
Economy Is a Myth

The reality is that an American in today's workforce is just as likely to experience *downward* mobility as he or she is to move up in the world. A study conducted by Julia Isaacs, a fellow with the Economic Mobility Project, measured two kinds of economic mobility: "absolute mobility," which is the degree to which one generation does better than the one before it, and "relative mobility," or how easy it is for an individual to climb the social ladder through smarts, talent, hard work, and so on. She used a unique set of data that allowed her to directly compare the incomes of Americans in the late 1990s and the early 2000s with the incomes of their parents' generation in the late 1960s.

The data on absolute mobility are mixed. Isaacs, using family income data, found that the current generation as a whole is doing better than the previous generation—that's absolute mobility. But the nation's income is distributed much less evenly than it was a generation ago, so looking at aggregated family incomes tends to obscure the overall degree of mobility—recall that much of the last three decades' growth in household income was a result of more women joining the workforce.[13]

When the Brookings Institution's Isabel Sawhill and John Morton looked at four generations of income data for men alone, they came up with a very different picture. They compared men ages thirty to thirty-nine in 1994 with their fathers at the same point in their careers and found that median incomes had increased by only 0.2 percent annually during the last three decades. But, they noted, "the story changes for a younger cohort." Men in their thirties in 2004 had a median income that was, on average, *12 percent less* than that of their fathers' generation at the same age. The scholars concluded, "The up-escalator that has historically ensured that each generation would do better than the last may not be working very well."[14]

It's relative mobility, however, that really speaks to the health—or the lack thereof—of the American dream, and Isaacs's conclusions are stunning. "Contrary to American beliefs about equality of opportunity," she wrote, "a child's economic position is heavily influenced by that of his or her parents."

Isaacs categorized American families as belonging to one of four groups: the "upwardly mobile," who do better relative to their parents; those "riding the tide," families that earn more than their parents did but remain in the same relative position on the economic ladder; those "falling despite the tide," a small group who are earning more than their parents did but who nonetheless fell into a lower position on the ladder; and those who are "downwardly mobile." The key take-away is that American families are just as likely to be downwardly mobile—33 percent fall into this group—as they are to join the 34 percent who move up.

It's crucial to understand the relationship between inequality and immobility, and central to that relationship is the concept of "intergenerational assistance." That's a fancy way of saying that a person's chances to advance economically are very much impacted by whether his or her family can help with expenses such as tuition payments, a down payment on a house, or seed money to start a business. The wealthy don't pass on their status to their kids through inheritance alone, but also by smoothing the way for their ascent to the top of the pile.

Dalton Conley, the director of NYU's Center for Advanced Social Science Research, compared two hypothetical kids—one from a family with some money and the other from poor parents. Both are born with the same level of intelligence, both are ambitious, and both work hard in school. In a meritocracy, the two would enjoy the same opportunities to get ahead. Yet the fact that one might graduate from college free and clear, while the other is burdened with $50,000 in debt makes a huge difference in terms of their long-term earnings prospects. That's only one of the myriad ways that parents pass their economic status on to their children, Conley explained. "When you are talking about the difference between financing their kid's college education, starting a new business, moving if they need to move for a better job opportunity—[differences] in net worth might make the difference between upward mobility and stagnation."[15]

Blame the "New Economy" for Hindering Upward Mobility

Unlike the issue of vast income disparities, which many conservative pundits dismiss as irrelevant, there's broad agreement across the ideological spectrum about the importance of upward mobility. In the United States, where we take for granted levels of poverty that would be a front-page scandal in most advanced economies, the stakes are that much higher. It's one thing to live in a new Gilded Age if we all have a fair shot at ending up among the "haves," but it's altogether different when a nation's wealth is concentrated at the top of a rigidly stratified society. As Dalton Conley put it, our lack of mobility "very manifestly displays the anti-meritocracy in America—the reproduction of social class without the inheritance of any innate ability."[16]

The interplay of a number of factors determines social mobility, and there's been heated debate about what has caused these changes in the U.S. economy and what the policy implications might be. Three trends help explain why it's so much harder to get ahead in the United States today than it was for previous generations of working people and why it's apparently easier to get ahead in more socially oriented countries: differences in education, the decline in union membership—and the loss of good manufacturing jobs—and a relatively weaker social safety net.

It should come as no surprise that roughly speaking, the decrease in relative mobility from generation to generation correlates with the rise of "backlash" conservatism, the advent of Reaganomics, and the series of massive changes in industrial policies that people loosely refer to as the "era of globalization."

The United States is the only advanced country in which the federal government is not directly involved in higher education. That has helped drive dramatic increases in the average cost of a college education since the post–World War II era. In 1957, for example, a full-time student at the University of Minnesota paid $111 per year in tuition, which, in today's dollars, is about $750.

During the 2005–2006 school year, in-state tuition at the University of Minnesota was $8,040. As education writer Naomi Rockler-Gladen noted, that's an inflation-adjusted increase of 1,000 percent since 1957. At more than $7,000 in average yearly costs (in 2009), a public university education in the United States is a lot more difficult to finance than it was a generation ago.[17] That negatively affects mobility; a college degree is still a bootstrap, even if it's somewhat less sturdy than it was during the last century.

Isabel Sawhill looked at the relationship between education and mobility and concluded, "At virtually every level, education in America tends to perpetuate rather than compensate for existing inequalities."[18] She pointed to three reasons for that. First, we have a relatively weak K-12 system. "American students perform poorly on international assessments," she wrote. "Colleges are forced to provide remedial work to a large share of entering freshmen, and employers complain about workers' basic skills." A society with a weak education system will, by definition, be one in which the advantages of class and family background loom large. Second, the U.S. education system is largely funded through state and local property taxes, which means that the quality of a kid's education depends on the wealth of the community in which he or she grows up. This, too, helps replicate parents' economic status in their kids. Finally, Sawhill notes, in the United States, unlike in other advanced economies, "access both to a quality preschool experience and to higher education continues to depend quite directly on family resources."

Another major factor is the decline in organized labor and solid, good-paying manufacturing jobs. Those jobs once represented another bootstrap that is now disappearing.

There's also an inverse relationship between how robust a country's social safety net is and the degree to which working families face the prospect of *downward* mobility. For example, countries that have generous unemployment benefits show a clear trend: offering displaced workers more assistance (a) extends the period of unemployment (which tends to be the focus of most conservatives) and

(b) also means that when working people do reenter the workforce, they do so at a higher average wage. There's a similar dynamic in terms of health care: people with access to paid sick leave and other health benefits switch jobs less frequently than do those who don't enjoy those bennies, and as a result, they have longer average tenure and higher earnings.

In these areas, the United States has felt Jacob Hacker's "great risk shift." Hacker stated that the U.S. "framework of security has unraveled, leaving Americans newly exposed to the harshest risks of our turbulent economy: losing a good job, losing healthcare, losing retirement savings, losing a home—in short, losing a stable, financial footing." All of those hardships offer unique opportunities to fall out of the middle class—opportunities for downward mobility that simply don't exist for the Canadian or French worker, people who can rely on a more progressive state to help preserve their income levels when disaster strikes.

Ultimately, the take-away from the decline in American upward mobility is that the existence of a middle class is not a natural phe-nomenon. It was created by providing good-quality public educa-tion, mandating minimum wages, and guaranteeing working people the right to organize.

Conservatives have spent the last three decades unraveling those kinds of protections—all have been subjected to death "by a thousand small cuts" since Reaganomics hit the United States. As a result, it has once again become true that the accident of one's birth dictates one's life chances to a very large degree, and that is a wholly predictable result of the rise of the conservative backlash.

Is the Value of
Education Declining?

In 2007, George W. Bush tried to explain why the gap between the haves and the have-nots had widened so dramatically during his presidency. "The reason is clear," he said, "we have an economy that increasingly rewards education and skills because of that education."[1]

He was only halfway wrong! In the middle of the last century, at the height of America's industrial dominance, there were a number of ladders that people could use to climb out of poverty and into the middle class. One of them was higher education. After World War II, the GI Bill sent millions of vets to college (and lent them money to buy homes and start new businesses). The middle class was thus born of very direct "government intervention" in the economy. And for those who earned a college degree, economic security was all but guaranteed.

There were also opportunities for people without degrees. They could land apprenticeships or otherwise work their way up to stable and secure jobs that paid enough to provide for a family and maybe send the kids to college. Each generation was doing better than their parents had before them.

But then something changed. For decades, the economic boost one can expect from earning a college degree has fallen (even while the cost of getting that degree has skyrocketed, as we saw in chapter 2). This isn't a new phenomenon. Writing in *The Review of Economic Statistics* in 1977, economist R. B. Freeman noted that during that decade, "The once sizeable premium to the college graduate diminished; attainment of professional and managerial job status became less frequent; and the rate of return to the college investment dropped after having risen in the 1960s."[2]

The trend appears to have accelerated in recent years. In 2008, the *Wall Street Journal* reported that during "the economic expansion that began in 2001 and now appears to be ending, the inflation-adjusted wages of the majority of U.S. workers didn't grow, even among those who went to college." When the article was published, people with bachelor's degrees were earning almost 2 percent *less* than they had in 2000. The economy was growing, but, as Jared Bernstein told the *Journal*, "The fruits of growth are flowing largely to a relatively small group of people who have a particular set of skills and assets that lots of other people don't."[3]

Economists attribute the decline in value of a college diploma to globalization—computer nerds in Seattle competing with programmers in Mumbai—to new technologies that have made many middle-level positions for college grads obsolete and, more than anything else, to a greatly expanded pool of workers holding a bachelor's degree.

At the beginning of the twentieth century, there were fewer than 1,000 colleges in the United States, with only 160,000 people enrolled.[4] In 1948, almost 15 percent of the adult population had a college degree,[5] and between 1973 and 2008, the share of 18- to 24-year-olds enrolled in college increased by more than 15 percent—almost 4 in 10 young adults were hitting the books that year.[6] Much of that increase can be attributed to the loss of those solid manufacturing jobs. In an "information economy," more and more kids rightly feel the need to get a decent education. But with an increase in supply—in this case, workers with bachelor's degrees—comes a drop in price, and that's manifested in the dwindling economic advantage of having a secondary education.

At the same time, the relative value of a high-school degree has risen, because the wages of high-school dropouts have fallen dramatically in real terms since the 1970s. Yet as economists James Heckman and Paul LaFontaine noted, "It is surprising and disturbing that, at a time when the premium for skills has increased and the return [on] high school graduation has risen, the high school dropout rate in America is increasing." The scholars added, "America is becoming a polarized society. Proportionately more American youth are going to college and graduating than ever before. At the same time, proportionately more are failing to complete high school."[7]

How to Train Wage Slaves

Higher education is obviously pretty important, but to understand how education shapes economic outcomes, you've got to start earlier, in primary schools. U.S. students don't stack up well against those in other advanced economies, in terms of being prepared for a good secondary education. According to a 2008 study, one-third of new college freshmen require remedial courses in math, English, and other basic academic skills.[8]

And although every wealthy country offers a basic education that results in very high literacy rates, the United States doesn't stack up well against its competitors when you look at the rate of *high-level* literacy (basic literacy simply means that you can read signs and fill out forms). A study of fourteen wealthy countries found that only one in five U.S. adults had a high level of literacy, half the rate in Sweden and the fourth-lowest rate in the group.[9] That shouldn't come as a surprise; a study of fifteen-year-olds ranked the United States twelfth out of seventeen advanced countries in high-level reading skills.[10]

Exactly why our kids do poorly in international comparisons—it's also true of math and science skills[11]—is a subject of much debate, but one thing is clear: it's not that we're trying to educate our children on the cheap. Among the thirty countries in the Organisation for Economic Co-operation and Development (OECD), only Norway spent more per student on primary education than the United States did.[12]

That's a nationwide average, however, and the quality of education in various school districts—and in public versus private schools—is anything but consistent. Just consider how kids in different districts are prepared to succeed in our high-tech economy. University of New Hampshire scholars Virginia Garland and Sara Wotton wrote that the tech gap separating students of different economic strata hasn't narrowed in recent years, despite being the subject of much discussion among education advocates:

> Unfortunately, the "digital divide" between the "haves" and the "have nots" is widening. While some well-financed suburban schools have installed "wireless" computers and have trained teachers to use the new technologies, poorer urban and rural schools are lagging behind with outdated computers and insufficient Internet access. This gap has serious negative consequences for the future of the next generation. Those students from urban and rural working-class families, largely racial and ethnic minorities, will be unable to compete with their wealthier, better educated, and more technologically advanced peers in the global marketplace.[13]

During the 1970s and the 1980s, researchers noticed something else: schools weren't only funded differently, they also took a different approach to teaching. Scholars noted that children from poorer neighborhoods spent more time doing rote learning and being taught how to comport themselves in a work environment, while children in more affluent districts spent more time developing higher cognitive skills and critical thinking. Researchers concluded that the universal education system—perhaps the greatest accomplishment of early progressive reformers—was separating kids into "tracks," with those in wealthy districts being prepared for managerial positions where they'll be required to think and act autonomously, and poorer kids being taught to follow instructions and be good wage slaves. Many researchers began to see our school system not as the great democratizing force that most people believe it to be—preparing all American children to reach their full potential—but as a means of "reproducing social class" from generation to generation.[14]

That was then. Now, in the era of No Child Left Behind, most kids are being taught to take tests, rather than to think. According to David Berliner, a professor of education at the University of Arizona, high-income kids "typically score well on the tests used to satisfy NCLB requirements," but, at the same time, "today may actually be worse for poor children in the U.S. than at any time in the last half century."

> This is because the lower classes are being kept from the liberal arts and humanities curricula by design. Using the argument that we must get their test scores up, we in the United States are designing curriculum for poor children, often poor children of color but certainly, numerically, for poor white children, that will keep them ignorant and provide them with vocational training, at best. Their chances of entrance to college and middle-class lives are being diminished, and this is all being done under the banner of "closing the gap," a laudable goal but one that has produced educational policies with severe and negative side effects.[15]

So, although George W. Bush was right that we live in a society that "increasingly rewards education," it's important to recognize that our educational system is still leaving many, many children behind.

THERE IS NO FREE MARKET

Don't believe that modern markets exist
without government

We actually need the tough medicine that the free market is
trying to force upon us. We need more capital freed up for
the private sector. We don't need more capital for the public
sector. . . . The stimulus is the worst thing they can do. It's
actually going to stifle the economy.

—"Free market" economist Peter Schiff, on why the 2009 stimulus plan
would send the United States into a deep depression

Perhaps the central and most enduring myth of conservative economics is that there exists an organically functioning "free market."
Conservatives like to portray themselves as self-reliant actors content
to brave the cutthroat world of unregulated capitalism and let the
chips fall where they may. And they like to portray liberals as timid,
always looking to the state to be their protective "nanny."

But economist Dean Baker, the codirector of the Center for
Economic and Policy Research, explained why that's a myth. "What
the conservatives have done is they've rigged the deck," he told me.
"They've made sure that certain people come out ahead, that income
flows upward, and that other people are put at a disadvantage—and
these things are built into the rules of the system. And then what

49

they want to do—in talking about 'free markets'—is they want to kick back and say, 'No, no, no; those are the rules, and we can't talk about them.'"

According to the dominant narrative, the free market may have some flaws, but it is ultimately such a dynamic force that the meddling of pasty government bureaucrats, no matter how well intentioned, can only throw a wrench in the works and ultimately screw us all.

The kernel of truth behind the mythology is that the free market's opposite—the centrally planned economy—has indeed proved disastrous. It's pretty clear that economies in which entrepreneurs have the ability to start new businesses, take risks on new ventures, and hopefully come up with a better mousetrap fare significantly better than do those that lack the relative freedom of liberal capitalism.

From that little nugget of truth, a number of commonly held myths have arisen. First, conservatives conflate the kind of public interest regulations that one finds in all liberal democracies with the central planning that's helped doom North Koreans to decades of destitution and famine. The reality is that although central planning has been a demonstrable failure, regulation in the public interest is absolutely necessary for markets to work. Greed may be a factor that motivates people to work hard, but *unchecked* greed—unconstrained by regulations that protect the public interest—is a disastrous force. As Robert Pollin, the codirector of the Political Economy Research Institute at the University of Massachusetts, put it, "It is time to recognize that unregulated financial markets always have, and always will, cause financial crises. There are no historical exceptions to this observation at all. This point has to be grasped."[1]

Second, listening to the free-marketeers, one might imagine that markets are like mushrooms: organic entities that would grow just fine without the intervention of a human hand. That may have been the case when there were actual physical markets where people came to trade sheep and chickens. But when we speak of the modern "market"—this complex system for distributing the fruits of a society's economic output—we're talking about an entity created by the government, with rules established by the government.

And it's the rules of the game, much more than some unseen but all-knowing "hidden hand," that ultimately determine who wins and who loses.

Why the Free Market Works for Nikes but Not for Fire-Fighting

Competition in a free market is the cornerstone of the "neoclassical" economics that's taught in every university program in the country—it is by no means exclusive to conservatives. In fact, it has historically been associated with liberalism (traditional liberal views were shaped by opposition to mercantilism).

All but the most ideologically driven economists understand that the market is very good at allocating certain goods and services. It's the most efficient way to distribute sneakers, bubble gum, and washing machines. There are, however, vitally important goods and services that the free market doesn't handle well at all. Yet the Right continues to see the market as a solution to problems it simply cannot address.

Consider fire-fighting. We now deem the task a "public good": something that individuals can't decide for themselves to forgo. But in the early years of our Republic, in cities such as Boston and New York, small, privately operated fire brigades vied for property-owners' business. You'd pay a small fee, and they'd give you a placard to hang on your door identifying you as a client. If a fire did break out, the company would—in theory, anyway—come and douse the flames.

It was a libertarian wet dream and it was utterly disastrous. Sometimes, several fires broke out simultaneously. Small independent fire companies could respond to only one or two—they were constrained by their own limited personnel and equipment.

It wasn't profitable to maintain the capacity to deal with a rare occurrence like multiple fires breaking out at once; if a fire company did devote the resources necessary to have that capacity, it would then be at a competitive disadvantage. In our current system, if a massive fire breaks out, fire companies from across a municipality can respond, together, specifically *because* they're not in competition.

And although one can live just fine without consumer goods—nobody ever died for lack of an iPod—society as a whole suffers great damage from less-than-ideal fire control. While hiring, or not being able to hire, a fire brigade was a private matter that accorded nicely with the principles of the free market, it was also a transaction that came with what economists call negative "externalities": effects that a transaction between two parties can have on a third (more on that in chapter 10). In this case, those effects are fairly obvious: a fire that isn't properly extinguished can spread rapidly to neighboring homes, potentially resulting in a disastrous conflagration that could consume the whole neighborhood.

Fire-fighting—and the military—are two commonly used examples of what the market can't accomplish, but only because they're so clear-cut. Yet the same holds true for other goods and services as well, as we'll soon see.

Living in a Libertarian Fantasy Land

The fact that the private sector doesn't serve our public needs well hasn't prevented libertarians from twisting themselves up in all sorts of logical contortions to make the market's square peg fit into the round hole of public goods.

Michael Kinsley, writing in the *Los Angeles Times*, cited an elaborate argument that he'd encountered for privatizing America's highways and byways. "This is a classic libertarian fantasy," he wrote. "Government auctions off the land, private enterprise pays for construction and maintenance, tolls cover the cost, competing routes keep it all efficient." But what about when roads cross—who owns the intersections?

> Well, markets would recognize that it is more efficient for
> one company to own the intersections, but it would have an
> incentive to strike the right balance between customers on
> each highway. And stoplights? Ultimately, the author had
> worked his way up to a giant monopoly that would build, own
> and maintain all the roads and charge an annual fee to people
> who wanted to use them. None dare call it government.[2]

To understand how deeply disconnected this belief system is from any discernible reality in our modern economy, consider for a moment the basics of the free market model. In order for a transaction to work, both the buyer and the seller need to have a good grasp of what the product being sold is worth elsewhere and what others are buying and selling. In other words, they have to have more or less equal access to information. There can be no misrepresentation by either the buyer or the seller in a free market transaction. And both parties have to enter into the transaction freely, without being coerced; neither side can exercise power over the other, whether implicitly or explicitly, through threats or other means.

This pristine market may have existed on the village green back in the day—you could wander around and get a good sense of the lay of the land. Sellers would have a disincentive to peddle crappy wares or sell mutton and call it lamb because people would remember those slights in the future. In that mythical marketplace of yore, the price of a good or a service was based on what buyers were willing to pay, as long as it was more than the cost of production.

But take that model for a spin in our modern consumer culture, where we're bombarded with messages suggesting that we'll be sexier people if only we buy the right brand of toothpaste. Consider the utter impossibility of having "perfect knowledge" of the market in this globalized world—what is the price of tea in China?

If the only cable provider in your area is Comcast, as it is in mine, what competition keeps that company on its toes? What about "loss leaders": goods priced below their cost of production in order to get you into the store? And what does it all mean when China can sell goods here at a price just above the cost of production *in China*?

There's Nothing Free about the Free Market

Let's say, for the sake of argument, that a truly free market could, in fact, address most of society's needs (I say "most," because even hard-core libertarians appreciate the government seeing to national defense and administering a neutral judicial system). Common sense should tell you that in order for that creature to exist, corporate lobbyists, major campaign donors, and industry groups would have to value a theoretical construct of what a market should look like over their own bottom lines.

But nobody would argue that lobbyists spent a total of $3.3 billion dollars in 2008 to make sure that the U.S. economy adhered to a pristine free-market model.[3] The government intervenes in the market all the time—we pay some farmers to grow crops, others not to; we promote specific industries' products in international markets; the government sets up the rules under which corporations negotiate with their workers; governments sign trade agreements that determine which workers will face competition from overseas firms, and which will not; they routinely dole out tax breaks and low-interest loans and waive environmental and other standards to promote regional growth; and on and on and on.

There are few impediments to a company moving its manufacturing capacity to, say, Mexico to exploit cheaper labor and then importing its products right back to sell to U.S. consumers. But what about doctors, lawyers, and economists? They're protected from foreign competition not only by immigration restrictions, but also by onerous licensing and educational requirements that often require even accomplished professionals to go back to school.

According to Dean Baker, if "instead of putting downward pressure on the wages of our auto workers, we'd be putting downward pressure on the wages of our highest earners," it'd be "a great free-trade story." Baker estimated that simply bringing down the wage scale of U.S. doctors to the levels of their Western European counterparts would save the U.S. health-care system $80 billion every year.[4]

There's a reason we haven't heard this great free-trade story: as we'll see in chapter 15, these deals are negotiated with tons of input from corporate lobbyists and trade attorneys but very little advice from people who represent U.S. consumers and workers or the environment.

The Veil Lifts, Exposing the Hypocrisy of the "Free Marketeers"

If anyone truly believed that the U.S. economy bore even a vague resemblance to a free market, surely the multibillion-dollar bailouts that Wall Street has enjoyed since the collapse of the debt-backed securities market came as an eye-opener. According to market theory, businesses that are poorly run—that take stupid risks—should crash and burn, and their workers, equipment, and capital are supposed to end up being absorbed by more productive enterprises.

In the lead-up to the crash, the giants of Wall Street—having relentlessly pushed for deregulation of the finance sector—thought that they'd stumbled across a formula for making securities backed by very risky loans risk-free (more on this in chapter 4). With the housing market booming through 2007, they figured they had a cash cow—that they could sit back and collect endless fees for putting together these shady securities. They told mortgage lenders that they'd buy up any loan the lenders could generate. This led to the creation of things such as "liar loans": mortgages that didn't require borrowers to prove that they in fact earned $100,000 a year at their $35,000 jobs.

Then everything went south in the housing market, as it was clear to some people that it inevitably would (a "bubble," after all, is when asset values rise well beyond what the laws of supply and demand would dictate). Yet despite the fact that the banks had lauded the power of "free markets" to correct themselves when lobbying for deregulation for years, when their businesses were threatened they didn't dream of taking their lumps according to the model. They screamed that they were too big to fail and turned to the taxpayers for a lifeline.

Even if we accept the logic that these big institutions' sudden collapse would have sent the United States—and the world—into another Great Depression, there were still a number of ways that federal officials could have intervened. The most "free market" thing to do would have been to seize the insolvent banks, liquidate their bad holdings in an orderly manner, and then return them, smaller, leaner, and more focused on their core business—lending and holding deposits—to the private sector. This would have wiped out the investors who took a risk buying shares in the banks and the management that had driven the financial sector into the ground and also would have come at a considerably lower price to Dick and Jane Taxpayer.

That happened to a degree in the United Kingdom, where British taxpayers' cash earned them a controlling interest in the banks they bailed out. In the United States, however, the bailout—under the guidance of former Goldman Sachs CEO Henry Paulson—was designed to leave those who had invested in Wall Street's ailing financial giants unharmed. Paulson injected $10 billion into Goldman Sachs, twice as much as superinvestor Warren Buffett did, but the U.S. taxpayers got a quarter of the value that Buffett received in exchange. According to Simon Johnson, the former chief economist for the International Monetary Fund, Paulson's bailout deals gave taxpayers less potential for profit when the banks recovered than shareholders such as Goldman Sachs chief executive officer Lloyd Blankfein and Saudi Arabian prince Alwaleed bin Talal, the owner of 4 percent of Citigroup Inc. Johnson called the transactions "just egregious."[5]

How could such a thing happen, when both Democrats and Republicans supposedly embrace the free market? As the *Washington Post* reported, "An army of accountants, financial advisers, asset managers, lobbyists and others descend[ed] on Washington as part of the government's attempts to rescue the economy and bail out industries."[6] In the last quarter of 2008 and the first of 2009, the top twenty-one recipients of bailout funds spent a whopping $18 million lobbying Congress.[7] And according to a report by Public Citizen, "Lobbyists, political action committees (PACs) and trade associations tied to the banks receiving the most federal bailout money [had] scheduled 70 fundraisers for members of Congress" in the eight months following the 2008 elections.[8]

With the helpful "guidance" of an army of lobbyists from Big Finance, the government decided to prop up the ailing banks with a bailout, rather than liquidating them. So the taxpayers took a big chunk of the dubious mortgage-backed paper off the banks' hands. The feds bought some directly, and they put the U.S. government on the hook for much more by offering guarantees on some dubious securities. This was because without guarantees, the mortgage-backed paper on the banks' books was impossible to sell, and they couldn't lend money until they got at least a portion of it cleared.

So, who bought these shady assets, now backed in part by the full faith and credit of the United States of America? Investors, among whom were the very banks that we had to rescue because they were "too big to fail." According to Bloomberg News, "Of the seven biggest owners of residential mortgage-backed securities, only San Francisco–based Wells Fargo & Co. reduced holdings of the debt on its trading book."[9] The rest added more of the paper to their books. Why? Because they knew there would be people who would buy these securities as long as the taxpayers had a piece of the downside risk. "Anytime people know there's a buyer coming, they position for that, and that's clearly what happened here," Steven Kuhn, the comanager of the Nisswa Fixed Income Fund, told Bloomberg.[10]

Now here comes the fun part. The prices of those dubious securities could well tank again, leaving the banks exposed to losses despite the bailout. "It's a trade that will likely work out, but it's still a speculative trade, which is not what a taxpayer should want from firms that have only recently come out of critical care," said Joshua Rosner, a managing director at New York–based Graham Fisher & Co. So, if it works out, Wall Street stands to make a bundle. And if it doesn't . . . would the banks again be deemed too big to fail?

The bailouts were the most visible evidence that the biggest players have a firm grip on the "free market" in the United States. They represented the height of crony capitalism—of socializing risk while privatizing profits, a perverse reverse socialism that protected the most comfortable among us. And the ultimate punch line is that this was a program designed by people whom the *Washington Post*'s Peter Whoriskey called the "most ardent disciples of free-market principles."[11]

TROUBLETOWN

FANNING THE FLAMES OF CLASS WARFARE

BY LLOYD DANGLE

59

4

HOW COULD ANYONE BELIEVE THE BIG BANKS ARE VICTIMS?

Don't believe that the housing crisis was caused by poor people

It wasn't greed that caused the mortgage mess. In large part, the mess was the product of government policies designed to increase home ownership among the poor and ethnic minorities.

—John Carney, a corporate lawyer who "primarily represented banks, hedge funds and private equity firms"[1]

Perhaps the most pernicious right-wing lie of late is that the Wall Street hustlers who came close to bringing the global economy to its knees in 2008 were just innocent victims of government-sponsored programs that forced them to lower lending standards in a misguided effort to increase home ownership among the poor (read: dark-skinned).

It's an alluring story line for those who are ideologically predisposed to blame "inner city" people instead of MBAs in suits roaming the executive suite. It's also patent nonsense—a Big Lie that has nonetheless become an object of almost religious belief for some on the Right.

Jeb Hensarling, a notably obtuse Republican back-bencher from Texas, wrote that "the conservative case is simple":

> The [Community Reinvestment Act] compelled banks to relax their traditional underwriting practices in favor of more "flexible" criteria. These subjective standards were then applied to all borrowers, not just low-income individuals, leading to a surge in lower-quality loans. . . . Blame should [also be] directed at Fannie [Mae] and Freddie [Mac], and their thirst for weaker underwriting to help meet their federally mandated "affordable housing" goals. . . . This distortion has had seismic consequences as market participants, wrongly believing GSE-touched loans were sanctioned by the government and therefore safe, began to rely on a government mandate as a substitute for their own due diligence.[2]

This tale has everything a conservative could want—Big Government overreach, well-intentioned but out-of-touch liberals causing devastating unanticipated consequences with their social tinkering, and even their favorite bogeyman, ACORN, and other low-income housing advocates who have pushed for increased home ownership among the poor.

The narrative gained steam with an influential op-ed in the *Wall Street Journal* by Peter Wallison, a fellow with the American Enterprise Institute (who, according to his bio, "had a significant role in the development of the Reagan administration's proposals for the deregulation of the financial services industry").[3] Wallison found that "Almost two-thirds of all the bad mortgages in our financial system, many of which are now defaulting at unprecedented rates, were bought by government agencies or required by government regulations."

The data shows that the principal buyers were insured banks, government sponsored enterprises (GSEs) such as Fannie Mae and Freddie Mac, and the FHA—all government agencies or private companies forced to comply with government mandates about mortgage lending.[4]

The sleight-of-hand here is pretty straightforward. The U.S. government regulates lenders and provides deposit insurance to banks, which means that a large chunk of all home loans—good, bad, and in between—have some connection to a government program. It's like saying that the government is responsible for pollution because the EPA regulates industrial emissions.

Yet no bank has ever been "forced to comply with government mandates about mortgage lending." There *are no* "government mandates," and there never were. In order to qualify for government-backed deposit insurance—a benefit that banks aren't forced to accept but enjoy having—the Community Reinvestment Act and similar measures designed to prevent discrimination in lending (to *qualified* individuals) only *encourage* banks to lend in all of the areas where they do business. And Section 802 (b) of the act stresses that all loans must be "consistent with safe and sound operations"—it's the opposite of requiring that lenders write risky mortgages.[5]

There are no penalties for noncompliance with CRA guidelines. The only "stick" hanging over banks that fail to meet those standards is that their refusal *might* be taken into account by regulators when they want to open new branches or merge with other financial institutions. What's more, there are no defined standards for CRA compliance, and within the banking community, the loose guidelines are considered to be somewhat of a joke.

As Sheila Bair, the chairwoman of the FDIC, asked in a December 2008 speech, "Where in the CRA does it say: make loans to people who can't afford to repay? Nowhere! And the fact is, the lending practices that are causing problems today were driven by a desire for market share and revenue growth . . . pure and simple."[6]

Fannie and Freddie: Tempted by Easy Profits

Fannie Mae and Freddie Mac were created by an act of Congress, but they are (or were, until being taken over in the wake of the housing crash) private, for-profit entities whose dual mandate was to increase the availability of mortgages to moderate- and low-income families, and at the same time turn a profit for their shareholders. Fannie and Freddie did end up with a very large portfolio of subprime loans, with a high rate of default, but they didn't get into the market because the government mandated it. They dived in deep because there were profits to be made as the housing bubble expanded. As Mary Kane, a finance reporter for the *Washington Independent*, put it:

> Neither the Community Reinvestment Act—the law most cited as the culprit—nor other affordable housing goals set by the government forced Fannie, Freddie or any other lender to make loans they didn't want to. The lure of the subprime market was high yields and healthy profit margins—it's as simple as that.[7]

Contrary to the conservative spin, University of Michigan law professor Michael Barr told a congressional committee that although there was in fact quite a bit of irresponsible lending in low-income communities in the late 1990s and the early 2000s, "More than half of subprime loans were made by independent mortgage companies not subject to comprehensive federal supervision; another 30 percent of such originations were made by affiliates of banks or thrifts, which are not subject to routine examination or supervision, and the remaining 20 percent were made by banks and thrifts [subject to CRA standards]." Barr concluded, "The worst and most widespread abuses occurred in the institutions with *the least* federal oversight [italics added]."[8]

That's not to say that millions of Americans didn't bite off more than they would eventually be able to chew in the housing market. A lot of people looking to turn a quick buck by capturing the booming value of real estate in the mid- to late 2000s bought property with "teaser" loans that offered very low rates for the first few years; the investors assumed that they'd be able to turn a tidy profit before higher interest rates kicked in. Many of those individuals have since found themselves "under water"—owing more on their homes (and investment properties) than they're worth.

Yet it's worth noting that most of the *experts* also didn't identify the real estate bubble as a problem, even as home prices far surpassed values that could be reasonably explained by the laws of supply and demand. Irrational exuberance was the theme of the day. In 2006, David Learah, the former head of the National Association of Realtors, wrote a book titled *Why the Real Estate Boom Will Not Bust—And How You Can Profit from It: How to Build Wealth in Today's Expanding Real Estate Market*. The book made quite a splash at the time.

In 2010, former Fed chairman Alan Greenspan offered a bit of historical revisionism to a House committee investigating the causes of the financial crisis, telling lawmakers, "In 2002, I expressed concern . . . that our extraordinary housing boom, financed by very large increases in mortgage debt, cannot continue indefinitely. . . . I warned of the consequences of this situation in testimony before the Senate Banking Committee in 2004."

Writing in the *Washington Post*, Dana Milbank offered a corrective with some of the highlights of Greenspan's congressional testimony at the peak of the housing bubble. In 2005, Greenspan told lawmakers, "A bubble in home prices for the nation as a whole does not appear likely." He added, "Home price declines . . . were they to occur, likely would not have substantial macroeconomic implications," and explained that "nationwide banking and widespread securitization of mortgages make it less likely that financial intermediation would be impaired."

In English, that last bit meant "banks won't get into serious trouble even if things do go to hell," and we know how well that prediction turned out. If Greenspan could be so wrong and the smart people at the *Washington Post* and the *New York Times* couldn't see this huge, dangerously inflated housing bubble, how was your average couple trying to get a place to live or the small investor looking for a few bucks in rental income supposed to make a rational decision about how much debt to take on? That's not a defense of individuals who got in over their heads; it's simply an important bit of context.

The narrative that the real estate crash and the subsequent recession were the fault of borrowers, especially poor and middle-income borrowers—while members of the financial community were innocent victims—is not only revisionism of the worst kind, but it's an especially egregious lie.

The obvious sin of this claim is that it shifts responsibility for the mess away from those who created it. But what makes it even more disgraceful is that conservatives have long argued that efforts to increase home ownership among low-income families and communities of color was the "free market" thing to do (and, to some degree, that it negated the need for a decent social safety net). It was George W. Bush, not Vladimir Lenin, who said in a 2002 speech, "We have a problem here in America . . . a homeownership gap," and said, "we've got to work together to close [the gap] for the good of our country."[9] This was standard American Enterprise Institute–quality conservative fare.

Blaming individuals is easy, though—it's not hard to understand how people could borrow a bunch of cash they were later unable to pay back. The real cause of the housing crash is, of course, a far more complicated tale. Yet it's a story that ultimately represents the abject failure of conservative economic mythology, so it's important to understand.

How Wall Street Turned Home Mortgages into Economic WMDs

The bottom line: lenders used ludicrously lax standards to write loans to just about anybody, and people certainly got in over their heads. Yet as business reporter Andrew Leonard wrote, beginning in the 1990s, "The incentive for everyone to behave this way came from Wall Street . . . where the demand for [debt-backed securities] simply couldn't be satisfied. Wall Street was begging the mortgage industry to reach out to the riskiest borrowers it could find, because it thought it had figured out a way to make any level of risk palatable." He added, "Wall Street traders, hungry for more risk, fixed the real economy to deliver more risk, by essentially bribing the mortgage originators and ratings agencies to . . . make bad loans on purpose. That supplied [Wall Street] speculators the raw material they needed for their bets, but as a consequence threw the integrity of the whole housing sector into question."[10]

Although the U.S. housing market is worth somewhere in the neighborhood of $10 trillion, it was Wall Street's wheeler-dealers—with lobbyists and congressional allies keeping regulators out of their business—who built a house of cards out of "exotic" mortgage-backed products and other "derivatives" worth as much as sixty times that figure. It was paper wealth backed by little more than the irrational belief that what goes up will never come down.[11] These instruments, which Warren Buffett called "the real Weapons of Mass Destruction," were estimated to be "worth" roughly twelve times the output of the entire *global* economy.[12]

This is how a drop in the U.S. housing market could precipitate such widespread economic pain worldwide. It wasn't silly borrowers who were to blame—if not for the huge overhang of "toxic" securities Wall Street had created, even a ridiculously high rate of default in this country's subprime mortgage market wouldn't have stunned the entire global economy.

So, just what is a derivative? It's a piece of paper that can be bought and sold for real money but isn't attached to a real asset. Its value is simply derived from something tangible—hence the name. We often hear about the "real" nuts-and-bolts economy, and derivatives are in essence the exact opposite: they represent an unreal economy, created by financiers in New York and London, and it was this shadow economy that would bring the real one to the brink of collapse in 2008.

There are all sorts of derivatives. They are essentially bets—you can bet that a market will go up or down or that a particular company will do well or poorly. You can bet on interest rates or the value of a country's currency going up or down, or you can make more exotic bets on just about anything in the world—even what the weather will be like at some point in the future.

Yet the Great Recession was caused by debt-backed securities tied, at some point, to the U.S. housing market. When you buy a home, that's an asset. Presuming that you make your monthly payments, the mortgage held by the bank is an asset as well. But if your house loses 30 percent of its value and you stop making the payments, then your loan becomes a liability. When a number of mortgages are cut up and bundled together and then sold off in pools to investors, that's a security. Its value is based on future loan payments from homeowners like you.

Now, a derivative is a financial instrument that allows investors to essentially bet on whether the mortgages that are bundled up in some asset-backed security do in fact get repaid. The investors don't own the original mortgages, and they don't own the mortgage-backed security created from those loans. Writing in *Salon*, Andrew Leonard offered a useful metaphor. He suggested that we think of the real economy as a football game, with real flesh-and-blood players running around on a real field, hitting one another and moving a real ball toward a real goal post. All of those guys, the field, the equipment—they're tangible, just as your house is tangible.

There are some people who have a direct stake in the game— such as the teams' owners and the players, their families, agents, and so on. But there are also millions of people who might bet on the outcome of the game but are in no way directly involved in the play. It's these bets that parallel the trillions of dollars in debt-based derivatives that became so "toxic." They were making some people rich when the housing market was flying, but when the market tanked, they turned out to be bad bets, and the amount of money at stake was enormous—far, far larger than the entire value of the U S. housing market.

The financial industry first started to churn out derivatives in the early 1980s. Investors mostly gambled that interest or currency exchange rates would go up or down. Then during the 1990s, when interest rates were low around the world, the demand for more exotic "structured" investments (which are largely unregulated)—including various derivatives and swaps based on debt—skyrocketed.

By the beginning of the 2000s, the investment bankers were pushing those debt-backed derivatives hard to investors who were looking for big returns on their dollars—much better than they could get from putting their money in old-school investments like stocks and bonds. The bankers' hard sell created so much demand that lenders wrote loans to just about anybody for just about anything; loans, after all, were the raw material for the alphabet soup of exotic investment vehicles: the "collateralized debt obligations (CDOs)," "credit default swaps," and other innovative products that turned "toxic" toward the end of the decade. Wall Street had little to lose by giving investors more of these fancy new bets; Wall Street traders made their fees, and as long as the housing market—the hard assets underpinning all of the theoretical wealth that was created—held up, everyone was happy.

Even today, the banking industry warns of the need for "creativity" in devising new financial products. The seed of the Great Recession was a bunch of bankers figuring out a novel way to take a pile of iffy loans and effectively launder them of risk, at least so it would seem. They did it by slicing those mortgage-based derivatives up into different classes, with what they call the more "senior" slices getting paid first if there was a profit, and the more "junior" classes of securities lining up behind them to get paid in order afterward.

Theoretically, the senior slices are therefore much more secure: if the market were to go down, but not by too much, they'd get paid first and the more junior classes would be left holding the bag. But the reality—and here's where we would have been well served by some good old-fashioned common sense—is that they were still dealing with pools of *very risky* loans. The bankers, however, were thrilled to create new sources of revenues and got the ratings agencies to give the senior slices AAA ratings, declaring them the safest kinds of investments. And this is key: municipalities, pension funds, and many other institutions are prohibited from stashing their money in *anything but* the highest-rated investments. Many dived in, only to get burned when the whole thing came apart.

The most important point here is that the bankers *knew they were playing with fire*. The *Los Angeles Times* reported, "Before Washington Mutual collapsed in the largest bank failure in U.S. history, its executives knowingly created a 'mortgage time bomb' by making subprime loans they knew were likely to go bad and then packaging them into risky securities."[13] According to the *Wall Street Journal*, U.S. prosecutors are, as of this writing, "investigating whether Morgan Stanley misled investors about mortgage-derivatives deals it helped design and sometimes bet against."[14] And the Securities and Exchange Commission charged Goldman Sachs with "defrauding investors by misstating and omitting key facts about a financial product tied to subprime mortgages as the U.S. housing market was beginning to falter."[15]

They needed some help laundering the risk out of those shaky loans, and they got it. A Senate panel investigating the roots of the crash "unveiled evidence that credit-ratings agencies knowingly gave inflated ratings to complex deals backed by shaky U.S. mortgages in exchange for lucrative fees."[16]

Wall Street Rules

Nobel Laureate Joseph Stiglitz neatly summed up the environment in which this took place:

> The mortgage brokers loved these new products because they ensured an endless stream of fees. They maximized

their profits by originating as many mortgages as possible, with frequent refinancing. Their allies in investment banking bought them, sliced and diced the risk and then passed them on—or at least as much as they could. Our bankers forgot that their job was to prudently manage risk and allocate capital. They became gambling casinos—gambling with other people's money, knowing that the taxpayer would step in if the losses were too great.[17]

They wouldn't have been able to do it without reckless deregulation for deregulation's sake—a bipartisan affair fueled by the right-wing noise machine. Greed and the herd mentality are constants, after all; without regulations that protect the public interest, they can only lead to disaster.

As financial reporter Gillian Tett detailed in the *Financial Times*, a crucial moment in the development of the crisis occurred back in the mid-1990s, when JP Morgan was struggling to deal with the huge number of loans on its books and needed large reserves of cash in case those loans went bad. It was at that moment when two groups of young JPM hotshots—one that was creating those exotic new investments and another that was knee-deep in "subprime" loans—started to talk to each other and realized that they could launder the risk out of sketchy home loans by securitizing them.[18]

This discussion, which would lead to so much economic pain for millions of people around the world, could not have come to fruition without the demise of the Glass-Steagall Act in 1999. It forced firms to choose between writing loans and investment banking, but it was done in by a massive lobbying effort by investment bankers after the tech bubble had collapsed in 2000.

In the early 1990s, betting on interest rates was all the rage among higher-risk investors. But, as Tett noted, in the middle of the decade, "The interest rate climate suddenly changed, unleashing wild market turbulence and causing many of the derivatives contracts to produce huge losses—or 'blow up,' as traders call it."

In the aftermath, these exotic investment products had a bad name, and there were widespread calls to regulate them.

But the International Swaps and Derivatives Association fought back furiously, arguing that a regulatory clampdown would not only run counter to the spirit of capital markets, but also crush creativity. Their aggressive lobbying campaign was effective: By the mid-1990s, regulatory pressure had died away.[19]

Then, as the new century dawned, with little public debate, a group of lawmakers—Republicans and "blue-dog" Democrats— led by John McCain's future chief economic adviser, Phil Gramm (who would gain some infamy by saying that the Great Recession was overblown and America had become a "nation of whiners), pushed through the "Commodity Futures Modernization Act of 2000," which put the final nail in the regulatory coffin. The legislation provided us with what became known as the "Enron Loophole"— which exempted most energy trading from oversight—and it also assured Wall Street's whiz kids that their new products would be free of pesky regulation. The popularity of those investments soon exploded.

Part of the reason for their popularity was that because they were unregulated, they could be highly leveraged. "Leveraging," using a limited amount of cash to buy a much larger position in an invest- ment, is a common investment tool. Yet there are rules in effect in regulated markets—in the major stock and bond markets—that limit the amount that an investor can leverage. For example, the SEC says you have to put up at least 50 percent of the cost to buy a stock on American stock exchanges. These fancy debt-backed investments, however, were contracts between two gamblers and therefore not subject to the rules.

We also have to give a nod to the influence of the large hedge funds, which have grown like kudzu in recent years (in 1999, it was estimated that hedge funds held about $450 billion in assets; by

2008, the total amount invested in hedge funds was estimated to have been as much as *$4 trillion*).[20]

A hedge fund is like a mutual fund that allows rich investors to cover their bets by putting a little wager on the other team. But unlike a mutual fund, which has to follow a whole slew of regulations, hedge funds, because they're open only to an elite club of "qualified investors"—people with $5 million or more in investments—are almost totally unregulated, the assumption being that these big shots are savvy enough to watch out for themselves and don't need much oversight. They're free to play fast and loose with the market, buying into speculative, risky investments that have the potential to turn a high yield, and they can be (and generally are) highly leveraged. There are few institutions that are less transparent than hedge funds, which rely on keeping their activities under wraps to avoid getting beaten by their competitors.

With all of this in mind, let's look again at the chain of events that began with some shaky mortgages and progressed to a financial meltdown. First, the financiers took those loans and made them into mortgage-backed securities. Then they sliced the securities up into derivatives—collateralized debt obligations—which got sold off and repackaged again and again. During that process, investors' cash got leveraged further and further, to the point at which the whole thing was based on little more than vapor—paper wealth that could, and did, disappear in a flash with a market downturn.

NYU economist Nouriel Roubini, known as "Doctor Doom" for accurately predicting the crash, described it like this:

> Today any wealthy individual can take $1 million and go to a prime broker and leverage this amount three times; then the resulting $4 million ($1 equity and $3 debt) can be invested in a fund or funds that will in turn leverage these $4 million three or four times and invest them in a hedge fund; then the hedge fund will take these funds and leverage them three or four times and buy some very junior tranche of a CDO that is itself leveraged nine or ten times. At the end of this credit

chain, the initial $1 million of equity becomes a $100 million investment out of which $99 million is debt (leverage) and only $1 million is equity. So we got an overall leverage ratio of 100 to 1. Then, even a small 1% fall in the price of the final investment (CDO) wipes out the initial capital and creates a chain of margin calls that unravel this debt house of cards.[21]

The lack of transparency in this "speculative economy" is such that nobody knew precisely who was holding onto what securities and derivatives, and the complexity of the investments meant that they were almost impossible to accurately value in the real world. That uncertain combination resulted in a kind of panic among the investor class, with everyone fearful that all of these exotic bets might be called in. That in turn made it tough for the banks to raise cash and led to hoarding of whatever reserves they had—the "lending freeze." That, in turn, added to problems on "Main Street," with businesses large and small unable to get their hands on the money they needed to weather the turbulent economic seas and, in some cases, to stay afloat.

This is hardly an academic discussion of where to lay the blame for the financial crisis, because there is one thing that's as sure as death and taxes: Big Finance's lobbyists will continue to resist calls to re-regulate the financial sector. And absent effective regulation of the financial markets, we can expect to continue to suffer through an endless series of booms and busts, while the fat cats of Wall Street just continue to get fatter.

Were the Titans of Finance Really Too Big to Fail?

As they sifted through the wreckage of our economy following the financial crash of 2008, regulators and lawmakers were faced with a conundrum. Would they let the big banks that had gone out on a limb with those newfangled debt-backed securities take a beating, as the "logic" of the free market would dictate?

The received wisdom was that the really big financial services firms couldn't be allowed to simply crash and burn, no matter how appropriate that outcome might have been. They were "too big to fail"; we were told that their demise would halt the flow of capital throughout the economy, depriving it of its lifeblood. Panic was running through the capital markets, and the "credit crunch" could only be alleviated with a massive government bailout—hundreds of billions to "recapitalize" the banks and restore liquidity to the system.

That was a highly debatable proposition. Economists at the Federal Reserve Bank of Minnesota crunched some numbers and found that lending between banks at the time had been "healthy" and "bank credit [had] not declined during the financial crisis." The Minnesota Fed's economists saw "no evidence that the financial crisis has affected lending to non-financial businesses." The researchers called on lawmakers to "articulate the precise nature of the market failure they see, [and] to present hard evidence that differentiates their view of the data from other views."[1]

The Minnesota Fed's conclusions were backed up by a study of Treasury Department data by Celent Financial Services, a consulting firm. According to Reuters, Celent's researchers concluded that the "data actually suggest world credit markets are functioning remarkably well." Rather than a widespread banking problem, Celent found that the rot was limited to "a few big, vocal banks and industries such as car manufacturing, which would be in difficulty anyway."[2]

There was no question that banks had been writing far fewer loans and money wasn't flowing, but some economists pointed out that Americans had lost millions of jobs, several million homes, and trillions of dollars in stock market wealth, and as a result fewer people were looking to finance new big-ticket purchases. And businesses, seeing their customers tighten their belts, weren't terribly eager to borrow money to expand. In other words, Washington was focused on Wall Street as if its problems were disconnected from the immense pain being experienced in the brick-and-mortar economy.

Others, however, noted that the financial services sector— banking and insurance—employed more than 6 million people. Not all were rich traders; there were secretaries and janitors, too. In late 2008, Citigroup announced it would lay off 53,000 employees, the second-largest workforce cut by a single company in U.S. history.[3] That brought the number of people who lost finance jobs to 180,000 that year, and those people would spend less and pay fewer taxes, and many would have trouble paying their own mortgages. The sector's unemployment rate rose from 3.9 percent to 4.6 percent in just four months in late 2008.[4] Could Washington really let the financial services industry decline even further in the midst of a recession?

While this debate about "too big to fail" played out, a very relevant point was lost in the furor: there was scant discussion of the fact that our financial sector had become bloated during the previous decade and was swimming in capacity the rest of the economy didn't need.

Here's a fun fact about the finance industry. Historically, it grew and contracted with the business cycle. When the economy was going gangbusters and businesses were expanding, it was there to provide capital and insurance and connect investors with entrepreneurs and innovators. Then, when the business cycle took an inevitable downturn, it would contract. Financial firms would stop hiring. The number of bankers and insurers would shrink.

But a funny thing happened on the way to the financial meltdown. As the Associated Press noted, "When the Internet bubble burst in 2000, the [financial] sector never stopped growing. Instead, it ballooned over the past eight years to around 10 percent of the U.S. economy, puzzling economists."[5] It's not such a puzzle, though. In large part, the continued growth of the sector was based on the explosion in derivatives—high-value vapor, as we saw in chapter 4—rather than on anything connected to real growth in the "nuts and bolts" economy.

When the recession of 2001 began, the financial services sector employed 5.7 million people. At the time, the total value of derivatives held by U.S. commercial banks was thought to be around $42 trillion.[6] By the third quarter of 2007—before the crash—the financial sector was employing almost 6.2 million people, and the estimated value of derivatives held by U.S. banks had skyrocketed to almost $170 trillion—almost three times the value of the entire world's economy.[7] During the intervening period, the "real" U.S. economy was in the doldrums: from 2000 to 2007, the economy added jobs at the lowest rate in the post–World War II era.[8]

"The financial sector," wrote Dean Baker, "has nearly quadrupled as a share of the private sector, yet it provides no obvious benefit that was not available 30 years ago":

> Finance is an intermediate good; like trucking, it provides no direct benefit in itself. Rather, its benefit is in its support for the productive economy. If we had four times as many employed in trucking (relative to the size of the economy) as we did 30 years ago, people would be very concerned about our grossly inefficient trucking sector.[9]

It was this incredibly bloated sector of the economy providing "an intermediate good" that we had to rescue—keep that in mind.

When the Financial Tail Wags the Corporate Dog

The financial sector's size isn't the only issue to consider. Its influence on the behavior of the rest of our corporate culture is something that we take for granted, but maybe we shouldn't.

Consider for a moment how often you've heard that "the markets" are happy—or unhappy—about something that is occurring? You know, "The markets reacted with enthusiasm to an announcement by the Fed today . . ." Not enough people ask the very logical question "Just who are these markets and why the hell should I care if they're enthused?"

"Markets," in this sense, means how owners of stocks and bonds feel about their prospects of making a nice return on their investments down the road. And because we're talking about owners of stocks and bonds, we're talking about America's economic elite. According to economist Edward Wolff, those in the top 1 percent of the population controlled almost half of our financial wealth in 2007 (excluding tangible assets like homes, boats, and cars). The top 5 percent owned 72 percent; the top 10 percent of the distribution were holding onto 83 percent of the nation's financial wealth, and so on. The bottom 80 percent—eight out of ten Americans—owned just 7 percent of the nation's financial wealth.[10]

In America's executive suites, "the markets" are all-powerful, but it wasn't always so. The modern system of finance developed during the progressive era—from the late 1890s through the 1920s—and its creation was heavily influenced by prevailing anger at the power of huge private trusts. Dispersed ownership and new forms of finance—through stocks, corporate bonds, and other securities— were seen as an antidote to the influence of the robber barons, that handful of dynastic families who controlled large swaths of the U.S. economy.

Since then, the original function of the financial markets—to link investors' capital with innovative firms—has been turned on its head. Today, says Lawrence Mitchell, a professor of business law at George Washington University, corporate behavior is very much dictated by the financial markets—quarterly earnings, stock prices, and the like—and not the other way around. That's not a good thing.

In his book *The Speculation Economy*, Mitchell cited a recent survey of CEOs who run major U.S. corporations. It found that almost 80 percent of them would have "at least moderately mutilated their businesses in order to meet [financial] analysts' quarterly profit estimates."

> Cutting the budgets for research and development, advertising and maintenance and delaying hiring and new projects are some of the long-term harms they would readily inflict on their corporations. Why? Because in modern American corporate capitalism, the failure to meet quarterly numbers almost always guarantees a punishing hit to the corporation's stock price.[11]

And corporate managers' own fortunes are tied to their companies' share prices through bonuses, stock options, and other incentives. The desire to make the financial sector happy often dwarfs other imperatives; Mitchell calls it "short-termism" and suggests that making a company's balance sheet look good, quarter to quarter, also drives CEOs to sacrifice values such as worker safety, environmental protection, and other social goods.

This dynamic, too, was completely absent from the debate over whether the Titans of Wall Street were really "too big to fail."

TAX CUTS AREN'T A SOLUTION TO EVERY PROBLEM

Don't believe the conservatives' magic bullet for economic woes

> There are two ways you can put money into the economy, by spending more or by taxing less. But if it's stimulus you want, taxing less works best. That's why permanent tax cuts should be the centerpiece of the economic stimulus.
>
> —*Likely 2012 presidential candidate Mitt Romney, during the debate over Obama's stimulus package*

It's difficult to know where to start deconstructing conservative rhetoric on taxing and spending. This is such a central part of their worldview, and it's informed by a whole slew of falsehoods.

In order to make sense of it all, it's necessary to understand four key concepts behind the Right's rhetoric. First, they say they have a laserlike focus on "small" government and lower taxes as goals unto themselves, but when they're in power, government always seems to get bigger. Second, when they decry government "spending," they're really talking about the government spending money for things they don't like. Third, they make it seem like the poor don't pay taxes, and therefore only businesses and those at the top need "relief." And, finally, they still make the classic "voodoo economics" argument: giving tax cuts to the wealthy can only lead to Limousine Lifestyles for everyone!

1. Shrink the Government and Drown It in a Bathtub

Conservatives believe in small government as an ideological end unto itself. They believed Reagan when he said, "Government is the problem," and they think that shrinking that problem down so that it becomes small enough, in the words of antitax activist Grover Norquist, to "drown in a bathtub," is a virtue.

They naturally tend to assume that their political opponents must take the opposite view: that liberals want to expand government and raise taxes because they prefer bigger government and higher taxes. That's a serious distortion; progressives see policy goals and aren't afraid of pursuing solutions to problems through government, the private sector, or a combination of the two. When a real problem can't be addressed by the private sector—poor kids lacking health insurance is a perfect example—then we look to the public sector for the answer.

And then we pay for it, rejecting the reckless "borrow-and-spend" approach that George W. Bush used to turn a tidy budget surplus left by Bill Clinton into a deep sea of red ink. The bottom line is that progressives and liberals couldn't care less about how big or small the government may be in the abstract, only whether it functions well and solves the problems we ask it to address.

2. Conservatives' Favorite Programs Don't Count as Wasteful Spending

Despite conservatives' ideological devotion to limited government, make no mistake that when they say "government," they are talking about limiting corporate regulation and reducing the amount of money spent on the relatively meager social safety net that takes the hard edges off America's brand of unbridled "turbo-capitalism." In practice, almost everybody, from across the political spectrum, is happy to spend money and expand government in pursuit of his or her own objectives. Spending projects are wasteful "pork" only when they're in another lawmaker's district. Republicans rarely object to spending tax dollars on the military, our intelligence agencies, law enforcement, or border security, to name a few. To state the obvious: these things cost money, too—a lot of it.

3. The Poor Don't Pay Taxes

Contrary to the right-wing narrative, everyone pays taxes. Conservatives insist that the tax system is highly progressive and that anyone who suggests otherwise is just whining. Rush Limbaugh put it this way: "The bottom 50 percent is paying a tiny bit of the taxes, so you can't give them much of a tax cut by definition. Yet these are the people to whom the Democrats claim to want to give tax cuts. Remember this the next time you hear the 'tax cuts for the rich' business. Understand that the so-called rich are about the only ones paying taxes anymore."[1]

That's true, however, only when you do a little sleight of hand. You have to look at the federal income tax in isolation and then pretend that it represents the government's entire take. It's true that the bottom 40 percent of U.S. households don't pay much in *federal income taxes*. And, according to a Congressional Budget Office (CBO) analysis, the wealthiest 1 percent do pay more in federal income taxes than the bottom 90 percent combined.[2]

Yet that's a far cry from the claim that the "poor don't pay taxes." Rushbo won't tell you, but the CBO also said that if you look at state and local taxes, the top 1 percent of Americans paid 5 percent of their incomes, while the bottom 50 percent (many of them among those who paid no federal income taxes) shelled out 10 percent, twice as much proportionately.[3] In addition, the CBO found that the bottom 80 percent of the pile paid around 9 percent of their incomes in Social Security taxes, while the top 1 percent paid only 1.6 percent of theirs.[4] After the income tax, Social Security taxes represent the largest share of the federal take.

A 2009 study by the nonpartisan Institute on Taxation and Economic Policy looked at state taxes (including sales taxes) and concluded, "Nearly every state and local tax system takes a much greater share of income from middle- and low-income families than from the wealthy. That is, when all state and local income, sales, excise and property taxes are added up, most state tax systems *are regressive* [emphasis theirs]."[5] The top 1 percent of earners paid around 5 percent of their incomes in state and local taxes, while the poorest fifth of the population paid almost 11 percent of theirs.[6]

When the institute looked at excise taxes—on gas, cigarettes, alcohol, and other goodies—they found that the "average state's consumption tax structure is equivalent to an income tax with a 7.1 percent rate for the poor, a 4.7 percent rate for the middle class, and a 0.9 percent rate for the wealthiest taxpayers."[7]

When you add it all up—state and local taxes, federal taxes, and excise fees—it turns out that the rich, the poor, and those in between all end up with about the same tax rate. That's the conclusion of a 2007 study by Boston University economists Laurence J. Kotlikoff and David Rapson. They summarized, "The average marginal tax rate on incomes between $20,000 and $500,000 is 40.3%, the median tax rate is 41.8%, and the standard deviation of all of those rates is 5.3 percentage points. Basically, most of us pay about 40%, plus or minus 5.3 percentage points."[8]

That brings us to an important point: It wasn't always that way. According to a 2010 study by Wealth for the Common Good, an organization of deep-pocketed progressives, "Over the last half-century, America's wealthiest taxpayers have seen their tax outlays, as a share of income, drop by as much as two-thirds. During the same period, the tax outlay for middle-class Americans has not decreased." The study found that the nation's "highest earners— the top 400—have seen the share of their income paid in federal income tax plummet from 51.2 percent in 1955 to 16.6 percent in 2007, the most recent year with top 400 statistics available." Between 2001 and 2008 alone, tax cuts for the wealthy cost the U.S. Treasury $700 billion.[9]

4. Tax Cuts for the Rich Will Also Help the Rest of Us

Republicans use the lie that the poor don't pay taxes to justify big cuts for the wealthy. The bad news is that those cuts *raise* taxes for everyone else. You won't read that in the legislation, but it's the real-world result of cutting taxes without taking on the politically unpopular task of identifying services to be cut.

Even when revenues drop, people expect the cops to come when called and the streetlights to burn. Budgets become stretched, and communities tighten their belts—perhaps laying off some workers. But then—and this is key—state and local governments also *make up much of the shortfall* with higher fees for various services, higher tuition at public colleges, and increases in sales, excise, and property taxes, all of which fall disproportionately on the poor and the middle class.

Most government spending is locked in—for Social Security and Medicare, the defense budget, and a host of other programs that would be politically unpopular to cut. The Right has done an excellent job of pushing the notion that they're for tax cuts, but remember that they are talking about corporate taxes, capital gains taxes on investments, and taxes for the top earners. When those revenues dry up, the rest of us have to pick up the tab.

So keep in mind that the Right actually loves to raise taxes, just as long as they're hiked on the backs of ordinary working people. Barack Obama's first budget made the Bush tax cuts permanent for every couple making less than $250,000 and every individual taking in less than $200,000, while allowing those cuts targeted at the richest Americans to expire. This effectively cut the tax bills of about 98 *percent of the population*. The response from House Minority Leader John Boehner, a long-time advocate of tax cuts? "The era of big government is back, and Democrats are asking you to pay for it," he told the *Washington Post*.[10]

Government Is Always Big, Whether Republican or Democratic, but Who Foots the Bill?

On the GOP's Web site, a common refrain from the Right:

> America's producers can compete successfully in the inter-
> national arena—as long as they have a level playing field.
> Today's tax code is tilted against them, with one of the highest
> corporate tax rates of all developed countries. That not only
> hurts American investors, managers, and the U.S. balance of
> trade; it also sends American jobs overseas.[11]

In the real world, however, looking at the *total* U.S. tax burden, we're in great shape compared to our competitors. Out of the thirty countries that belong to the Organisation for Economic Co-operation and Development (OECD)—sometimes called the "rich countries' club"—the United States comes in fourth from the bottom.[12] And although we have relatively high corporate income taxes, the over-all rate that "America's producers" pay—corporate taxes combined with taxes on capital gains—ranks twentieth out of the thirty OECD countries.[13]

As we'll see in the next chapter, the share of the economy represented by government spending (at the local, state, and federal levels combined) has also been remarkably consistent during the last forty years or so, regardless of which party controlled the White House or Congress. In the two years that Gerald Ford presented budgets, government spending as a share of the gross domestic product averaged 31.4 percent; in ultraliberal Jimmy Carter's four years, it dropped to 30.7 percent; Ronald Reagan, the patron saint of fiscal conservatism, came into office, and it rose to 32.2 percent. It nudged slightly higher during the first George Bush's term in office, then dropped to an almost Nixonian 30.3 percent during the

Clinton years, before rising to 31.6 percent during the second Bush administration (that's the average of his first seven budgets—as of this writing, the data only go up to 2008).[14]

Looking at the other side of the ledger, overall government *revenues* have also remained relatively stable, but the pattern is reversed. The government's take, as a share of GDP, dropped during the Ford era, rose again under Carter, and fell again under Reagan. Revenues rose by almost 2 percent under Clinton and fell by a percent and a half under George W. Bush. (The only exception: government revenues rose from 27.3 percent of GDP during the Reagan years to 27.6 percent under George Herbert Walker Bush.)[15]

So, as we'll see in chapter 6, although the government taxes and spends at fairly similar rates, under Republican leadership the nation shells out *a bit more* for government services and takes in just *a bit less* in taxes. With a $15 trillion economy, those little differences add up to pretty big deficits, and this, rather than hot school lunches for poor kids, is responsible for a large chunk of our federal debt. Yet conservatives have managed to convince the mainstream media and much of the country that they're the fiscally responsible ones who are always ready to step in and clean up the nation's budgetary mess.

Abusing the Laffer Curve

If you can get a lot of people to repeat the same specious claim often enough, it effectively becomes "true." Here's an example. The Right can't admit that their tax cuts will bust the budget and still claim to be good fiscal stewards. So, instead, they try to dazzle us with magical thinking: cutting taxes, they say, actually brings more money into the government's coffers! See, they don't want to slash and burn popular government programs—their tax cuts will raise more cash to fund 'em!

In 2007, *Time* magazine's Justin Fox sampled some Republican opinions on this interesting dynamic and concluded, "If there's one thing that Republican politicians agree on, it's that slashing taxes brings the government more money."

> "You cut taxes, and the tax revenues increase," President Bush said in a speech last year. Keeping taxes low, Vice President Dick Cheney explained in a recent interview, "does produce more revenue for the Federal Government." Presidential candidate John McCain declared in March that "tax cuts . . . as we all know, increase revenues." His rival Rudy Giuliani couldn't agree more. "I know that reducing taxes produces more revenues," he intones in a new TV ad.[16]

The spin is premised on an egregious distortion of "Laffer's curve," the conservative media's favorite economic theorem. The idea, first scribbled on a cocktail napkin by economist George Laffer (at least, according to lore), is pretty simple. It holds that you can raise income taxes to a degree, but when the top tax rate exceeds a certain point, people will go to such extraordinary lengths to avoid paying the piper that the government will actually end up collecting less revenue.

The thing about Laffer's curve is that it makes perfect sense in theory, but it completely defies reason in practice, at least in the context of modern America. Most economists agree with Laffer's argument that there is a point of revenue "maximization," after which hiking rates will lead to fewer tax dollars coming in. If you were to tax income at a rate of 100 percent, it wouldn't make much sense for anyone to go to work—at least not on the books.

The hot air hisses out of the balloon when politicians and pundits use the theory to advocate tax cuts in the United States, which is among the more lightly taxed countries in the developed world. The fallacy is simple: top personal and business tax rates have decreased for years, and there's no evidence whatsoever to suggest that we're anywhere *close* to being above Laffer's curve today. And if you're below the curve when you cut taxes, you're not going to generate that surge of new income.

For his *Time* article, Justin Fox followed up with a survey of what people who understand basic math were saying about this bit of conservative spin:

> If there's one thing that economists agree on, it's that these claims are false. We're not talking just ivory-tower lefties. Virtually every economics Ph.D. who has worked in a prominent role in the Bush Administration acknowledges that the tax cuts enacted during the past six years have not paid for themselves—and were never intended to. Harvard professor Greg Mankiw, chairman of Bush's Council of Economic Advisers from 2003 to 2005, even devotes a section of his best-selling economics textbook to debunking the claim that tax cuts increase revenues.

Andrew Samwick, now at Dartmouth, was the chief economist on Bush's Council of Economic Advisers during that period. But in 2007, after Bush had claimed yet again that it's "a fact that our tax cuts have fueled robust economic growth and record revenues," Samwick responded with a plea to the Bush administration to stop making that claim. In an opinion column in the *Wall Street Journal*, he wrote, "You are smart people. . . . You know that the tax cuts have not fueled record revenues. You know what it takes to establish causality. You know that the first order effect of cutting taxes is to lower tax revenues."[17]

Yet pointing out that simple truth is anathema in conservative circles. In 2007, Megan McCardle, then an up-and-coming libertarian writer with the *Atlantic Monthly*, wrote about the editorial higher-ups of an unnamed "conservative publication" spiking a book review she'd written because she hadn't toed the party line. "Even while otherwise expressing my vast displeasure with the (liberal) economic notions of the book I was reviewing," she wrote, the editors killed the piece "because I said that the Laffer Curve didn't apply at American levels of taxation." She added, "This isn't me looking for an alternative explanation for the spiking of a bad review: the literary editor accepted it, edited it, and then three hours later told me it couldn't be published because it violated their editorial line on taxation."[18]

The Reality: Undertaxation

Nobel Prize–winning economist Paul Krugman argues that the success of the Right's crusade against taxes has resulted in "a fundamental mismatch between the benefits Americans expect to receive from the government and the revenues government collects."[19]

New York Times reporter David Leonhardt looked at the consequences of that disconnect. He noted that during the postwar years, the United States had adhered to "Wagner's Law," which holds that as countries become wealthier, their citizens demand more government services, and tax rates tend to rise. "Over the last couple of decades," Leonhardt wrote, "we have repealed Wagner's Law—or, more to the point, only partly repealed it. Taxes are no longer rising. They fell to 18 percent of G.D.P. in 2008 and, because of the recession, to a 60-year low of 15.1 percent last year. Yet our desire for government services just keeps growing."[20]

We are, as a result, now *undertaxed*, given what we expect the government to do. According to the Congressional Budget Office, federal tax revenues as a share of the economy have hit their lowest point in sixty years.[21] In 2009, the federal government took in the equivalent of 15 percent of the GDP, while spending 26 percent! Much of that was driven by the economic crisis, but the CBO estimates that even after the recession, the gap will still be significant.[22] By 2020, the federal government's spending is projected to equal 26 percent of the GDP, while taxes are on pace to equal only 19 percent.

Closer to home, the economic crisis, which eviscerated state and local budgets, is giving us a pretty clear vision of what conservatives' limited-government, low-tax utopia really looks like when put into practice. Consider just a few anecdotes.

Joining Arizona in eliminating health insurance for the poor was Tennessee, which cut 100,000 people from its Medicaid rolls, including 8,000 children. One of those people was Jessica Pipkin, who lost the use of her arms and legs in a car accident in 2005. Pipkin requires round-the-clock care—at $37 per hour—but was told that she would lose her benefits because she and her husband earn too much to qualify. Are they rich? Well, her husband makes $19,000 as a satellite television repairman, and Pipkin receives another $14,000 in Social Security benefits.[23]

In Minnesota, Governor Tim Pawlenty, a possible contender for the 2012 Republican presidential nomination, submitted a budget that slashed funds from student aid, financial assistance to counties and municipalities, a job program for the blind and the mentally ill, low-income housing programs, mass transit in the Twin Cities, and a state program that helps insure people with costly preexisting medical conditions. It was approved by a Democrat-controlled legislature; lawmakers justified their budget by pointing out that they'd rejected Pawlenty's proposals for deeper, more painful cuts.[24]

Clayton County, Georgia, a mostly African American suburb of Atlanta, eliminated its bus service into the city, leaving tens of thousands of Georgia's working poor without a way of getting to their jobs. "I don't know what I'm going to do," a fifty-seven-year-old worker told the *Los Angeles Times*. "So many people here, they're going to be sure enough messed up. We need this bus bad."[25] As of this writing, Oregon, Florida, New Jersey, and Maryland were also looking at deep cuts to public transportation systems to make up budget shortfalls.

Perhaps the most striking vision of the libertarian utopia comes from Ashtabula County, Ohio. It reduced the number of sheriff's deputies patrolling the 720-square-mile county from 112 to 49 and cut the number of prisoners in detention from 140 to 30. More than 700 people were put "on a waiting list to serve time in the jail," including, according to Sheriff Billy Johnson, some violent offenders. When a county judge was asked what citizens should do to protect their families "with the severe cutback in law enforcement," he responded, "Arm themselves. . . . Be very careful, be vigilant, get in touch with your neighbors, because we're going to have to look after each other." A gun instructor told the local news station he agreed with the sentiment. "You don't have any other option," he said. "We don't have the law enforcement out here to handle it right now."[26]

I write this from California, the scene of a devastating budget crisis that's firmly rooted in the Right's antitax crusade. In the summer of 2009, California lawmakers agreed on a budget with Governor Arnold Schwarzenegger that contained "a vast array of spending cuts that will soon be felt throughout the state. The K-12 education budget, which also includes community colleges, lost $6.1 billion from its roughly $58 billion base, and higher education took a $2 billion hit. . . . The state will save $1.3 billion by furloughing state workers three days out of the month. Medicaid took a $1.3 billion cut, along with a $129 million trim to the state's program that insures children whose families make too much for them to receive Medicaid."[27] As a result of the cuts, the University of California raised tuition 32 percent. *Time* magazine noted that "Public universities from Michigan to Arizona to North Carolina have [also] slashed budgets and hiked tuition."[28]

In 2010, conservative pundit George Will wrote a column bemoaning California's fiscal woes. "It took years for liberalism's mania for micromanaging life with entangling regulations to make California's once creative economy resemble Gulliver immobilized by the Lilliputians' many threads," Will wrote.[29]

What he omitted were the words "Prop 13." Proposition 13, passed by voters in 1978, rolled back property taxes to their 1975 levels and exempted homeowners from future increases in their tax assessments, even as the value of their houses skyrocketed— and it required a two-thirds supermajority in both chambers of the state legislature to pass a tax increase, allowing a Republican minority to strangle California's revenues. As Paul Krugman noted, "The result was a tax system that is both inequitable and unstable. It's inequitable because older homeowners often pay far less property tax than their younger neighbors. It's unstable because limits on property taxation have forced California to rely more heavily than other states on income taxes, which fall steeply during recessions. Even more important, however, Proposition 13 made it extremely hard to raise taxes, even in emergencies."[30]

The Right has been pushing similar laws in dozens of states, but with California offering a clear illustration of the damage these measures can do, they've had only limited success so far.

The Gradual Collapse of America's Infrastructure

America's core infrastructure has been falling apart in very visible ways during the last decade.

In 2010, the *New York Times* reported, "Thousands of water and sewer systems may be too old to function properly." On average, a major water line bursts every two minutes somewhere in the country. "For decades," the *Times* noted, "these systems—some built around the time of the Civil War—have been ignored by politicians and residents accustomed to paying almost nothing for water delivery and sewage removal. And so each year, hundreds of thousands of ruptures damage streets and homes and cause dangerous pollutants to seep into drinking water supplies."[31]

In 2007, a Minnesota bridge spanning the Mississippi River collapsed, killing 13 people and injuring almost 150 more. Republican governor Tim Pawlenty reacted to the disaster by calling a press conference, where, with a steely look of determination, he lied to the American people. Pawlenty insisted that inspections in 2005 and 2006 had found no structural problems with the overpass. But the *Minneapolis Star-Tribune* reported that the bridge "was rated as 'structurally deficient' two years ago and possibly in need of replacement." The bridge was borderline, with a 50 sufficiency rating. If a bridge scores less than 50, it needs to be replaced.[32] When the bridge collapsed, more than a hundred others in the

Gopher State had a rating below that number.[33] According to the *Pioneer Press*, the bridge's suspension system was supposed to receive extra attention with inspections every two years, but the last one had been performed in 2003.[34]

The governor had every reason to obfuscate; in 2005, he'd vetoed a bipartisan transportation package that would have put more than $8 billion into transit fixes during the subsequent decade.[35] Pawlenty was applauded by fellow Republicans for his staunch fiscal "conservatism."

The Minnesota bridge tragedy occurred just weeks after an eighty-year-old steam pipe in Manhattan blew up, killing one person and injuring dozens more.[36] A year before that, hundreds of thousands of Americans became refugees after New Orleans's pitiable levees collapsed—a graphic illustration of shortsighted public policy if ever there was one. More than seven hundred bodies were found in the Crescent City during the following months.

It's all part of a larger picture. We have a crumbling power grid[37] and are falling behind the rest of the world in broadband technology.[38] The American Society of Civil Engineers (ASCE) talks of "congested highways, overflowing sewers and corroding bridges" that are "constant reminders of the looming crisis that jeopardizes our nation's prosperity and our quality of life." Every year the engineering society issues a report card grading fifteen categories of America's once-premier physical plant. In 2009, we got a "D." The ASCE called the state of the infrastructure in one of the wealthiest countries in the world "a disgrace."[39]

The organization estimates that it would take an investment of $2.2 trillion during the next ten years to bring our infrastructure up to modern standards. That investment would create thousands of decent jobs and might unleash a new wave of productivity growth.

Nobody seriously believes that the hidden hand of the market is going to step in and inspect and repair our bridges and water systems. When lawmakers don't fund that work, they know full well that it won't get done. And the evidence that infrastructure investments result in increased economic productivity is strong; some studies have estimated that every dollar invested in public infrastructure yields a 104 percent return through increases in productivity.[40]

This is a very clear example of relentless tax cuts resulting in *reduced* economic activity, not the opposite. And it's a predictable outcome of the rise of "backlash" conservatism. We've swallowed thirty years of small-government rhetoric, and it's led us to a point in which our infrastructure, once the pride of the developed world, is falling apart around us. We're reaping what we've sown.

No, Tax Cuts Don't Always
Generate Jobs and Prosperity

Howard Kurtz, a media critic for the "liberal" *Washington Post*, offered a glimpse at how deeply conservative ideas about taxation have permeated the mainstream when he said in an online chat with readers,

> The argument over tax cuts is always over how large they are (can the economy afford them?) and who gets the benefits. . . . *But there is no dispute among economists that tax cuts stimulate the economy* by putting more cash in people's pockets [emphasis added].[1]

Kurtz has no doubt heard the mantra that "tax cuts" always spur growth repeated ad nauseam at dozens of D.C. cocktail parties, from "sensible" Democrats, wild-eyed right-wingers, and everyone in between. It's an article of faith that "cutting taxes" just spurs growth and creates jobs.

I put "tax cuts and "cutting taxes" in quotes because the central flaw in Kurtz's facile claim is this: although there is little dispute among economists that certain tax cuts can spur growth in specific economic situations, those same economists spend an extraordinary amount of time debating, sometimes heatedly, *which* tax cuts boost the economy, *when* they're the appropriate tool, and *how much* they can add, compared to other kinds of stimulus spending or direct job creation.

The basic problem with the claim that "tax cuts stimulate the economy" is that "taxes" aren't generic. You can cut taxes on companies or individuals or dole out cuts that fall more heavily on the rich or the poor. You can target tax cuts at investors or low-income families with young children. You can cut taxes on specific goods—food or yachts—and services, or in a specific geographic zone to encourage investment. And various recipients of those breaks—whether companies or individuals—will respond to those cuts with different kinds of changes in their economic behavior.

Yet another problem also exists. As we'll see in chapter 11, there simply isn't much correlation between various countries' tax burdens and the relative strength of their economies. Some economic powerhouses have relatively low tax rates; others' rates are relatively high.

A few years back, Larry Beinhart wrote a book called *Fog Facts*. "Fog facts," he explained to me, are things that "have been published or are easily known but have disappeared in the fog." They should be part of the conventional wisdom but aren't. He added, "I'm talking about things that are important—that once you bring them to the foreground it changes your picture of reality."[2]

In his 2008 article "Tax Cuts: The B.S. and the Facts," Beinhart took a look at a fog fact about taxes. He compared two sets of data, historic income tax and GDP growth rates in the United States, and concluded, "The brute facts" are as follows:

- High income taxes correlate with economic growth.
- Income tax increases are followed by economic growth.
- Moderate income tax cuts are followed by a flat economy.[3]

Here's how Beinhart explains each of the three:

- **High taxes correlate with strong economic growth.** The four periods of greatest economic growth in U.S. history, by pretty much any measure, are
  - World War II (1941–1945): The top tax rate varied from 88 to 94 percent.
  - Postwar under Truman and Eisenhower: The top rate bounced around from 81 to 92 percent.
  - The Clinton years: Clinton raised Bush's top rate of 31 percent to 37 percent and then to 39 percent.

- The first two Roosevelt administrations (1933–1940). When Roosevelt came into office, Hoover had already raised the tax rate in 1932 from 25 percent to 63 percent. Roosevelt raised it again in 1936 to 79 percent.

  A lot of ink, sweat, and ranting have gone into proving that the New Deal did not end the Great Depression. Nonetheless, the economy grew 58 percent from the time Roosevelt came into office to when the United States entered the war. Some of that anti–New Deal rhetoric also claims that the recovery began under Hoover. Perhaps, but to say so is also to say that it began with tax hikes.

  Likewise, many right-wing critics insist that the Clinton boom actually started under Bush the First. It is necessary to remember that Bush the First also raised taxes (from 28 percent to 31 percent) and was soundly thrashed by the conservatives for doing so. Stephen Moore of the Cato Institute called it "The Crime of the Century" and explained at length how it had brought ruin to America.

- **Tax increases are followed by economic growth.** Three of the four high-growth periods cited previously followed significant tax hikes. The fourth, the Truman-Eisenhower years, began with a top tax rate of 91 percent—it couldn't get much higher.

- **Moderate cuts are followed by flat growth.** John F. Kennedy is generally credited with starting the tax-cut craze. He proposed it, but, as with all of his ideas, it was Lyndon Johnson who actually got it enacted. The top rate was cut from 91 percent to 77 percent, then to 70 percent, on all income more than $200,000 for a single person and more than $400,000 for a married couple. That's where it stayed, through the Nixon, Ford, and Carter administrations. The Dow Jones average was pretty much the same when that period ended as when it began. Median personal income stayed roughly the same.[4]

I should note that Beinhart isn't saying that high taxes *cause* faster growth—just because B follows A doesn't mean that A *led to* B. Correlation isn't the same as causation. Obviously, all kinds of factors other than the top tax rate helped drive those growth spurts. Just one example is the huge competitive advantage the United States enjoyed for several decades following World War II, simply by virtue of the fact that it had developed a ton of industrial capacity during the war, while its major competitors had seen half of their infrastructure blown to pieces. But if B stubbornly *refuses* to follow A in every circumstance, then you can be pretty sure that A *isn't* responsible for B. A lack of correlation disproves causation.

So when Kennedy cut the top rate from 91 percent to 70 percent, that may have unleashed a lot of economic activity, but, as we saw in chapter 5, all but the sketchiest economic thinkers agree that when George W. Bush cut the top rate from 39.6 percent to 35 percent, he only succeeded in leaving a big hole in the budget.

Tax cuts, properly targeted, can be effective tools of public policy. The idea that cutting taxes *always* spurs growth, creates jobs, and leads to magic rainbows and puppies, on the other hand, is pure fantasy.

6

REPUBLICANS HAVE NEVER CARED ABOUT THE DEFICIT

Don't believe there's a budget apocalypse just over the horizon

> Current challenges in heal/th care are driven largely by fundamental problems in existing Federal Government entitlement programs. These include a $38-trillion unfunded liability in Medicare . . . that will grow to $52 trillion . . . and a Medicaid Program that is the leading cause behind State budget crises. But the Majority's legislation layers on yet another Washington-based medical program.
>
> —*Representative Roscoe Bartlett (R-MD), announcing his opposition to House Democrats' health-care reform package in 2009*

One thing practically everyone understands is that what have become known as "entitlements"—Social Security, Medicare, and other programs that provide a cushion of sorts for working families—are quite popular.

This presents a challenge for conservatives: you just don't get very far in U.S. politics on the promise of cutting grandma's health benefits. It's worth restating that although people respond positively to the idea of limited government in the abstract, when it comes to specifics, people *love* big government and most, if not all, of what it does.

They want a government that will educate their children, put out forest fires, pay for their million-dollar cancer treatments, make sure that big chemical companies aren't poisoning their water, and keep them from having to eat cat food after busting their asses for fifty years in the U.S. workforce. They expect cheap student loans and meat inspections and smooth highways, and even the lowest of "low-information" voters know they're not going to get that stuff from the private sector.

So the Corporate Right has had to frame the debate on different terms. They've come up with a Big Lie to do it, claiming that the United States is headed toward a gazillion-dollar deficit just around the corner, and the only way to stave off this looming budgepocalypse is to swallow the bitter medicine of "entitlement reform."

It's not that they oppose popular programs like the State Children's Health Insurance Program—perish the thought; they're compassionate!—it's just, they claim, that they have the kind of clear vision that's needed to make the hard choices necessary to "save" the Republic over the long haul.

Everyone Wants Big Government
(at Least, the Parts They Like)

Even the most hawkish of deficit hawks are quite fond of some aspects of big government. Most are military hawks as well. So, even though they warn of economic destitution coming over the horizon unless we tear more holes in an already threadbare social safety net, they rarely mention the enormous amounts of money that are spent on the security state and national "defense." It's as if money for guns is somehow different from money spent on butter.

If you want to look at long-term budget busters, however, there's no better place to look than our military spending. Never mind what we're paying for today's wars—the $685 billion defense budget tells only part of the story.[1] The little-discussed truth is that we're still paying for Korea, Vietnam, Grenada, Panama, the first Gulf War, Somalia, the Balkans, and on and on.

Estimates of just how much of our national debt payments are due to past military spending vary wildly. Economist Robert Higgs calculated it like this:

I added up all past deficits (minus surpluses) since 1916 (when the debt was nearly zero), prorated according to each year's ratio of narrowly defined national security spending— military, veterans, and international affairs—to total federal spending, expressing everything in dollars of constant purchasing power. This sum is equal to 91.2 percent of the value of the national debt held by the public at the end of 2006.[2]

In 2006, he came up with an annual figure of $206.7 billion for interest payments alone on our past militarism. Add it all up, and we're talking about at least a trillion dollars in military and homeland security spending. If there were a million-dollar bill, you'd have to stack a million of them to reach a trillion dollars. It's almost three times the entire budget for the Department of Health and Human Services, which is tasked with protecting the well-being of all Americans.

So the stark reality is that what poses as a debate between advocates of "big government" and fiscal conservatives is actually a debate about priorities, because we're going to spend a lot of money on government regardless of who occupies the White House and who's running Congress. The questions come down to what those massive piles of dollars are going to buy, and whether we'll raise enough taxes to cover it or simply borrow the cash from the Chinese and let future generations worry about paying it back.

The Reality: Conservatives Spend Like Drunken Sailors

Because budgetary debates are actually about priorities, rather than about how big the government will be—between 1960 and 2010, federal spending as a share of overall economic activity has bounced around within a fairly narrow range of between 17.7 percent

(Eisenhower) and 21.8 percent (Poppy Bush)—progressives often answer conservative deficit hawks by pointing out their hypocrisy. Since the middle of the last century, the truth, contra the "tax-and-spend" label, is that Democrats have been *far* more conservative when it comes to keeping deficits under control than their Republican counterparts have.

Although Congress has to share credit or blame for the budget situation at any given time, the numbers are fairly clear. As financial analyst Hale Stewart noted after George W. Bush's first term,

> Ronald Reagan started his term with total debt outstanding of 930 million and increased total debt outstanding to 2.7 trillion. This is a 13.71% compound annual increase. He never balanced a budget.
>
> Bush I started his term with outstanding debt of 2.7 trillion and increased total debt to 4 trillion. This is a 10.32% compounded annual increase. He never balanced a budget.
>
> Clinton started with total debt outstanding debt of 4 trillion and increased total debt outstanding to 5.6 trillion. This is a 4.2% compounded annual increase. He balanced his last three budgets.[3]

George W. Bush started with $5.6 trillion total outstanding debt and increased total outstanding debt to $10 trillion. That works out to a 9.8 percent annual increase. He never came close to balancing a budget.[4]

Barack Obama came into office during a period of unprecedented economic upheaval, with tax revenues in the tank and economists from across most of the ideological spectrum calling for deficit spending in the short term to prop up an economy that was in real danger of collapse. But, nonetheless, as the conservative *Washington Times* noted in early 2010, "President Obama notched substantial successes in spending cuts last year, winning 60 percent of his proposed cuts and managing to get Congress to ax several programs that had bedeviled President George W. Bush for years."[5]

Yet arguing that progressives are better fiscal stewards is inherently difficult. The Corporate Right has so effectively framed the debate that most political reporters—and certainly most ordinary citizens—take it as an almost scriptural truth that progressives like "big government" and spending tax money for the sake of spending tax money. It's unlikely that the discourse will ever fully embrace the hard fact that when conservatives are in power, they are more likely to spend like drunken sailors on shore leave (with a Visa card) than their more liberal counterparts are. As we saw in the last chapter, taxes fell for 98 percent of U.S. households in 2009, but a poll found that only 12 percent of the population believed that the Democrats had cut their tax bills.[6]

Because it's taken for granted by so many people that progressives raise taxes, the Right has a perfectly flexible avenue of attack: when a Democrat such as Bill Clinton reduces the deficit for the first time in a half-century, conservatives say that it was only because Newt Gingrich's right-wing Republicans controlled Congress for most of his presidency. But when George W. Bush, for the most part presiding over a GOP-controlled Congress, sent deficits spiraling into the heavens, that simply became evidence that he wasn't a *real* conservative (which, for many on the Right, explains his unpopularity far better than the disastrous wars he started, his administration's lackadaisical response to Hurricane Katrina, the corruption that became endemic in the GOP-controlled Congress on his watch, or a dozen other failings).

So progressives are damned if they do and damned if they don't. A better approach is to educate the public about how the federal budget works, what our tax dollars buy, and why we can in fact afford to have a progressive society if we so choose.

The Reality: There Is No Entitlement Crisis

Here's a testament to the power of conservative economic propaganda: Social Security is not only popular, it's also in *sound fiscal shape*. It's got a surplus that will run out in 2037, but even if nothing were to change by then, it could still continue to pay out 75 percent of scheduled benefits seventy-five years from now, long after the surplus disappears, and those benefits would *still* be higher than what retirees receive today.[7] Yet polls consistently show that younger people are pessimistic about the program's stability and fear that it won't be there when they reach retirement. They've drunk deeply of the conservative "entitlement crisis" Kool-Aid.

In part, that's the result of some fast and loose talk about how the system was designed to operate. Take the Social Security Trust Fund—established during the Reagan era to cushion against a wave of baby boomers now hitting retirement age. Fiscal scare-mongers make a great deal of fuss about the fact that by 2016, the total benefits paid out of the program will exceed Social Security tax revenues, and the fund will have to be tapped to make up the difference.[8]

Yet that's exactly what it was always supposed to do. That's why Congress created it—to ease the boomers into the system without shock. (And because the bonds in the Trust Fund earn interest, the total value of the fund will actually continue to grow after that date. If nothing else changes, the total paid out in benefits won't exceed tax revenues combined with interest on the bonds until 2024.)[9]

Another part of the narrative of a weak and unsustainable Social Security program stems from the idea that the Social Security Trust Fund is being constantly "looted" and is now little more than a pile of worthless paper. But that worthless paper is in fact a pile of United States Treasury bills, considered among the safest invest-ments in the world. As Dean Baker put it,

> Under the law, the federal government is obligated to repay the government bonds held by the Social Security trust fund, just as it is obligated to repay other government bonds. While tax revenue will be needed to repay these bonds, it is slated to come from personal and corporate income taxes, both very progressive forms of taxation. By contrast, the Social Security tax is a highly regressive wage tax. The meaning of the trust

fund is that workers effectively prepaid their Social Security taxes. Now, the government is obligated to tax the Bill Gateses and Pete Petersons of the world to repay this debt.[10]

Another common refrain is that there will be "only" 1.8 workers in the United States for each retired person come 2075, compared with 3.4 workers for each retiree today. That's true but largely irrelevant: in economies with fewer workers per retiree, productivity per worker tends to be higher. What's more, it's an argument unrooted from our economic history—nobody mentions that there were almost four *nonworkers* for every wage-earner during the nineteenth century; the ratio reversed itself during the last century.[11]

The *Real* Crisis: Health Care

Now, there *is* a crisis looming, but it has nothing *directly* to do with federal spending on popular social programs. We spent more than eight times as much on health care in 2007 than we did in 1980.[12] In just ten years, from 1995 to 2005, average health-care spending increased by 77 percent.[13]

That kind of growth outpaces the overall growth in the economy by a mile—the share of America's total economic output being sucked into health care has increased from just under 14 percent in 2000 to more than 16 percent this year and is expected to top one-fifth of the total economy in ten years.[14]

One would be hard-pressed to argue that we aren't facing a looming crisis in health-care costs. And Medicare and Medicaid—the two primary public health programs in the United States—are indeed headed for a day of reckoning if this country can't get those costs under control.

This is not a crisis of government spending—Medicare and Medicaid face the same cost pressures as do businesses that provide coverage for their employees. Conservatives would have you believe that these programs are in trouble because they're administered by the government, but, as is often the case, the opposite is true: between 1970 and 2003, Medicare spending grew by an average rate of 9 percent per year, while private-sector health costs rose by 10.1 percent annually.[15]

And, according to the Congressional Budget Office, the administrative costs for the public Medicare program, at 2 percent, are a fraction of the 16.7 percent that go into nonmedical costs—and profits—in the private plans offered under the Medicare Advantage program.[16]

A Trillion Here, a Trillion There: Pretty Soon You're Talking about Real Money

Let's look at the makings of a Big Lie. In the quote that opened this chapter, Roscoe Bartlett, a GOP representative from Maryland, talked of a "$38-trillion unfunded liability in Medicare" that "will grow to $52 trillion."

As New Hampshire Republican senator Judd Gregg noted, "It's hard to understand what a trillion is. I don't know what it is." This is what conservatives are counting on—using numbers big enough to simply derail any discussion of how we prioritize our spending. Given that the entire federal budget is less than $3 trillion annually, an "unfunded liability" of $52 trillion is simply unfathomable.

Here's the kernel of truth on which these astronomical future deficits are based: according to the Congressional Budget Office, if everything remains exactly as it is currently projected for the foreseeable future—if health spending continues to rise at the current pace, the population grows as rapidly as expected, the economy expands by the rate it is projected to grow, the tax rates remain the same, and on and on, then over the next *seventy-five years*, we would be faced with a deficit of truly epic proportions.

Ordinarily, we don't project budgets that far out—it's pointless to do so. We'd never assume that U.S. forces would remain in strength in Afghanistan and Iraq for seventy-five years and project our military spending on that basis. In almost every other instance, we look at projected budgets over a ten- or sometimes twenty-year window, and for good reason: the likelihood that spending, revenues, demographic changes, and economic growth would all adhere to projections fifty years from now approaches zero. Even very modest changes to any of these factors, when extrapolated over a span of three-quarters of a century, can shift the entire super-long-term budget outlook quite dramatically.

Consider this argument in more accessible terms. Take a hypothetical individual who makes $50,000 per year, and imagine that this person spends what he or she takes home after taxes on rent, food, clothes, and the like. And after blowing through the paycheck, this person indulges in a daily mocha frappuccino that he or she can't quite afford—let's say that it puts him or her over budget by $2 every day.

The person is clearly running a deficit and, during the course of a year, will spend $730 more on fancy coffee than his or her salary allows.

It's technically accurate that during the course of this person's lifetime, with modest interest rates of 5 percent on his or her debt, we're looking at an irresponsible lunatic "projected" to face a coffee deficit that will run into the hundreds of thousands of dollars. Yet it is only technically accurate; in reality, individuals prioritize their spending, and if they really loved that frothy shot of coffee, they would pay for it by brown-bagging lunch once a week or going to the movies less frequently. Or, if they couldn't trim anywhere and simply couldn't give up that coffee, perhaps they'd do a little extra work on the side.

Let's further imagine that our coffee-lover's salary has grown by 2 percent per year during the previous five years, while a cup of frappuccino has gone up by 3 percent. If that trend were to continue for a couple of decades, it's likely that this person would develop a taste for tea. But it's also just as likely that the rate by which the cost of a frappuccino increases will slow, or that our poor caffeine addict will get a better job with a higher salary and not have to worry about his or her cup of joe.

Any way you slice it, there's no way that everything would remain constant until our hypothetical coffee addict woke up one day to face a $100,000 coffee bill. Yet this is precisely the spin that conservatives have adopted toward entitlement spending.

Although everyone agrees, for example, that if rising health-care costs can't be contained in some fashion, we would eventually end up with an unsustainably large tab, it's also universally accepted that something has to give, that health-care costs *cannot* continue to grow at their recent pace indefinitely. And as far as Social Security goes, minor tweaks are all that are required to shore up a popular program's long-term financial health.

The Gazillion-Dollar Fake Entitlement Crisis

The Heritage Foundation, arguably the premier voice of the Corporate Right, warns that "Social Security, Medicare, and Medicaid threaten to swamp the federal budget" and promises that the "long-term tab" for these programs works out to $40 trillion, or "$400,000 for every full-time worker in America today."[17]

Whether the "gap" is $38, $40, or $53 trillion, it's always based on a seventy-five-year projection, and it always conflates Social Security, which is on sound footing, with our public health programs, which face the specter of ever-rising costs. And here's a key point: the assumptions that are used to make those projections are remarkably gloomy. Specifically, the Social Security Board of Trustees, which issues annual reports on the state of our public retirement program, assumes that during the next seventy-five years the U.S. economy will grow by *half the rate* of the last seventy-five years. That may well prove to be the case, but it's an *ahistoric* assumption.

Yet that's not all. As economist Doug Henwood noted of the projections for Social Security,

At every turn there's a bearish assumption in the Trustees' numbers. At 0.4% a year, the projected population growth through 2075 represents quite a deceleration from the 1.2% average of the last 75, and well under the Census Bureau's

0.7% projection for the next 50 years. The workforce is slated
to grow even less—by just 0.2%. Not only is the youthful share
of the population expected to decline, the Trustees project
that fewer of them will be working: the share of the population aged 20–64 at work (the employment-population ratio) is
projected to decline, a violation of all historical precedent.

Henwood concludes that if you "rerun the projections with more
reasonable—though still conservative—projections," the "'crisis'
largely or fully disappears."[18]

Armed with these massive and wholly unlikely numbers—projected
deficits so great that they shock and awe—the Heritage Foundation
then offers us a false choice: we can either (A) do nothing and face
certain doom; (B) raise taxes, which they argue would be foolhardy,
given that "the United States owes much of its economic success to its
policy of low taxation and low government spending" (another lie to
which we'll return later); or, (C) "rein in spending."[19]

But, they caution, making modest adjustments to these programs—or trimming other spending—is "like trying to bail out the
Titanic with a Dixie cup." The only solution, they say, is to "tackle
the real problem," which "means reining in the huge costs of Social
Security, Medicare, and Medicaid."

If we were to use a different set of assumptions in our projections, however, we would see a problem that can be addressed
with any number of relatively painless fixes. Right now, Americans
pay Social Security taxes on the first $106,800 they earn. But
because the distribution of income has skewed toward the
wealthy for the previous three decades, the amount of income
falling under the cap has shrunk—in 1982, when the payroll tax
was last tweaked, 90 percent of all income fell below the cap; by
2006, that number had fallen to 84 percent.[20]

Eliminating the cap would instantly close the "Social Security
gap" over the long run. Yet according to economist John Irons,
even rejiggering the number so that it again captured 90 percent of
Americans' wages would narrow three-quarters of the gap. And in

the process, only 6 percent of the population—all high-earners— would feel any tax bite at all.[21]

Health-care costs are a systemic problem. As far as Social Security goes, minor tweaks are all that's required. When you project a shortfall over three-quarters of a century, you're going to come up with a big number, but keep this really salient point in mind: if we don't do anything at all with Social Security. that "huge" gap—tens of trillions of dollars—works out to just 0.7 percent of our gross domestic product, a drop in the proverbial bucket.

Finally, we don't necessarily need to raise taxes to increase revenues. According to the federal government, the amount of taxes owed but not collected—the so-called "tax gap"—is around $300 billion.[22] David Cay Johnston, arguably the best tax reporter around, believes it to be a conservative number. And, as Johnston explained in his book *Perfectly Legal*, most of the gap isn't due to waiters not reporting tips:

> Historically, we thought of the tax gap as being people at the bottom. You know, the guy who cuts lawns and gets paid in cash. That underground cash economy. But . . . a lot of the underground economy is at the top. It involves people with enormous incomes, who are not reporting these incomes, or are underreporting them.[23]

Johnston noted that in 1983, 10 percent of American companies' incomes were funneled through offshore tax havens to avoid paying corporate taxes here at home. By 2009, the share had increased to 25 percent. He pointed to tax deferrals that allow wealthy earners and corporations to delay paying their tax bills, sometimes for decades in some cases. Johnston called deferrals "one of the major tools for redistributing wealth upward," explaining:

> While most of us must pay each time we get a paycheck, executives and corporations can defer their taxes for years,

even decades. When the treasury finally gets the money, inflation has eroded its value; in the meantime, government must borrow more, pay more interest, and collect more from everyone else.[24]

Johnston estimated that eliminating most tax deferrals alone would bring an additional $100 billion in revenues each year without raising tax rates. Simply closing the loopholes in the tax system that allow very wealthy people to avoid paying their fair share would more than eliminate the seventy-five-year deficit.

Enter the Doomsayers

Talk of mammoth shortfalls is not only ubiquitous in conservative circles, it's become firmly entrenched in the mainstream discourse (as these things are wont to do). What makes this meme particularly worthy of note is that few ideas can be credited to a single powerful individual quite as much as America's dreaded "entitlement crisis" can.

That individual is Peter Peterson, the former commerce secretary under Richard Nixon and cofounder of the Blackstone Group, a private equity firm that got fat on leveraged buyouts during the go-go 1990s. Peterson claims to be working desperately to save America from itself. He's written four books on the horrors of our future fiscal prospects, founded the "nonpartisan" Concord Coalition in 1992 (with former Republican senator Warren Rudman), and in 2007, he shelled out $1 billion of his own money to start the Peter G. Peterson Foundation, which is dedicated to raising awareness of our crushing debt burden. As of early 2010, the Peterson Foundation had come up with the figure of $62 trillion as our "true national debt."

Dean Baker calls him the country's leading "granny-basher" for his years-long crusade to "reform" Social Security and Medicare and notes that Peterson, who opposed Clinton's efforts to reform a bloated health-care system in 1993 (saying, of course, that we couldn't afford it) never concedes that it's *spiraling health-care costs* that pose the greatest threat to future budgets and future generations' prosperity. "The agenda of Peter Peterson and his ilk," wrote Baker in 2009, "never had anything to do with generational equity. The point was always to gut Social Security and Medicare. These programs stand out as key targets precisely because they are hugely effective and popular programs."[25]

What's remarkable is how successful Peterson has been in obscuring his agenda in a cloud of supposedly sensible bipartisanship. He hired Bill Clinton's (and subsequently George Bush's) comptroller, David Walker, to run his foundation. Walker, a bean counter's bean counter, is a rarity: a pithy, charismatic accountant. In 2006, under his leadership, the General Accounting Office (GAO) patiently explained to Congress that "Today's fiscal policy remains unsustainable" and added, for clarity, "what is unsustainable will not be sustained."[26]

Walker resigned in 2008, five years before his term was up, to spread the gospel. In a much-discussed 2007 interview, Walker compared the United States to Rome before its fall, warning not only of irresponsible fiscal management, but also of our "declining moral values."[27]

Peterson has invested heavily in his own media, and he's done a remarkable job of inserting his agenda into the mainstream media as well. He founded the *Fiscal Times*, a paper dedicated to spreading the word. On New Year's Eve 2009, the *Washington Post*—a paper that has a unique place in creating and disseminating D.C.'s conventional wisdom—was caught up in a controversy after running an article produced entirely by Peterson's *Fiscal Times* in its news pages without disclosing that its source was an arm of a conservative think-tank. The article furthered the "sky is falling" narrative, naturally, without offering any competing perspectives.[28]

Peterson bought the film *I.O.U.S.A.*—a piece of right-wing agit-prop written by Addison Wiggin, an analyst at Agora Financial

Services. The *New York Times* called it a "resolutely nonpartisan movie that tracks America's 'fiscal cancer' through centuries of budgetary highs and lows."[29]

In 2009, CNN, supposedly a "liberal" counterpart to Fox News, broadcast the film in its entirety, along with a panel discussion. Jamison Foster, a fellow with the watchdog group Media Matters, wrote of the broadcast, "Viewers were treated to two hours of gloom and doom about the speed with which the sky is approaching the earth, interspersed with grave warnings that we must do something and self-congratulating statements that politicians must have courage to take unspecified unpopular steps to get the deficit under control and begin to pay down the debt."[30]

In 2010, Peterson's institute joined with the Pew Charitable Trusts to push a bipartisan "deficit commission" to study "entitlement reform"—an idea adopted by Barack Obama. It should come as little surprise that the fiscal narrative pushed by Peterson and his fellow granny-bashers has been embraced by members of both major parties; as Jamison Foster put it, "the media's coverage of public policy debates presents a narrow spectrum of opinion—basically, ranging from 'moderate' 'pragmatists' who advocate 'entitlement reform' (which, coming from the mouth of a Beltway insider, tends to be code for 'benefit cuts') to conservatives who advocate tax cuts at every turn (resulting in deficits that, the conservatives and the 'moderates' agree, will require 'entitlement reform')."[31]

The result of all of this is what economist Robert Kuttner called a "disabling . . . bipartisan echo chamber on the alleged entitlement crisis."[32] Don't fall for its ubiquitous projections of imminent budgetary catastrophe—they represent a Big Lie.

And don't believe we have to close the rather manageable deficit we do face on the backs of Grandma and Grandpa, the poor, widows and orphans, or the disabled. Ultimately, there is no "entitlement crisis" because there are so many ways we can choose to pay for that extra frappuccino.

How More Government (of One Sort) Brings Greater Individual Liberty and Personal Choice

In April 2010, the Pew Trust released a poll that got pundits' tongues wagging. "By almost every conceivable measure Americans are less positive and more critical of government these days," Pew told us.

According to the polling firm, Americans' distrust of government had increased dramatically since 1997. "Over this period, a larger minority of the public also has come to view the federal government as a major threat to their personal freedom. . . . 30% feel this way, up from 18% in a 2003 ABC News/*Washington Post* survey."[1]

In part, Pew's findings were a sign of the success of the "conservative noise machine." They also touched on an important and largely unexamined assumption in our political discourse: that when "government" grows, our individual freedoms and personal choices decline by definition.

To see how facile that equation really is, you have to disaggregate what we mean by "government." You can divide it up, roughly, into a "security state," a "social welfare state," a "public infrastructure state," and a "regulatory state" (there's obviously some overlap with such broad categories). The security state can and does add to our personal freedom. If there's no competent police force and you're afraid to leave your house for fear of assault by marauding bandits, then you're not really free.

Having said that, I certainly agree that the expansion of the security state—criminalizing more behavior, increasing law enforcement's surveillance of the public, and locking up more people—is a real threat to our personal liberties. A security state is necessary, but there's a lot of potential for abuse, and people are right to be wary of its growth.

The regulatory state is obviously subject to fierce debate. Conservatives are right when they point out that it has the capacity to overreach. But in theory, at least, the regulatory state constrains the "freedom" to harm others, which is an entirely good thing. Most of us don't want companies to have the "liberty" to sell us defective products, tempt us with grossly misleading advertising, hire children to toil away in sweatshops, or spew toxic sludge into our water.

But let's turn to the largely unexamined belief that more government leads to less personal liberty in relation to its other tasks. Maintaining our public spaces and infrastructure enhances our personal freedoms. Tomorrow, I can choose to go to a national park or a public beach that I know is safe and clean. I don't drive a car, but thanks to our government-funded public transportation system, I can get around freely. I have a choice of paying the top rate to catch a cab—a convenient private sector transaction—but if I can't afford that, I'm still able to take the (government-subsidized) bus. Having reliable delivery of fresh water to my home liberates me from the task of trudging to a river to fetch it by bucket, as people do in many places. It'd be hard to name something that added more to Americans' individual freedom and choice than the establishment of the Eisenhower Interstate Highway System, a massive socialist undertaking by the standards of today's conservatives.

And now we come to the social welfare state. Although one obviously can't opt out of financing one's share for it—you have to pay your taxes—it provides us with an enormous amount of individual liberty and freedom of choice. And I'm not just talking about the "freedom from want" that is common to Marxist thinking. Consider a few examples.

In the United States, it's not uncommon for people to stay in dead-end jobs or crappy relationships for fear of losing their health coverage. In Canada or France or any other industrialized country, a citizen's health care is his or her own. People in those countries have the very real freedom to quit that lousy job or dump that asshole without worrying about losing their coverage. In this example,

Americans are slaves not to an overarching state, but to the way our private insurance system works.

Or consider the millions of people who want to go to college but can't afford to pick up the tab for tuition and living expenses. Many still have the choice to get a higher education through federal education grants and subsidized student loans. That's a personal choice that the private sector has no incentive to provide to citizens.

There are also programs that help people start new businesses or buy homes that they couldn't otherwise afford. There are programs that offer them new job skills. Even if you're dirt poor, you can still get into a program to help you kick a drug addiction. You can go to the library and read a book or search job listings on the Internet. All of these things give people real choices they wouldn't otherwise have.

I could go on and on. The young researcher working on an NIH-funded science project, the farmer who has the choice to maintain his or her family's tradition only because of agricultural subsidies, or the actor performing in an off-off-Broadway play that couldn't be produced without a grant from the National Endowment for the Arts—all of these are living examples of people who have the freedom to pursue options that would be closed to them without Big Government "intervention" in the economy.

When progressives advocate for better public transportation, they're trying to increase ordinary Americans' freedom of movement. When they promote the wonders of municipal WiFi, they're talking about the freedom to work anywhere in a city, anytime you want, without having to pay to suck down a cup of stale Starbucks coffee.

Once again, governance all comes down to a question of priorities. And, in rough figures, we spend about a fifth of our federal budget on the social welfare state, around 5 percent on the regulatory state, and about 10 percent on the infrastructure state.

And the security state? It sucks up around two-thirds of the national budget.

7

AMERICA HAS NO RESPECT FOR FAMILY VALUES

Don't believe that women choose motherhood over work (or vice versa)

Because men are more likely to take jobs that are unpleasant, dangerous or dull in exchange for higher pay, they reap the financial benefit. Another reason women's average earnings are less than men's is that they take more time out of the work-force for care-giving. Scholars can debate whether it is societal pressure or innate desire that makes women elect to spend more time with their children. But so long as these decisions are a reflection of women's expressed preferences, this isn't a problem that needs to be solved.[1]

—*Arrah Nielsen, of the Independent Women's Forum, a right-wing "feminist" group*

Most people are aware of the "glass ceiling" that keeps women out of the top spots at big firms, and of the "gender pay gap"— the fact that women make 78 cents for each dollar earned by men with similar qualifications.[2]

Conservatives minimize not only the damage these inequities cause for women, but also the economic toll they take on tens of millions of households in which women are the primary breadwinners.

It's estimated that during a forty-year career, the average American woman gets short-changed $434,000 in earnings.[3] That's not chump change.

The kernel of truth in conservative arguments is that in 2010, it's no longer the case that women face frequent discrimination based on the old belief that they can't do the jobs as well as men can, although that still happens. The reality is that in the U.S. economy, women are more often simply victims of their *biology*.

Conservatives like to talk about "what women themselves want." British columnist David Green, in an article titled "The Gender Pay Gap Does Not Exist," wrote, "From ages 18–29 there is hardly any difference [in men and women's pay] . . . women aged 22–29 are paid on average slightly more per hour than men. . . . Having children is the decisive factor," Green concludes, "not being a woman."[4]

That's pretty much true, but it misses the point entirely. When women choose to have children, as most will, they lose seniority, their career paths take detours, and they end up taking home smaller paychecks than their male counterparts do. That's why the pay gap doesn't manifest itself in the very early years of a person's career— these are the years before working women start to have children.

Follow the logic of the "women's choice" argument to its ridiculous conclusion, and this is where you end up: we *can* have equal pay, but only if women wise up and stop pumping out those babies. Of course, it is an immutable law of nature that women bear children—half of whom, the last time I checked, will grow up to be men—so what they're actually saying is that we could have equal pay for the final generation of humans before the species dies out.

The Big Lie that is implied in every argument in support of the status quo is that this is a natural law of the workplace—when one takes a break from one's career, for whatever reason, one must accept the consequences: slower advancement and lower pay.

The reality is quite different. Women have entered the work-place in huge numbers in every advanced economy during the last fifty years, but the United States is *alone* among the wealthy nations in basically telling women to suck it up. Every other wealthy country—and most poorer ones—offers some form of flexible workplace policy that allows women (and men!) to take time off to have a baby without sending their careers back a step.

Women are also penalized for cultural assumptions about gender. As the designated caregivers for sick children and elderly parents, women are expected to put *their* careers on hold, and they take a financial hit when they do. There's no earthly reason this burden shouldn't fall on men as often as it does on women, but that's the reality and women pay the price.

And here's a very important thing to understand about the gender wage gap: it varies quite a bit from country to country, and the United States has one of the largest. Dutch economist Remco Oostendorp studied the effect during a sixteen-year-period in eighty countries. Among the thirteen "high-income countries," the United States tied for the fourth-greatest disparity in earnings between men and women.[5]

For the most part, those national differences can be explained by workplace policies that either allow or prevent women from hanging onto their jobs when life demands that they take some time off. These differences are discussed at length in this chapter. The wage gap is also related to how much power workers have in general. Economists Francine Blau and Lawrence Kahn looked at the wage gap in twenty-two countries during a ten-year period and found that when unions play a larger role in determining pay scales, the gender wage gap shrinks.[6]

Women play a greater role in the U.S. economy today than at any time since Rosie the Riveter gave up making bombers and went back home to make babies after World War II, but U.S. corporations—enabled by a political class still dominated by men—continue to punish them for the high crime of being female.

The American workforce has one of the highest rates of female participation in the world. Between 1955 and 2002, the percentage of working-age women who had jobs outside the home almost doubled, while men's workforce participation fell by more than 10 percent.[7] Women went back to work as it became harder for a single earner to keep a family afloat. Economist Doug Henwood showed that a worker making an average manufacturing wage had to work 62 weeks in order to earn the median family income in 1947. By 1973, that had risen to 74 weeks, and in 2001, it was 81 weeks.[8]

So, we can thank women's participation for a significant chunk of the U.S. economy's much-vaunted "dynamism." Highly educated women entering the workforce in the 1990s added to America's "productivity miracle." Harvard economist Richard Freeman studied labor stats in 1998 and found that women moving into the workforce increased the employment rate by almost 10 percent. Forget about "business-friendly" regulatory environments and the wonders of "Rubinomics"—the injection of female workers into the workforce accounted for almost two-thirds of the difference between the unemployment rate in the United States and other advanced economies (more on those data later).[9]

Yet despite all that women contribute to our economic health, the United States was one of only 4 countries out of 173 studied by McGill University's Project on Global Working Families that doesn't mandate some form of paid maternal leave. That puts the United States—among the wealthiest nations on the planet—in the company of desperately poor Liberia, Papua New Guinea, and Swaziland.[10]

What's more, 145 of those 173 countries mandate that employers provide paid leave for workers who become ill or who have to care for a sick child or an elderly parent, but the United States is not among them. The best we do is require some U.S. employers to offer *unpaid* leave under the Family and Medical Leave Act (FMLA).[11] This doesn't cover all workers—only 40 percent of the private-sector workforce fall under the act—and conservatives fought tooth-and-nail against the measure when it was passed during the Clinton administration.[12] Conservatives continue to oppose family leave policies to this day.

Regardless of how enlightened we believe we are, the yoke of housework, child rearing, and elder care still falls disproportionately on women. The legendary progressive economist Marilyn Waring was the first to consider the economics of unpaid housework in the 1980s. Waring estimated that if what has traditionally been thought of as "women's work" were counted economically, it would constitute the world's single largest service and production sector.[13] Suzanne Bianchi, a sociologist at the University of Maryland, found that working mothers spent an average of twelve hours a week on child care in 2003, an hour more than stay-at-home moms did in 1975.[14]

The economic penalties imposed on working women when they take time off for family responsibilities create a double whammy that lowers fertility rates and impacts the wealth of both single women and two-income families in myriad ways. Inflexible workplaces offer socially mobile women a devil's choice: they can advance in their careers or they can have families. According to *BusinessWeek*, female corporate execs are twice as likely to be child-free as are women in the population as a whole. Those making $100,000 per year are two-and-a-half times more likely to be childless.[15]

Yet more often, women don't have a choice, and they take the financial hit. Karen Kornbluh noted that women without children made 90 percent of what their male counterparts earn, but working mothers earn less than 75 percent. A first child lowered a woman's earnings by an average of 7.5 percent, a second child by 8 percent more.[16]

It's not that women leave the workforce permanently to have kids or care for a sick child or parent; it's that when they leave their jobs, they usually can't return (or they lose their seniority when they do). According to economist Heather Boushey at the Center for American Progress, "If women have paid leave they are much more likely to go back to their jobs, and much less likely to quit or switch jobs."[17] Not having it creates a ripple effect in their working lives, costing them seniority, raises, and future promotions and benefits. Former Clinton adviser Gene Sperling pointed out that the average time a worker needs to stay on the job to get pension benefits—if people get them at all in our wonderful "New Economy"—is 5 years. Men's average time working the same job is 5.1 years; for women it's less than 4.[18]

According to the Employee Benefits Research Institute, women older than sixty-five who have income from pensions and annuities pull down, on average, $10,866 per year, while their male counterparts enjoy an annual income of $16,933—56 percent more.[19] And with our uniquely inflexible workplaces, a third of U.S. women work in "nonstandard" or part-time jobs with no pension benefits.[20] Both of those factors help explain why women older than sixty-five are twice as likely to live in poverty as men.[21]

Pretty much every aspect of women's reproductive work is punished economically in the U.S. workplace, and that affects all two-earner nuclear households—the ideal to which we're all supposed to aspire. It doesn't need to be this way. We're so far behind the rest of the world in commonsense, pro-women, and pro-family policies that we don't need to reinvent the wheel to figure out what works. Yet just about every measure to close the wage gap or mandate parental leave policies is opposed by the dead-enders of a cranky old patriarchy whose views are increasingly out of step with the realities of modern life and the imperatives of a global economy. When Bill Clinton managed to squeeze the Family and Medical Leave Act through Congress, the late Strom Thurmond warned that similar measures in Europe had "contributed to a stagnating economy and unemployment." The Chamber of Commerce has been fighting the FMLA ever since and has formed a fake grassroots group called the National Coalition to Protect Family Leave, the goal of which is to, well, destroy family leave legislation. Yet in fact, among the ten countries with the most competitive economies (according to the World Economic Forum's annual rankings), only the United States lacks generous family leave policies.

The truth is that family-friendly policies are also good for business. In his book *The Pro-Growth Progressive*, Gene Sperling reviewed the gains made by firms that have gotten ahead of the curve in workplace flexibility. He cited a study of a hundred U.S. businesses that found paid parental leave to be associated with a 2.5 percent increase in profits. He mentioned another study that concluded that employees who participated in one company's "work-life" programs were 45 percent more likely to say they'd "go the extra mile" for their employers than were workers who didn't take part in the program. Sperling concluded that giving employees more flexibility resulted in improved "motivation, making workers more productive," and ended up cutting costs by reducing employee turnover.[22]

The return on investing in working families is high. A study of the impact of an after-school program in North Carolina found that enabling parents—primarily mothers—to work a full day before picking up their kids added $590 million to the state's economy. The Department of Education estimates that the cost of universal after-school programs nationwide would be between $5 billion and $10 billion annually, a drop in the bucket as far as federal spending goes.[23]

Women and the families they support—with wages and unpaid labor—have every reason to feel beleaguered by a culture that doesn't care about their values. They have a clear choice between progressive and conservative solutions; they can support the right-wingers who whine about sex on TV but never do anything about it, or they can support liberals fighting for the United States to catch up with Mexico and Greece in terms of family-friendly public policies. Arguing for an economy that works for women and their families is the type of politics that once upon a time fueled the New Deal Coalition—it represents the promise of a humanist economy.

The Myth of the Pipeline:
Why Women Aren't Poised to
Shatter the Glass Ceiling

In chapter 7, we saw that the gender pay gap doesn't appear immediately, right after college, when young women earn pretty much the same salaries as their male counterparts.

It's also true that more women than men are earning college degrees. In 2003, there were 1.35 women graduating from a four-year college for every man. That year, women earned half of the business degrees awarded in this country, up from only 9 percent in 1971.[1]

These two trends have led to a widespread belief that once women achieve a critical mass in the lower echelons of corporate management, they'll begin to move up the "pipeline," eventually achieving something like parity in the nation's executive suites. According to the theory, senior management is just that—senior—and even if women hold very few of the top positions today, the next generation of movers and shakers will naturally be a more diverse crowd. But in 2010, a major study by Catalyst, a nonprofit business consulting group, suggested that the pipeline that many have been counting on is in fact a myth.[2]

Rather than look at the average salaries of all men and women, as we did in the last chapter, researchers Nancy Carter and Christine Silva studied the subset of the population that is most likely to end up becoming tomorrow's corporate leaders—"high potential women and men MBAs for whom much was paid and from whom much was expected." They were the "best and the brightest," having gotten advanced degrees "at twenty-six leading business schools in Asia, Canada, Europe, and the United States" between 1996 and 2007.

What they found was that the women in this rarified group fell behind the men right away and stayed behind during the early years of their careers:

Among this highly talented group, women lag men in advancement and compensation from their very first professional jobs and are less satisfied with their careers overall. Furthermore, women are more likely to have left their first post-MBA job because of a difficult manager and to have paid a penalty for pursuing a nontraditional career pathway, such as working in the nonprofit, government, or education sectors; being self-employed; or working part time before returning to work full time in a company or a firm.

The researchers found that even "after taking into account number of years of experience, industry, and global region," women "still were more likely than men to start in a first post-MBA job at a lower level." Right out of business school, men were given more responsibility and earned an average of $4,600 more than their female counterparts did.

When men and women started at similarly low positions, men got promoted faster and had an easier time moving up the ladder. And whatever their starting salaries, men saw greater increases than women did in their first years after earning an MBA.

It's been argued that men and women have different aspirations and exhibit different degrees of ambition. Yet the researchers found that the results were the same even when they looked only at those who said they aspired to be CEOs. And they adjusted for childbearing, finding that the pattern remained the same when they looked only at men and women who hadn't yet had children.

After testing every possible explanation for the differing outcomes, what they were left with was old-school sexism. "I was shocked," Catalyst CEO Ilene Lang told ABC News when asked about the findings. "This really ate away, undermined my confidence that important change had taken place."[3]

Lang called the study an important wake-up call for young women who thought the battle for equality in the workplace had been fought and won by their mothers. "We've raised them to think they can do anything," she said. "There are still a lot of inequities. They need to be armed and vigilant."

8

OUR HEALTH-CARE SYSTEM IS A HUGE RIP-OFF

Don't believe we have the greatest health care in the world

We do not have 47 million Americans who don't have health-care. There are *no Americans* who don't have access to health-care. Everybody in this country has access to health-care. We do have about 7.5 million Americans who want to purchase health insurance who cannot afford it, [but] we do not need a plan that destroys what is good about health-care in this country [in order] to give the government control over our lives.

—*Representative Virginia Foxx (R-NC)[1]*

In 2009 and 2010, the debate over health care unleashed some sheer unmitigated craziness from the Right that far surpassed the usual boilerplate about "tort reform" and standard warnings that the proposal would blow up the national debt. The American people, trying to figure out what the complicated legislative proposals would actually mean, were treated to extreme and sometimes bizarre arguments about our health-care system.

What made the ocean of crazy surrounding the debate so remarkable is that the overheated—and decidedly ill-informed—spew was coming not only from the likes of Rush Limbaugh or Sean Hannity, but also from the mouths of elected public officials, people who are tasked with creating legislation. When asked what he didn't like about the bill as it was working its way through the Senate, Senator James Inhofe (R-OK) appeared to be proud of his ignorance of the details. "I don't have to read it or know what's in it," he told the *Grady County Express Star*. "I'm going to oppose it anyways." According to the *Star*, "Information provided by news media have [*sic*] helped [Inhofe] become a staunch non-supporter of the bill"—in other words, his opposition was firmly grounded in whatever he picked up from the fair-and-balanced conservative media.

Representative Steve King (R-IA) warned that the House reform bill "cancels every [health insurance] policy" in America and added for emphasis, "[House Speaker Nancy] Pelosi's agenda takes every [policy] away." King was speaking on MSNBC. Not to be outdone, Minnesota Republican representative Michele Bachmann told Fox News that the House bill would make private insurance illegal. And Representative Paul Broun (R-GA) warned that the Democrats' incremental, rather business-friendly reforms would "destroy America as we know it today."

House Minority Leader John Boehner (R-OH) warned that health-care "rationing" is inevitable. Sue Myrick, a cancer survivor and a GOP representative from North Carolina, said, "Make no mistake, [the proposals in Congress] are all gateways to government-run health care." And when decrying the bill's "socialism" failed to stir up popular ire, conservatives simply upped the ante and promised everyone that the Democrats were bent on nothing short of killing off U.S. citizens in order to control health-care costs.

The rumors about the infamous "death panels" were started by veteran wing-nut Betsy McCaughey, a former lieutenant governor of New York, and they were soon being touted by GOP heavy-hitters such as John Boehner and Chuck Grassley, who said, "We should not have a government program that determines if you're going to pull the plug on Grandma."

What was the actual provision that started the death-panels nonsense? In the real world, the bill simply directed Medicare to reimburse doctors for consulting with patients who want help drawing up a living will: a way to control *their own health care* if they become incapacitated. That was it—the substance of the "death panels" meme.

How Conservatives Framed the Debate

While madness was the order of the day on the airwaves and the blogs, more serious discussions were occurring among policy wonks and lawmakers on *Meet the Press* and in the pages of the Beltway press.

As always, if you can frame the terms of a debate, you've gone a long way toward winning it before you've even begun. And tragically, Republicans, the health-care industry, and business-friendly "blue dog" Democrats were largely able to do exactly that. With a substantial assist from the corporate-owned media, they successfully focused the debate on the short-term costs to the federal government's bottom line. In fact, they did such a good job that much of the discussion revolved around what was arguably one of the least-relevant aspects of the proposals being debated in Congress at the time: whether they "cost too much" or were "deficit neutral" in terms of their impact on the federal budget during the ten years to follow.

There were a number of problems with that question. First, we were talking about proposals that would extend health care to tens of millions of uninsured Americans. Why such a significant improvement in the health and economic security of so many people should be expected to come without cost to the government's balance sheet is a mystery. Second, the narrative focused on the impact of the proposals on the federal budget in isolation, all but ignoring the larger effect that fixing the system (if done right) might have had on the economy as a whole. Under consideration were various proposals that were designed to rein in the spiraling cost of health care across the entire system, investments that analysts expected to have a *significant* payoff.

For example, a study by David Cutler of Harvard and the Rand Corp.'s Melinda Beeuwkes Buntin estimated that just three elements within the larger proposals offered by the Democrats in 2009—all of which entailed early start-up costs—would have resulted in $550 billion in savings to the larger health-care system during the following ten years.[2]

In 1960, we spent less than 5 percent of the gross domestic product on health care, and all but a small number of working-age Americans had access to care. Today, health-care spending represents around 18 percent of our economic output, and about one in six citizens lacks coverage. According to virtually every projection available to lawmakers as they debated the bill, the situation was only going to get worse unless we made substantial reforms. So the more salient question would have been: how can we possibly afford *not* to fix the health-care system?

In order to dodge that discussion, some on the Right undertook the difficult task of defending the status quo. Perhaps one of the most brazen lies to pass conservative lips during the debate was also the simplest. As Senator John Barrasso (R-WY) put it, "I do believe we have the best health care system in the world."[3] Barrasso followed that jaw-dropping statement with an anecdote. "That's why the premier of one of the Canadian provinces came here just last week to have his heart operated on," Barrasso noted. "He said, 'It's my heart, it's my life. I want to go where it's the best.' And he came to the United States."

Barrasso wasn't alone in using anecdotes to make his case. We were regaled with an endless series of stories about the supposed horrors of living in a country where everyone is covered—the tyranny! The genre took a comical turn when *Investor's Business Daily*, a rabidly right-wing rag, argued that if famed physicist Stephen Hawking, who has suffered for more than forty years with Lou Gehrig's disease, had been in a country with "socialized medicine," he surely wouldn't have survived.[4]

Hawking replied by noting that as far as he knew, he was still a Briton who had lived his entire life with socialized health care. "I wouldn't be here today if it were not for the [British National Health Service]," he said. "I have received a large amount of high-quality treatment without which I would not have survived."[5]

Americans Can't Afford the Status Quo

We do have excellent health care in this country—perhaps the best—for those who can afford it. Say, for example, a Canadian premier. And it's also true that a majority of Americans have access to at least decent health care. The reason this is not good enough is simple: we spend a great deal more on health care than any other industrialized nation does, yet millions of Americans have terrible coverage—a 2008 study found that one in five people under the age of sixty-five was *under*-insured[6]—and tens of millions more can't get any health care outside of the emergency room.

If you spend $150,000 on a Ferrari and beat-up old Pintos consistently outrace you, the fact that you don't get beaten *too badly* is hardly something to brag about. In 2007, we spent $7,290 per American citizen on health care. Not only did that figure lead the world, it did so by a huge margin—number two, Norway, came in at a little more than $4,700 per person, three grand less than the United States.[7] For that money, we ranked between 15th and 37th out of the 153 countries studied by the American Society of Integrative Medicine in every single measure of health outcomes. As one of the authors noted, "Almost every major study of America's healthcare system has concluded that we could hardly do worse in terms of how much well-being is yielded for the resources currently expended."[8] The World Health Organization ranked the U.S. system 37th out of the 191 countries it studied in 2000.[9] We're paying for a Ferrari, and we're getting burned badly on the deal.

In addition, our costs are growing fast. According to government data, health-care spending almost *tripled* between 1990 and 2009. The costs per person grew by almost 50 percent just in the period between 2000 and 2005.[10] That kind of growth outpaces the overall growth in the economy by a mile—the share of America's total economic output being sucked into health care is expected to equal one-fifth of the total economy in ten years.[11]

Those costs are much higher than what other countries pay, and unlike every other advanced economy in the world, most of that burden is borne by U.S. companies and families, instead of being spread across society via a progressive tax system. That puts U.S. firms at a distinct disadvantage in terms of labor costs and encourages them to offshore and outsource as many jobs as possible. As we saw, the health-care sector added a lot of jobs to the economy in recent years, but those spiraling health costs also create a powerful incentive for employers to send jobs in most other sectors overseas.

The sky-high cost of health care hurts working families, both directly and indirectly. As we've seen, during the last thirty years, economic growth hasn't made its way into most working people's paychecks. But—and this is key—the amount that businesses have had to pay for an hour of work has *increased* pretty much across the board.

Conservative economists such as Greg Mankiw, the former chairman of Bush's Council of Economic Advisers (who infamously suggested that assembling cheeseburgers at McDonald's should count as a manufacturing job), argued that looking at wages isn't an honest measure of how workers are doing, because their overall compensation—including medical and other benefits—rose faster than inflation, even if wages didn't.[12]

Allan Hubbard, another Bush economic adviser, told the *Wall Street Journal*, "Employers are spending more money on healthcare, and that's robbing people of wage increases." The claim is controversial—corporate profits and executive pay have both increased, and fewer than half of all U.S. workers get coverage from their employers—but it is a simple fact that the gap between the cash that working Americans are pocketing and the money their employers pay for an hour of their time has been growing.[13] According to a study by the Kaiser Foundation, workers' pay rose by 18 percent between 2000 and 2006—not quite keeping up with the 20 percent inflation during that period—while employers' health-care premiums rose by *almost 90 percent*.[14]

Looking only at the George W. Bush years—and before the Great Recession gained steam—economists Lawrence Mishel and Jared Bernstein found that although average weekly wages for (nonsupervisory) workers increased by a paltry 1.7 percent annually, average total compensation—including health care and other benefits—increased by 5.1 percent per year. If we stay on our current trajectory—driving fast toward a cliff, as the baby boomers hit their "golden years"—it's going to get much worse.

A picture can be worth a thousand words, and the graph below, based on projections by the Council of Economic Advisers, shows

Projected Annual Total Compensation and Compensation Net of Health Insurance Premiums

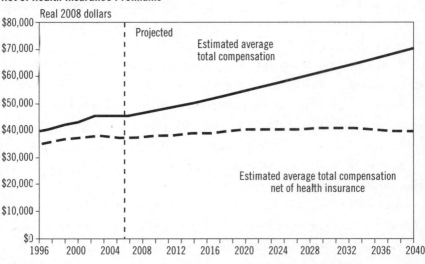

Source: CEA calculations.

that Americans' incomes will remain flat long into the future if rising health costs aren't controlled.

And then there are the direct costs. A study by the Commonwealth Fund found that families' out-of-pocket expenses (and premium copayments) rose in direct proportion to overall health-care spending.[15] In an ABC News/USA *Today* poll, one in four Americans said that their families had experienced a problem paying for medical care during the previous year, up 7 percentage points over the last nine years.[16] Almost half of those declaring bankruptcy in 2001 cited health-care costs as a "major contributor."[17]

We also pay a steep penalty—all of us—for our system's lack of universality. Studies show that people without coverage often put off medical care until the symptoms are so bad that they end up in emergency rooms, where they ran up about $65 billion in charges in 2005. According to a study by the advocacy group FamiliesUSA, the uninsured pay a bit more than a third of the costs out-of-pocket, the government picks up a third of the remainder, and the rest is paid by people with health insurance through higher premiums. According to the FamiliesUSA study, that adds up to almost $1,000 per fully insured family.[18]

So, What's Wrong with Us?

There are many reasons why our health-care costs are so bloated, and some are fiercely debated. Yet what is arguably the biggest problem is also one of the least discussed: the whole system is set up with perverse and essentially self-defeating incentives.

The United States has a *disease-care* system, where all of the emphasis is on treating people once they've gotten sick, instead of on keeping people healthy in the first place. It is reactive, rather than proactive, despite a large body of research that proves the old adage that an ounce of prevention is worth a pound of cure. Studies show that a dollar spent on preventive health will save up to four dollars by the fourth year that the data are tracked. But although public health experts preach the gospel, only about 1 percent of our spending—a penny of each U.S. health-care dollar—goes toward prevention.[19]

It's also the case that, as economist Josh Bivens of the Economic Policy Institute noted, "Health care is an area where the more costs are loaded up on the federal government, the more efficiently care tends to be delivered overall." Bivens pointed out that although the United States spends far more than other advanced countries do on health care, far fewer of those dollars are spent in the public sector. He suggests that this difference is a major reason we get far worse results than other wealthy countries do in terms of access, life expectancy at birth, our chances of living until age sixty, and most other meaningful metrics.[20]

To illustrate the savings that are built into public-sector health spending, he went on to cite an analysis by the Lewin Group of the impact that three competing approaches to reform would have had on the federal budget and overall health spending. The three plans included a conservative "limited government" proposal, a progressive plan that would have shifted most of the burden of paying for health care to the government, and the centrist, hybrid approach that was eventually embraced by congressional Dems in 2009.

The results are summarized in the table on page 135.

On the left is Representative Pete Stark's (D-CA) proposal for a single-payer system. As you can see, although it would have extended coverage to everyone—which obviously costs money—it was also the only approach that would have resulted in a reduction of health-care spending across the board.

In the middle is a plan along the lines of the Democratic proposals that were then working their way through the House. According to Bivens's analysis, although "federal health spending [would] rise" as the system is implemented, the "increases in federal spending . . . are accompanied by large reductions in spending by households and businesses. Net total health

Lewin Group Scoring of Three Health Reform Proposals

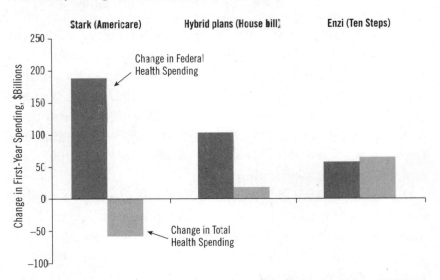

Source: Lewin group evaluation of congressional reform options, through the Commonwealth fund, www.commonwealthfund.org.

spending would rise by less than $18 billion, an amount that is more than explained" by new costs for covering the previously uninsured.

The right column, appropriately, shows the impact of a plan proposed by Senator Mike Enzi (R-WY), a boilerplate conservative proposal based on offering tax credits to help people purchase private insurance, deregulating the industry, and expanding the pool of Americans eligible for Medicaid. It would have increased federal spending by slightly less than the other two approaches, but in the process it also would have increased total health-care costs more than the amount of tax dollars required to implement the plan. And it would have insured only the relatively small number of people who made just a bit more than the cut-off for Medicaid.

Much of the difference between these approaches can be explained with a simple rule: when it comes to insurance pools, size matters. Having more people under a single umbrella results in more bargaining power with providers and greater economies of scale. And having a single insurer would eliminate the paperwork shuffling that's estimated to suck up as much as 30 percent of our health-care dollars.[21] This holds true not only on the systemic level. Today, most of the largest employers in the country self-insure: they pay their employees' claims directly and cut out the middleman. Big firms that don't self-insure buy insurance on the large-group market, where risk is spread out over a large pool. Large-group plans tend to be more or less comprehensive and, relatively speaking, affordable.

But those who are forced to purchase coverage on the individual or small-group markets have little buying power and are routinely forced to pay budget-busting premiums for the worst possible coverage: plans with high deductibles, caps on benefits, and strict limits on what is and isn't covered.

How the Public Option Was Killed by "Big Health" and Its Conservative Friends

Big pools were at the heart of the "public insurance option"—the most contentious point of debate in the reform battle, and one that progressives would eventually concede in the face of united opposition from the insurance industry and its supporters on both sides of the aisle in Congress. It would have worked like this: the government would have established regional exchanges, or "gateways," open to people who would otherwise be forced into the individual and small-group markets. These gateways would have had relatively large insurance pools, just as large employers—and public programs such as Medicare—have now.

Within these large purchasing pools, people would have been able to choose from among various insurance plans: one a government-run "public option" and the rest offered by private insurers. All of the plans would have had to conform to some minimal standards of coverage. The playing field would have been level for real competition between private insurers and the public insurance option, and advocates believed that eventually much of the population would have opted for the public option, expanding the insurance pool further and resulting in even greater cost savings over the long haul.

The public option died on the vine, however, withering under a heated assault by Republicans and "blue dog" Dems. Again, they killed it by successfully focusing the debate on the short-term costs of reform to the federal government's bottom line, obscuring the potential impact that a meaningful realignment of the health-care system would have had on the economy as a whole.

Yet the irony of the entire yearlong debate was this: the Obama administration and congressional leaders began with a proposal that was already a centrist, relatively business-friendly bill and then mollified self-appointed "fiscally conservative" Democrats by watering it down throughout the process so that what emerged from the legislative sausage-making was good as far as covering a lot of the uninsured, but very limited in its potential to contain the runaway health-care costs that represent the lion's share of our nation's "deficit crisis."

Instead of insuring a large pool of up to 130 million Americans, as candidate Obama suggested his public option would during the 2008 campaign, lawmakers started the debate with a public option whose eligibility was tightly restricted. The CBO's preliminary estimate suggested that only 10 million Americans would be enrolled in the public insurance plan by 2019. (That's out of about 30 million who could buy insurance—either public or private—through the insurance exchanges.) This shrunken public option was a nod to the power of the insurance industry—nothing more, nothing less. Then, after a bitter fight, the Obama administration dropped not only the public option, but also the large, federally run public "gateways." In their stead, we got exchanges with smaller purchasing pools organized at the state level.

As I write this in the middle of 2010, Americans are divided on the legislation. Many of the Affordable Care Act's benefits aren't scheduled to kick in until 2014, and that's part of the problem: people have heard a lot of criticism of the legislation but haven't had a chance to see what it actually does (and doesn't do—no death panels). This, too, was by design, in order to limit the short-term costs to the federal government and get the Blue Dog Coalition onboard.

Insurance Reform, Accomplished . . .
Health-Care Reform, Not So Much

Given the climate, it was a small miracle that Democrats were able to pass such an ambitious package at all. The Affordable Care Act was, as many observers noted at the time, the first major piece of social welfare legislation enacted in the United States in fifty years. Obama was the seventh president to try to codify the principle of universal health care into law in this country; Truman was the first, having attempted the feat almost seventy years earlier.

Yet, again, the reforms that eventually became law had been deeply compromised along the way. The legislation, which left the for-profit insurance industry largely unchanged, won't do nearly enough to control skyrocketing costs. Yes, it will cover tens of millions, which is a great accomplishment, but facing a crisis in health-care spending makes "bending the cost curve" downward an absolute economic imperative.

What Congress did in the end was pass a pretty good *insurance-reform* bill—it'll prohibit insurers from turning away people with previous conditions, dropping coverage for people once they get sick, and sticking them with onerous annual or lifetime caps on benefits. It offers people who can't afford coverage relatively generous subsidies and expands Medicaid eligibility for those who can't afford even a subsidized plan. And it requires all but very small employers to at least contribute to the cost of covering their workers.

We are still in desperate need of *health-care reform*, though. This means restructuring the way we pay for health care and changing the mix of incentives so that caregivers have an interest in keeping people healthy, rather than simply treating them when they're not. So, in the aftermath of the law's passage, it's important to understand a lesson from our recent history. We have to remember that other historic efforts that reshaped our society for the better weren't accomplished with the passage of a single law.

The Civil Rights Act of 1964 was a landmark measure, but activists at the time were disappointed that it didn't go far enough in guaranteeing minority voting rights. Yet its passage marked neither the beginning nor the end of the process—it was one of several key stepping-stones in the creation of today's civil rights laws. Two years earlier, Congress had taken up a proposal to amend the Constitution to prohibit states from imposing poll taxes—taxes that disenfranchised many of the poor and especially people of color—in order to vote in federal elections. It was ratified the same year as the Civil Rights Act's passage. Then, in 1965, many of the provisions that had been excluded from the Civil Rights Act—to the chagrin of civil rights supporters—were passed into law with the Voting Rights Act of 1965. Today, that law is widely seen as the most significant single piece of civil rights legislation passed by Congress.

We're at a similar juncture in terms of transforming America's health-care system. One way or another, the insurance reforms that were passed in 2010 aren't the end of the road. We can expect years of legislation that will shape what this "uniquely American" health-care system will look like. And those tweaks, depending on who's in power at the time and the political mood of the country, will either curb runaway health-care costs and assure decent coverage for all Americans, or they will result in the dilution of the already modest insurance reforms that were passed in 2010.

The worst parts of the act—the mandate to buy plans from private insurance companies and the fact that its potential to control costs is limited—are powerful arguments for a public insurance option that would be available on a national exchange and open to everyone. If the Affordable Care Act of 2010 was a starting point for major social change, similar to the Civil Rights Act of 1964, then fighting to add a robust public option could become something like the push for the 1965 Voting Rights Act in the years to come.

The Health-Care Economy

There's an old saw that says Americans don't make things anymore; we just sue one another and sell one another real estate.

Before the real estate market melted down, it accounted for many of the jobs created in the United States during George W. Bush's presidency. In the summer of 2005, the *New York Times* reported that the real estate biz—"everything from land surveyors to general contractors to loan officers"—had added 700,000 jobs to the U.S. economy during the previous four years, while the rest of the workforce had lost 400,000 jobs during the same period. Technically, the economy was in "recovery," when in fact most of it remained soft.[1]

So, a weak economy in most sectors was masked by an explosion in real estate sales, rocketing home values, and a surge of consumer spending as people took advantage of superlow interest rates and easy credit and grabbed chunks of equity out of their newly high-priced digs to go shopping.

Yet that wasn't all that was happening. At the same time, we saw the emergence of what could be called the "health-care economy." As Michael Mandel wrote in *BusinessWeek*, "Without [the health sector], the nation's labor market would be in a deep coma." Between 2001 and 2006, 1.7 million new jobs were added in the health-care sector. Meanwhile, the rest of the private sector added exactly zero new jobs (net) during that period.[2]

If current trends continue, 30 to 40 percent of all new jobs created in the United States during the next twenty-five years will be in the health-care business. Mandel argued that this trend is responsible in part for the low overall unemployment rate in the United States. "Take away healthcare hiring in the U.S.," he wrote, "and quicker than you can say cardiac bypass, the U.S. unemployment rate would be 1 to 2 percentage points higher."[3]

One could argue that this is precisely how a vibrant economy should work. A dynamic industry takes off and compensates for weaknesses in other sectors. When it cools, another field will explode, perhaps one we can't even imagine today.

What's more, those health-care jobs came at the same time that we were shedding millions of relatively high-paying manufacturing jobs. Wages in the health sector vary widely, but the average is slightly higher than incomes in the private sector as a whole. Health care is labor-intensive, so a lot of the more than $2.5 trillion we'll spend this year in the United States will end up in health-care workers' pockets. It's also an industry in which offshoring and outsourcing are uncommon; you might be able to schedule your colonoscopy with a guy at a call center in Mumbai, but ultimately your ass has to be in the same country as the medical personnel who do the procedure.

So, is a health-care economy a bad thing? It is; as we saw in chapter 8, our health-care system—a rip-off, by any reasonable measure—sucks up around a trillion tax dollars per year and threatens the competitiveness of U.S. firms. It's become a fabulously expensive jobs program that we simply can't afford.

9

OBAMA IS NOT A SOCIALIST

Don't believe that those poor, oppressed corporations need saving

> Revelations that the Republican National Committee urged fundraisers to shake the money trees by playing on fears about President Obama and "socialism" have ignited a classic Washington kerfuffle. But outside the Washington bubble, reaction to the document among Republican leaders has been decidedly less, well, worked up.
>
> —*National Public Radio, March 5, 2010: "Top Republicans: Yeah, We're Calling Obama Socialist"*[1]

The dominance of conservative economic narratives in our discourse has nudged the entire U.S. political spectrum to the right. Ronald Reagan, the Sainted King of modern conservatism, would have been considered a "RINO" (Republican In Name Only)—an apostate—if he served today. Reagan, after all, raised taxes to reduce the deficit, worked out a bipartisan bargain on Social Security reform, and signed an amnesty bill for undocumented immigrants. Sure, he railed against welfare queens, backed right-wing death squads in Latin America, and caused a lot of economic pain, but he also worked with the dreaded opposition to get things done.

And so it continues in the Obama era. The president's early years have presented an almost surreal situation: although many

143

liberals are deeply disappointed with the centrist course the administration has taken, a significant chunk of the population is convinced he's the reincarnation of Chairman Mao. Those who buy this aren't entirely to blame. Just as we saw with the "death panel" nonsense during the health-care debate, charges of socialism have come not only from feverish right-wing bloggers, but also from some of the most prominent leaders of the modern conservative movement.

When Newt Gingrich called Obama "the most radical president in American history" and urged a partisan crowd to block his "secular, socialist machine," it caused Norman Ornstein, a resident fellow with the über-conservative American Enterprise Institute (but also a very serious political wonk), so much embarrassment that he took to the pages of the *Washington Post* to push back against the former House speaker. "To one outside the partisan and ideological wars," he wrote, "charges of radicalism, socialism, retreat and surrender are, frankly, bizarre."[2]

Ornstein reviewed the health-care bill—he concluded it "would be fair to describe the new act . . . as a moderate Republican plan"—and also examined how Obama had administered Bush's Wall Street bailouts, the bailout of the auto industry, the administration's nuclear policy, and a few prominent appointments. "Looking at the range of Obama domestic and foreign policies," he wrote, "my conclusion is clear: This president is a mainstream, pragmatic moderate, operating in the center of American politics; center-left, perhaps, but not left of center."[3]

The "socialist smear," as Ornstein called it, is typical of the goal-post moving I touched on in the introduction to this book: we can all agree that the kind of heavy-handed government intervention that was typical of Eastern Bloc countries during the Cold War is a formula for economic disaster. Yet by decrying any center-left policy as a sign of creeping socialism, conservatives are saying, "Don't bother looking at whether this regulation or that new program is good or bad—regulation, taxes, and government programs are always bad simply by definition."

It's also part of a larger narrative: the Right would have us believe that capitalism, despite its apparent good health worldwide, is a delicate flower that, like liberty itself, could wither away and die at any moment. In announcing that the U.S. Chamber of Commerce was unleashing an $80–$100 million "war-chest" to defeat progressive candidates in 2008, CoC president Tom Donohue told reporters, "I'm concerned about anti-corporate and populist rhetoric from candidates for the presidency, members of Congress and the media. It suggests to us that we have to demonstrate who it is in this society that creates jobs, wealth and benefits—and who it is that eats them."[4]

According to that worldview, large corporations, the embodiments of American-style capitalism, are equally vulnerable to the meddling of know-nothing bureaucrats: the job-eaters. Again by definition, government intervention in the free market drives corporations away to sunnier locales or threatens their very existence. However well intentioned, it ends up costing workers their jobs.

You'll never see a corporate mouthpiece arguing on a cable news show that increasing the minimum wage will hurt fast-food companies' bottom lines; it's always about the jobs that will be destroyed.

What about Meddling in the Free Market of Ideas?

Everyone agrees that government intervention in the free market has the potential to overreach and, as a result, hurt free enterprise. Many of our political debates can be reduced to arguments over whether specific interventions serve the public well or are too heavy-handed. But we don't often turn that issue on its head. Democracy—which history has shown to be far more fragile than capitalism—requires a "free market" of ideas to function.

Americans tend to take the corporate-PR-media complex for granted, but its impact distorts the marketplace of ideas in both obvious and subtle ways. In 2010, the *Washington Post* reported that it had found "the influence peddlers of K Street" staking out space on social networking sites such as Twitter and Facebook. "Using their own names without mentioning that they work in public relations or as lobbyists," the *Post* reported, "employees of companies with interests in Washington are chattering online to shape opinions in hard-to-detect ways."[5]

Media critics will write a story when some corporate flack gets caught writing a column without disclosing that he or she has a financial interest in the subject at hand, but they rarely look at how corporate America's intervention in our marketplace of ideas results in the kinds of systematic distortions we examine in these chapters.

Private capital's meddling in our democracy isn't limited to influencing our political discourse and gaming the marketplace of ideas. Political scientists talk about "state capture": private interests effectively gaining control of one or more organs of state and using the power vested in those institutions—publicly financed and ostensibly serving the greater good—to feather their own nests. Usually, the term is applied to banana republics, and the means of capture are nefarious: corruption, threats, and even violence.

In the modern, democratic United States, our elites operate differently. Overt corruption—quid pro quo exchanges of votes for gifts or campaign contributions—happens occasionally. Yet it's rare, and when it occurs, the press is all over the story, and the public becomes outraged. Politicians do go to jail.

We have a private campaign finance system, however, that requires members of Congress to start raising hundreds of thousands of dollars to get reelected the moment they take office; a government overrun with well-heeled lobbyists, many of whom are ex-staffers visiting offices in which they once worked to call on former bosses; and a well-oiled revolving door between regulatory agencies and the industries they're supposed to be watching. Corporate America does more than merely fend for itself on Capitol Hill. Its efforts amount to state capture, even if subtle in form, and that has a measurable impact.

Call It Corruption: Unscrupulous Ties between Business and Government

Consider this: in a functional democracy—one where lawmakers pursue the public interest—the stock prices of politically connected companies or industries shouldn't be impacted by the changing fortunes of friendly politicians. But after the 2008 election, when Representative Henry Waxman (D-CA) wrested control of the influential House Energy and Commerce Committee from John Dingell (D-MI), auto stocks tanked on the news.

A *Washington Post* story headlined "Waxman Gains House Energy Committee, Auto Stocks Drop," didn't create any public outcry. "Struggling Detroit auto makers have lost a loyal friend in Rep. John Dingell," the *Post* reported. "In response, shares of GM and Ford fell following the news of Waxman's ascension."[6]

Dingell, who is relatively progressive in some areas, was also firmly in Big Auto's pockets and had clashed with Waxman on a number of issues over the years—issues like beefing up vehicle emission standards. During the course of Dingell's career, three of his top four contributors were GM, Ford, and Daimler-Chrysler; his wife, Debbie, was an industry lobbyist until their marriage in the early 1980s, and she continues to work for GM as of this writing. The couple owned more than a million bucks' worth of Big Auto stocks and options in 2006. After the last election, Dingell hired a Daimler-Chrysler lobbyist to be the Ways and Means Committee's chief of staff.

Waxman, one of the most liberal lawmakers on the Hill, had fought tenaciously against the Corporate Right on issues ranging from oversight of the "security contractors" who ran amok in Iraq to stronger environmental standards.

Most people wouldn't give that *Post* headline a second thought. Why *wouldn't* auto stocks take a hit when the industry "had lost a loyal friend" on a key regulatory committee? It's business as usual, of course, but it's also evidence of a corrupt government. What most people don't know is that forensic economists—the CSIs of the dismal science, people who follow economic clues to unearth crimes—don't take those kinds of stock fluctuations lightly.

In their book *Corruption, Violence, and the Poverty of Nations*, scholars Raymond Fishman and Edward Miguel noted that forensic economists look carefully at how ups and downs in the careers of government officials impact the stock prices of firms to which they're connected. They consider it to be among the more methodologically sound ways of rooting out government corruption.

In an article for *Foreign Policy* magazine, Fishman and Miguel laid out the rationale behind the approach:

> Whether through hefty campaign contributions or cushy jobs for former politicians, corporations are constantly accused of trying to profit through political ties. (Just think Halliburton or Russia's Gazprom.) But what's the real value of these companies' connections? If you ask politicians or investors, you're likely to hear a lot of denials. To get the truth, we could ask insiders to put some money where their mouths are, making them bet some of their own cash on whether particular companies are making back-alley deals with politicians to increase their profits. In this political betting pool, raw financial self-interest would lead bettors in the know to reveal their true beliefs about corruption.[7]

That betting pool is, of course, the stock market. The scholars wrote, "If connections buy tax breaks, valuable licenses, and advantages in bidding for government contracts, then strengthening political ties should boost profits. These higher profits translate directly into higher stock prices, and conversely, removing those ties should send profits—and stock prices—tumbling."[8]

Purdue University economist Mara Faccio studied those ties in every country that had a functional stock market. Not surprisingly, Faccio found strong connections between business and government across the board, but she also noted that the value of those connections in terms of stock prices varied greatly.[9] In the United Kingdom, for example, stock prices don't move at all when a firm's political ties wax or wane. When Rolls-Royce chairman John Moore was appointed to the House of Lords, Rolls-Royce's stock price remained unchanged. But in Italy, the picture is quite different. When Fiat chief Giovanni Agnelli was appointed to the Italian Senate, the automaker's stock soared by 3.4 percent, adding millions of dollars in value to the company in a single day.[10]

Now consider that headline once more—"Waxman Gains House Energy Committee, Auto Stocks Drop." It says we're a lot closer to Italy's infamous level of public corruption than we are to that of our British cousins. And, as Fishman and Miguel noted, that's already been pretty well established in this country:

> Numerous studies have found that the economic fortunes of well-connected U.S. companies mirror the political fortunes of their connections. When U.S. Sen. Jim Jeffords defected from the Republican Party and handed Senate Democrats a slim majority in 2001, Democratically connected companies benefited in the immediate aftermath. Similarly, the stock value of companies with former Republican lawmakers on their boards increased an average of 4 percent when the Supreme Court handed the 2000 election to George W. Bush, while companies with former Democratic politicians on their boards declined.

Most people have probably never heard of a "forensic economist," but we all know the score. The two words that political headline writers pair most frequently are "lobbyists" and "swarm." As in: "Lobbyists Swarm onto Cable Issue" (*Los Angeles Daily News*); "A Finance Overhaul Fight Draws a Swarm of Lobbyists" (*New York Times*); "Credit Card Industry Lobbyists Swarm Congress to Defeat Reform Bills" (*Colorado Independent*); "Lobbyists, Bankers Swarm US Agricultural Committee" (Reuters); "Lobbyists Swarm Capitol to Influence Health Reform" (Center for Public Integrity);

and so on ("hordes" and "lobbyists" also frequently share space in snappy political headlines).

Between 2000 and 2005, the number of registered lobbyists in Washington more than doubled, to more than 34,750, while the amount that they charge their new clients increased by as much as 100 percent. The *Washington Post* reported, "Only a few other businesses have enjoyed greater prosperity in an otherwise fitful economy."[11] During the health-care debate of 2009, the Center for Public Integrity, a watchdog group, found that there were eight lobbyists roaming the halls of Congress trying to influence the legislation for every lawmaker who would eventually vote on it.[12]

There's nothing inherently wrong with lobbying—it's how interested parties present ideas and information to legislators. But combined with a very expensive and, for the most part, privately financed election system, it gives those with deep pockets a disproportionate voice in our political debates, which is a major reason they always seem to do so well. The most basic laws of economics dictate that if corporate America weren't getting good value, it wouldn't drop vast sums of money on hiring lobbyists—peddling influence represented a $3.5 billion industry in 2009.[13]

There is also the "revolving door." The Center for Public Integrity keeps a database of former members of Congress who are now raking in big bucks working as lobbyists. It's constantly growing, but as of this writing, the center has profiled 148. If those lobbyists were still serving, they'd have just thirty fewer seats than the Republican Party currently holds. The database of former *staffers*-turned-lobbyists runs into the thousands.[14]

The revolving door at the regulatory level is an even more pernicious form of state capture. When people working for government paychecks at regulatory agencies are looking forward to cushy, high-paying gigs in the industries they regulate (and when people with good corporate jobs know they can put in a few years at a regulatory agency and then land a much cushier job in the industry down the line), it means that even when corporate America loses a battle in

Congress, it can still have its way at the agency level, where the rubber meets the road.

Two of the bigger news stories of 2010 illustrate just how badly this can undermine regulation that should have protected the public interest. When news broke that Toyota was recalling more than 5 million vehicles that were prone to taking off before their drivers touched the gas, it caused a political firestorm. The glitch had been responsible for more than a hundred deaths.[15] Public anger intensified when news surfaced that the company had covered up reports of the problem for quite some time.

A subsequent investigation by Bloomberg News revealed, "At least four U.S. investigations into unintended acceleration by Toyota Motor Corp. vehicles were ended with the help of former regulators hired by the automaker, warding off possible recalls, court and government records show."[16] The former regulators, Christopher Tinto and Christopher Santucci, both joined Toyota directly from the National Highway Traffic Safety Administration (NHTSA). Tinto became vice president of regulatory affairs in Toyota's Washington office, and Santucci landed a job beneath him.

Bloomberg reported that during the six years before the recall, the NHTSA had opened eight investigations into the sudden acceleration issue. Five were closed after the NHTSA found no evidence of a defect, and, "In four of the five cases that were closed, Tinto and Santucci worked with NHTSA on Toyota's responses to the consumer complaints the agency was investigating."

Another big story in April was a horrific explosion at a West Virginia coal mine that killed twenty-nine miners. It was the worst mining accident in more than twenty-five years. While the search was still on for the bodies of the missing, the Associated Press reported that the mine's operator, Massey Energy Corporation, "had been cited for 600 violations in less than a year and a half, some of them for not properly ventilating methane—the highly combustible gas suspected in the blast." The AP described Massey as "a powerful and politically connected company in Appalachia known for producing big profits, as well as big piles of safety and environmental violations and big damage awards for grieving widows."[17]

A few weeks later, the *Washington Post* reported that "More than 200 former congressional staff members, federal regulators and lawmakers" had gotten cushy jobs in the mining industry, "including dozens who work for coal companies with the worst safety records in the nation." Dozens of others had gone from the coal industry "into government as policy aides in Congress or officials of the Mine Safety and Health Administration (MSHA), which enforces safety standards."[18]

And, according to the *Post*, "The movement between industry and government . . . has led to a regulatory system tilted toward coal company interests. That, [critics] say, has put miners at risk and left behind a flawed enforcement system that probably contributed to this month's Massey Energy mine explosion in West Virginia." As of this writing, Massey Energy is reportedly being investigated by the Federal Bureau of Investigation on suspicion that it bribed safety regulators to look the other way.[19]

Remember that our tax dollars were paying for the agencies to regulate these industries—we were picking up the regulators' salaries. We should be calling this what it is: corruption. And maybe even screaming about it from the rooftops. But we don't—it's business as usual.

You'll never hear a speaker at a Tea Party event discussing campaign finance or lobbying reforms or the corporations on the other side of those revolving doors in Washington. You will, however, definitely encounter some powerful fears of socialism.

The Corporate Civil Rights Movement

One reason that people tend to accept private capital's constant interventions in our democracy is that there's little political pressure for true systemic reform. Sure, decrying Washington's "business as usual" may be popular on the campaign trail, and there are certainly "good government groups" (aka "goo-goos") issuing plenty of reports about these issues, but when it comes to real lobbying and campaign finance reform or slowing that revolving door, we've taken two steps back for each step forward.

In 2010, we actually took three steps back with the landmark Supreme Court decision *Citizens United v. FEC*. The ruling overturned several of the already limited checks on corporate campaign financing that we had in place. The conservative majority specifically killed off parts of the McCain-Feingold Campaign Reform Act that prohibited corporations from broadcasting "electioneering communications"—infomercials for or against a candidate—within sixty days of an election. The decision held that the limits had intruded on corporations' right to free speech under the First Amendment.

Harvard legal scholar Lawrence Tribe wrote that the decision "marks a major upheaval in First Amendment law and signals the end of whatever legitimate claim could otherwise have been made by the Roberts Court to an incremental and minimalist approach to constitutional adjudication, to a modest view of the judicial role vis-à-vis the political branches, or to a genuine concern with adherence to precedent."[20]

Looking narrowly at the details of the decision, Tribe was right. Michael Waldman, the director of the Brennan Center for Justice at NYU School of Law, wrote that the ruling "matches or exceeds *Bush v. Gore* in ideological or partisan overreaching by the court."[21] Looking at the broader landscape of U.S. history, however, the ruling did in fact follow a twisted sort of precedent. The *Citizens United* decision simply advanced a bizarre legal doctrine, developed during the last 150 years, that effectively codifies the power of corporate interests. Ultimately, it is based on an Orwellian concept known as "corporate personhood."

"Corporate personhood" gives businesses—entirely artificial entities created by the state—the same individual rights that the framers fought and died to secure for flesh-and-blood citizens (or at least for white male property holders, but you get the idea). The doctrine's origin in English law was reasonable enough; it was only by considering companies "persons" that they could be taken to court and sued. You can't sue an inanimate object.

During the nineteenth century, however, the robber barons, aided by a few corrupt jurists deep in their pockets, took the concept to a whole new level in the United States. According to legal textbooks, the idea that corporations enjoy the same constitutional rights as you or I was codified in the 1886 decision *Santa Clara County v. Southern Pacific Railroad*. But historian Thom Hartmann dug into the original case documents and found that this crucially important legal doctrine actually originated with what may be the most significant act of corruption in history.

It occurred during a seemingly routine tax case: Santa Clara sued the Southern Pacific Railroad to pay property taxes on the land it held in the county, and the railroad claimed that because states had different rates, allowing them to tax its holdings would violate the Equal Protection Clause of the Fourteenth Amendment. The railroads had made the claim in previous cases, but the courts had never bought the argument.

In a 2005 interview, Hartmann described his surprise when he went to a Vermont courthouse to read an original copy of the verdict and found that the judges had made no mention of corporate personhood. "In fact," he told the interviewer, "the decision says, at its end, that because they could find a California state law that covered the case 'it is not necessary to consider any other questions' such as the constitutionality of the railroad's claim to personhood."[22]

Hartmann then explained how it was that corporations actually became "people":

> But in the headnote to the case—a commentary written by the clerk, which is *not* legally binding, it's just a commentary to help out law students and whatnot, summarizing the case—the Court's clerk wrote: "The defendant Corporations are persons within the intent of the clause in section 1 of the

Fourteenth Amendment to the Constitution of the United States, which forbids a State to deny to any person within its jurisdiction the equal protection of the laws."

The discovery "that we'd been operating for over 100 years on an incorrect headnote" led Hartmann to look into the past of the clerk who'd written it, J. C. Bancroft Davis. He discovered that Davis had been a corrupt official who had himself previously served as the president of a railroad. Digging deeper, Hartmann then discovered that Davis had been working "in collusion with another corrupt Supreme Court Justice, Stephen Field." The railroad companies, according to Hartmann, had promised Field that they'd sponsor his run for the White House if he assisted them in their effort to gain constitutional rights.

Hartmann noted that even after the ruling, the idea of corporate personhood remained relatively obscure until corporate lawyers dusted off the doctrine during the Reagan era and used it to help reshape the U.S. political economy.

Nike asserted before the Supreme Court . . . as Sinclair Broadcasting did in a press release last month, that these corporations have First Amendment rights of free speech. Dow Chemical in a case it took to the Supreme Court asserted it has Fourth Amendment privacy rights and could refuse to allow the EPA to do surprise inspections of its facilities. J.C. Penney asserted before the Supreme Court that it had a Fourteenth Amendment right to be free from discrimination—the Fourteenth Amendment was passed to free the slaves after the Civil War—and that communities that were trying to keep out chain stores were practicing illegal discrimination. Tobacco and asbestos companies asserted that they had Fifth Amendment rights to keep secret what they knew about the dangers of their products. With the exception of the Nike case, all of these attempts to obtain human rights for corporations were successful, and now

they wield this huge club against government that was meant
to protect relatively helpless and fragile human beings.

Socialism or Corporatism: Which Is the Greater Threat?

The corporation is an entity created by government. It limits
investors' liability to the amount of money they pony up, even if the
corporation incurs liabilities that are far greater. This has enormous
value and is why more businesses don't operate as partnerships,
which would free them from corporate income taxes and a whole
slew of regulations.

Corporations have no consciences and can't be jailed or executed
for committing grave crimes. They lack the responsibilities of
citizenship but have successfully argued that they should enjoy its
rights. They play a dominant role in our political and economic
discourse and enjoy disproportional influence over the formulation
and execution of our laws.

An analysis of federal data by the Center on Budget and Policy
Priorities showed that outsize influence has "pushed corporate
income tax receipts down to historically low levels, both relative
to the size of the economy and as a share of total federal revenues."
Projections also revealed that "corporate [tax] revenues will remain
at historically low levels even after the economy recovers, and even
if the large . . . corporate tax breaks enacted in 2002 and 2003 are
allowed to expire on schedule."[23] As we saw in chapter 5, the
government always spends money, so when corporate tax revenues
decline, American families pick up the difference. At the same time,
corporate America enjoys all kinds of direct and indirect subsidies,
as well as the very valuable fruits of taxpayer-funded research and
infrastructure investments.

The take-away from all of this is simple: progressive policies
don't pose a risk of tilting the country into totalitarian socialism,
and liberals aren't "anticorporation."

What we see is that just as overarching government intervention in the free market can have disastrous consequences, so, too, does excessive corporate influence over our democratic institutions. Everyone agrees that business should have a seat at the table—it has every right to have its interests weighed in the formulation of public policy—and it should be protected from regulatory abuses. But it is not the only stakeholder that matters, and society doesn't fare well when economic power overwhelms the public interest.

It's no coincidence that as the political and legal playing fields have tilted further toward the interests of investors—with the rise of the conservative communications machine and the success of the "corporate civil rights movement"—the economic security of most working Americans declined and the country's wealth became highly concentrated at the top.

Or, to put it another way: understanding the dangers of corporatism doesn't make you a socialist.

Corporate America Had a Dream, Too

10

GREEN JOBS ARE A GREAT IDEA

Don't believe that environmental activists
want to ruin the economy

U.S. Sen. Lamar Alexander warned Monday that proposed
Senate climate change legislation would "'deliberately kill jobs
and make Americans poorer.'"
—*From an October 26, 2009, news report in Kentucky's* Kingsport Times

Since global warming became a front-burner issue, conservatives
have taken the old argument that environmental protections
hurt the economy to dizzying new heights. According to some of
the more feverish voices within the movement, it's not just that
protecting the environment comes with painful "unintended consequences." They argue that *the entire point of environmentalism*—
and the raison d'être of environmentalists—is to bring capitalism
to its knees.

No, *really*. Senator James Inhofe (R-OK), who called the science
of global warming the "greatest hoax ever perpetrated on the
American people," put it best when he argued that "the real purpose"
of the Kyoto Climate Accord was not to curb carbon emissions but
to "harm Americans, especially the poor and minorities, causing
higher energy prices, reduced economic growth, and fewer jobs."[1]
Long-time Alaska representative Don Young went a step further.

"Environmentalists," he told Alaska Public Radio, "are a socialist group of individuals. . . . I'm proud to say that they are my enemy. They are not Americans, never have been Americans, never will be Americans."[2]

Yet it was Jeffrey Kuhner, an entertainingly unhinged columnist for the right-wing *Washington Times*, who best spelled out this fascinating conspiracy theory in a column titled "A Convenient Lie." "Radical environmentalists," he wrote, "are forging a new socialist post-democracy that is slowly undermining representative government." He continued,

> The myth of global warming along with the Environmental Protection Agency have become the hammer and sickle of eco-Marxism—the new green-red alliance that seeks to destroy capitalism and the sovereign nation-state.[3]

Again, this dark conspiracism is simply the logical extension of the long-standing conservative argument that environmental regulations impose crushing costs on businesses.

Nobody disagrees that protecting the environment comes at a cost to firms' bottom lines. To the degree that they can, these businesses pass some of those costs on to consumers. But after that, anything that hurts a company's profit margins can certainly impact the growth of a business and limit new hires.

Yet that entire narrative asks you to look at only one side of the ledger. It's a Big Lie of *omission*. What they don't tell you is that environmental regulations are necessary for the free market to function. Without them, polluters can impose massive costs on the rest of society in order to derive a tidy profit for themselves. Robust environmental protections fix a significant "market failure," and even the most devout worshippers of Randian economics acknowledge that addressing market distortions is an appropriate role for the government. For many years, this has been the central progressive argument: that you have to count the external costs of *under*regulation as a kind of hidden tax that we all end up paying. Strong environmental protections force polluters themselves to absorb the costs of whatever damage they cause. It's really the "free market" way.

In recent years, progressives have also turned the environment versus jobs narrative on its head. Transitioning to a new, more sustainable, green economy, they argue, will not only protect the delicate rose of capitalism for future generations, it'll represent a new source of economic growth in the twenty-first century, creating millions of high-paying green jobs for industrious Americans.

As we'll see in chapter 15, there are a few obstacles to creating a greener economy, but both arguments have been validated by recent history.

Why Do We Pick Up after Our Dogs?

I have a puppy named Daisy. She poops, and I clean up after her. It's the right thing to do. She's my dog. I feed her, I enjoy her company, and if I don't pick up her leavings, then either someone else has to do it or my neighbors will end up paying a price. It would be great to live in a society where everyone routinely did the right thing, but that's not realistic. Picking up after one's dog is pretty gross, and some people simply don't want to do it. So my city, like most, mandates it, and if I don't do the right thing, then I risk a penalty, a fine.

At the heart of environmental economics is a basic question: what happens with the poop of our industrialized society? Will the dog owners of corporate America clean it up on their own dime or will the rest of us be forced to make a choice between hiring someone to pick up the crap or stepping in it when we sally forth? In economic terms, if they don't clean up after themselves, we as a society pay an externalized cost. It's a market failure because we're not part of the decision-making process. We can't make a rational cost-benefit analysis weighing the burden of regulation against the pollution costs of an industrial activity. And because we—rather than the firms that pollute—bear much of the costs for the damage they do, the polluters themselves don't weigh the costs and benefits accurately either.

The World Bank notes, "The effects of pollution can generally be classified into four major categories: health impacts, direct and indirect effects on productivity, effects on the ecosystem, and aesthetic effects." The World Bank authors continued,

> For example, a factory may emit soot that dirties surrounding buildings, increasing maintenance costs. The higher maintenance costs are a direct result of the factory's use of a resource—air—that from the plant's point of view is free but that has a cost to society.[4]

The World Bank, which was not populated by dirty socialists when I last checked, concluded with a commonsense statement that the Corporate Right refuses to acknowledge: "Such externalities are real costs and benefits attributable to the project and should be included" in the cost-benefit analysis every time.[5]

Progressives favor robust environmental protections not to undermine capitalism or hurt businesses, but to force firms to "internalize" those externalities. We want those regulations for the same reason that most communities require dog owners to pick up their own poop: it's not only the neighborly thing to do, but it's also fundamentally wrong for people to get to enjoy playing with their cute little puppies while the rest of us have to pay the street-cleaners' overtime.

A Calamity of Light Regulation

As I write this, there's a vivid example of the potentially *staggering* costs of inadequate environmental regulation in the Gulf of Mexico, fifty miles off the coast of Louisiana. In the dead of night on April 20, 2010, a fire broke out on the Transocean Deepwater Horizon oil rig. A massive explosion rocked the platform, killing 11 of the 126 workers who were stationed on the drill rig.

The structure sank, and a huge slick containing thousands of barrels of heavy crude oil began to drift toward the shores of Louisiana, Texas, Mississippi, and Florida. The Associated Press called it "the latest blow to a unique marine environment already fragile after decades of human encroachment and natural upheavals—at a time of year when some of its most vulnerable species are nurturing their young."[6] Nancy Rabalais, a scientist who heads the Louisiana Universities Marine Consortium, said, "The magnitude and the potential for ecological damage is probably [greater] than anything we've ever seen in the Gulf of Mexico."[7]

The slick threatened not only flora and fauna, but also the livelihoods of unknown numbers of Americans who work in fishing, tourism, conventions, and a host of other gulf industries. And the well, submerged five thousand feet beneath the gulf, was still spewing heavy crude. First estimated to be "leaking" oil at a rate of a thousand barrels per day, it was soon discovered that an automated system that was supposed to cap the well in the event of a calamity had malfunctioned. A second "fail-safe" system had as well. The wellhead was in fact "spewing" five thousand barrels of oil per day. Officials predicted that the disaster might continue for months, until a second "relief well" could be drilled into the ocean floor.[8]

British Petroleum, which operated the well, had made a mess of breathtaking proportions. It'll take years to understand the full impact of the disaster. As the *Christian Science Monitor* reported, "Federal officials speaking about the Gulf of Mexico oil spill . . . appeared to be steeling the Louisiana coast—and the nation—for consequences that could be 'catastrophic.'"[9] Ten days after the explosion, authorities shut down all commercial and recreational fishing in the gulf.

The worst-case scenario, according to independent analysts, was that the wellhead might give way entirely, which could release as much oil into the Gulf as *forty-five Exxon Valdez* disasters before a relief well could be drilled.[10] In that scenario, the spill would become the greatest human-caused catastrophe ever, after the bombings of Hiroshima and Nagasaki.

David Kotok, an investment analyst with Cumberland Advisers, described the almost inconceivable economic and ecological devastation if the worst should come to pass:

> [If] this spew stoppage takes longer to reach a full closure [then] the subsequent cleanup may take a decade. The Gulf becomes a damaged sea for a generation. The oil slick leaks beyond the western Florida coast, enters the Gulfstream and reaches the eastern coast of the United States and beyond. Use your imagination for the rest of the damage. Monetary cost is now measured in the many hundreds of billions of dollars.[11]

Even if the wellhead holds and the worst-case scenario is averted, analysts said that the estimated $12.5 billion in cleanup costs alone would be "only a start."[12] Louisiana's fishing industry might take a hit of $2.5 billion; Florida's sandy coasts could lose $3 billion in tourist dollars. The total, if the wellhead holds, might reach almost $15 billion, not including the pile of tax dollars being eaten up in government services as federal agencies work to contain the damage.[13]

BP went on a PR offensive. Chief executive Tony Hayward assured reporters, "Given the current conditions and the massive size of our response, we are confident in our ability to tackle this spill offshore."[14] He noted that "the Gulf of Mexico is a very big ocean" and said "the amount of volume of oil and dispersant we are putting into it is tiny in relation to the total water volume."[15] And Bill Salvin, a company spokesman, said of the company's effort to contain the wellhead and clean up the spill: "It's just an amazing effort, truly an *Apollo 13* effort 5,000 feet below the surface of the ocean trying to stop this spill."[16]

Both federal officials and BP executives agreed that the oil giant would take full responsibility for any damages to gulf communities and for the costs of cleaning up the mess. Homeland Security chief Janet Napolitano told *Good Morning America*, "They are the responsible party. They are going to end up paying for the federal government's cost, for the states' and, most importantly, for the individuals and communities that are going to be most directly impacted."[17]

According to BP, it was a terrible disaster that nobody could have predicted—with a "fail-safe" system failing miserably—but the company was mounting a Herculean effort to contain the damage and would ultimately absorb the costs. We were told that the story might eventually have a relatively happy capitalist ending for everyone except some seabirds and fish and the eleven workers killed in the explosion.

None of that is actually true. First, the calamity was indeed predictable, and most likely wouldn't have happened if the oil industry hadn't lobbied hard against regulations that would have protected the environment and saved the lives of the workers killed on the rig.

The *New York Times* reported, "Federal regulators warned offshore rig operators more than a decade ago that they needed to install backup systems to control the giant undersea valves known as blowout preventers, used to cut off the flow of oil from a well in an emergency." The *Times* article continued,

> Agency records show that from 2001 to 2007, there were 1,443 serious drilling accidents in offshore operations, leading to 41 deaths, 302 injuries and 356 oil spills. Yet the federal agency continues to allow the industry largely to police itself, saying that the best technical experts work for industry, not for the government.
>
> Critics say that, then and now, the minerals service has been crippled by this dependence on industry and by a climate of regulatory indulgence.[18]

The *Wall Street Journal* reported that oil-producing countries such as Norway and the Netherlands require offshore drillers to install "acoustic switches"—remote-controlled shut-off mechanisms that can be used to clamp down a well if the first lines of defense fail.[19]

U.S. regulators had considered requiring the switch since a smaller accident in 2000, when the Minerals Management Service— the agency tasked with regulating offshore drilling—issued a safety notice saying that a back-up system is "an essential component of a deepwater drilling system."[20] A spokeswoman for Norway's Petroleum Safety Authority told the *Journal* that the switches have a good track record in the North Sea. "It's been seen as the most successful and effective option," she said.[21] But the industry opposed it tooth-and-nail. According to ABC News, BP "spent years battling federal regulators over how many layers of safeguards would be needed to prevent a deepwater well from this type of accident." In a 2009 letter to the Department of the Interior, the company argued that mandating the use of an acoustic switch would be an example of "extensive, prescriptive regulations" that were unnecessary, because the "industry's current safety and environmental statistics demonstrate that the voluntary programs . . . continue to be very successful."[22]

The industry prevailed, and in 2003, the Minerals Management Service decided that the systems required "more study." A spokesman for Senator Ben Nelson (D-FL) told the *Journal*, "What we see, going back two decades, is an oil industry that has had way too much sway with federal regulations. We are seeing our worst nightmare coming true."[23]

Although BP had "urged the minerals service to allow operators to define the steps they would take to ensure safety largely on their own," the company had in fact violated its own safety protocols on the rig.[24] During a congressional investigation into the disaster, "A parade of witnesses at hearings last week told about bad decisions and cut corners in the days and hours before the explosion of the rig." But potential problems with the platform were identified much earlier and ignored by BP. According to internal documents obtained by the *New York Times*, "The problems involved the well casing and the blowout preventer, which are considered critical pieces in the chain of events that led to the disaster on the rig." The *Times* article continued,

> The documents show that in March, after several weeks of problems on the rig, BP was struggling with a loss of "well control." And as far back as 11 months ago, it was concerned about the well casing and the blowout preventer.

On June 22, for example, BP engineers expressed concerns that the metal casing the company wanted to use might collapse under high pressure.

The company went ahead with the casing, but only after getting special permission from BP colleagues because it violated the company's safety policies and design standards. The internal reports do not explain why the company allowed for an exception.[25]

Big Oil had argued, as industry always does, that the cost of the regulation would be too high and would hinder competitiveness and cost jobs. The price of the back-up system in question? A half-million dollars, on a rig that cost $270 million to build.[26] And as far as the industry's "voluntary programs," which are often used as an argument to fend off regulation, let's just say they've been less than impressive.

According to ProPublica, after a 2005 explosion at a British Petroleum refinery in Texas that killed fifteen workers, investigators "determined that the company had ignored its own protocols on operating the tower, which was filled with gasoline, and that a warning system had been disabled." BP pleaded guilty to federal charges arising from the incident and paid a $50 million fine[27]—a drop in the bucket for a company that turned a windfall $21 billion profit from sky-high oil prices that year.[28]

As I write, another BP rig, the Atlantis, is also causing concern after the *Washington Post* reported that it is currently operating "with incomplete and inaccurate engineering documents, according to records and interviews, a deficiency that one company official warned could 'lead to catastrophic operator errors.' "[29]

Screw Regulations! Bring On Private Enforcement!

Some conservatives argue that we don't need those pesky regulations, because we have lawsuits! They say that a company that causes a lot of destruction will face a flurry of litigation. That potential for liability "internalizes" those negative externalities another way. It's a "free market" fix, with free people suing other free people, instead of nosy regulators telling virtuous businessmen what to do. The concept is known as "private enforcement."

In practice, private enforcement is also a joke. A jury awarded thousands of Alaska residents $5 billion in damages after the *Valdez* disaster. But Exxon's legal eagles spent twenty years fighting the verdict in court, and the award was eventually reduced to just $500 million.

When toxic gas was released at a Union Carbide plant in Bhopal, India, killing as many as twenty thousand people, the Indian government pressed the company to compensate the victims for losses estimated at $3.3 billion. After five years of legal skirmishing, India settled for less than a sixth of that amount.[30]

The story gets even worse in the gulf. Let's go back a few years, to 1990. It was just after the Exxon *Valdez* disaster, and energy companies had gotten a taste of how high the costs of a major spill could be. As Mathew Wald detailed in the *New York Times*, Big Oil cut a sweet deal with the federal government. The oil companies would accept a very modest tax of 8 cents per barrel of oil—which works out to a rate of around a tenth of 1 percent—to finance the Oil Spill Liability Trust Fund, $1.6 billion that would be set aside to deal with disastrous spills. And in exchange, Congress agreed to limit the companies' liability for damages (other than the direct costs of the cleanup) to only $75 *million*, a figure that was probably dwarfed in the hours, not days, following the Deepwater Horizon explosion.[31]

So, with damages that may reach into the tens, if not hundreds, of billions, BP is in fact on the hook only for the price of cleaning up the oil and the first $75 million in damages. After that, regardless of whether the firm tells reporters that it will assume responsibility for all claims related to the disaster, we the American people will get stuck with the rest. Or, as Ben Nelson put it to reporters, "BP says it'll pay for this mess. Baloney. They're not going to want to pay any more than what the law says they have to."[32]

Nelson was among a group of gulf state lawmakers who called for raising the liability cap. So, in order to be on the safe side, just days after the disaster, when the extent of damages wouldn't be known for some time, BP attorneys fanned out through the gulf states to offer coastal residents a $5,000 check in exchange for waiving all future claims against the company.[33] Following public outcry over the move, BP admitted that the waivers had been "a misstep." But CEO Tony Hayward was smug, telling the *Times of London*, "This is America—come on. We're going to have lots of illegitimate claims. We all know that."[34] He had even more contempt for the survivors of the explosion. According to the *Guardian*, they were reportedly kept in isolation for forty hours following their ordeal. During that period, they were prevented from contacting their loved ones while "Transocean, the owners of the rig, readied its legal defenses." "Lawyers say the isolation was deliberate and that Transocean was trying to wear the men down so they would sign statements denying that they had been hurt," continued the report. "'These men are told they have to sign these statements or they can't go home,'" an attorney for one of the survivors told the *Guardian*.[35]

Transocean did quite nicely in the disaster. The rig's owner had insured the $270 million structure for $560 million.[36] Its liability, like operator BP's, was capped—in Transocean's case, at $65 million—but it filed a request with officials to limit its exposure to $27 million.[37] In a conference call with shareholders, the company announced that even if it faced its full liability for the mess, it would still turn a profit of some $90 million from the disaster.[38] The rest of the bill would be left to the taxpayer, so it's worth pointing out that the company has worked hard to avoid paying U.S. taxes. Transocean is, in reality, based in Houston, where almost all of its fifteen hundred workers are located. But in 1999, it shifted its "headquarters"—which can be simply a post office box—to the Cayman Islands, a well-known tax shelter. (In 2008, the firm moved its "headquarters" to Switzerland.)[39]

As we saw in chapter 9, corporations are citizens, just like you and I. But they're also profit-driven entities without a human conscience. Economics is ultimately about incentives, and corporations simply don't have real incentives for defending the environment. That's why we regulate. The massive costs of environmental damage represent the other side of the ledger—the very real and potentially life-saving benefits of adequate regulation that conservatives simply refuse to acknowledge.

The "Green-Collar Economy": How Environmentalism Can Create Jobs and Spur Growth

As I mentioned at the beginning of this chapter, progressives have promoted the creation of green jobs not only to protect the environment, but also to disprove the claim that we have to sacrifice prosperity to protect our ecosystem.

The idea, broadly speaking, is to transform our carbon-based economy to one that is run on clean and sustainable power; it would include increasing our energy efficiency and cutting down on our waste. And it would require a lot of work, from manufacturing new and cleaner technologies to upgrading our electrical network with "smart grid" technology. It would create jobs, lessen our dependence on oil (domestic as well as foreign), and reduce climate-changing emissions before it's too late. Economist Robert Pollin and his colleagues at the University of Massachusetts–Amherst estimated that 1.7 million net new jobs could be created in just two years with an investment of $150 billion in new green infrastructure—less than the average cost of keeping troops in Iraq for the same amount of time. They identified six areas that are ripe for investment: retrofitting buildings, expanding mass transit and freight rail, building a smart electric grid, and investing in wind power, solar power, and next-generation biofuels.[40] I can't think of anyone anywhere on the political spectrum who believes these things are bad. Conservatives simply think that the private sector will get us there on its own, eventually, and it's true that many firms are investing in new technologies for the green market.

The question is: how long would the private sector take? Today, clean and sustainable energy technologies are far more expensive than burning coal or gas and will continue to be in the immediate future. In 2008, the European Commission did a study of the costs of generating electricity using various technologies. With today's fuel prices, the cost of a megawatt-hour is as follows: gas goes for 50–75 euros; oil costs between 95 and 125 euros, and coal is a bargain at 40–55. But biomass energy costs 80–195 euros, wind goes for between 75 and 140, hydropower costs as much as 215 euros, and solar costs between 170 and 880 euros for a megawatt-hour. (Nuclear energy is cheap, and its lobbyists have pushed it as a green energy source; the problem is they still don't know what to do with the radioactive waste.)[41]

So an efficient green economy that frees us from our dependence on fossil fuels is a good that most of us want, but the private sector won't be able to deliver it as soon as we'd like. It's a classic place for the government to intervene. And governments around the world, including our own, are doing just that. Yet it's also a race, and whichever economy leads that race will have a real advantage—with more leading-edge technology and a large market share—for decades to come.

Big Oil, however, with its fingers deep into congressional pockets, wants to drill, baby, drill—and it can rely on "free market" rhetoric to make it happen. Consider a case in point: the planned Cape Wind offshore energy project miles off the coast of Cape Cod. The "wind farm," with 130 high-tech turbines, is expected to create 1,000 jobs during the construction phase and 150 permanent new positions on Cape Cod and the surrounding islands. It will also generate 420 megawatts of power, enough to meet 75 percent of the needs of Cape Cod, Martha's Vineyard, and the surrounding islands.[42]

It faced stiff opposition, ostensibly of the Not In My Backyard variety from residents who thought the wind turbines would be an eyesore and ruin their ocean views (the late Senator Ted Kennedy, sadly, was part of the effort to kill the project). But *Forbes* noted where a good chunk of the money behind the campaign was coming from. William Koch, an oil mogul and one of the most prominent conservative philanthropists in the United States, had put up $1.5 million to oppose the wind farm. *Forbes* noted the "irony" of his opposition:

Koch, through his Oxbow Group ($1.5 billion sales), had once made a mint off eco-friendly power plants by using laws that required power companies to buy Koch's power for above-market rates. He sold them for $660 million in 2000.

But, alas, he now says the project's economics, requiring heavy government subsidies, don't add up.[43]

Subsidies, of course, are the only way that moving to clean, renewable energy in the near future *does* "add up." Phillip Warburg and Susan Reid of the Conservation Law Foundation responded to the claim by stating the obvious. "Federal and state subsidies for renewable energy projects," they wrote, "have been created for the express purpose of helping wind and other forms of clean energy compete with long-subsidized conventional fuels, such as coal and oil, as well as nuclear power."[44]

The Big Race to a Green Energy Economy

Again, many governments, including our own, are already subsidizing renewable energy. According to a United Nations Energy Program report, it's a limited field:

So far, a small group of countries accounts for the bulk of renewables investments, R&D, and production. Germany, Japan, China, Brazil, and the United States play particularly prominent roles in renewable technology development, and they have so far garnered the bulk of renewables jobs worldwide. European manufacturers account for more than three-quarters of global wind turbine sales, but India's Suzlon also is a major force in the industry.[45]

In many respects, it's China, rather than the United States or Europe, that is poised to take the lead in renewable energy. According to MIT's *Technology Review*, China doubled its wind power capacity every year since 2004 and was on pace "to supplant the United States as the world's largest market for new installations." And "researchers from Harvard University and Beijing's Tsinghua

University suggest that the Chinese wind power industry has hardly begun to tap its potential. According to their meteorological and financial modeling, reported in the journal *Science*, . . . there is enough strong wind in China to profitably satisfy all of the country's electricity demand until at least 2030."[46]

In 2009, Chinese officials announced that they would build the world's largest solar power plant, a 30-megawatt project in the Qaidam Basin.[47] China already leads the world in hydroelectric power, according to the United Nations.[48] And after building one of the world's most extensive networks of high-speed trains, it is now looking to export that technology to the United States. The Chinese have signed "cooperation agreements with the State of California and General Electric to help build such lines," according to the *New York Times*. "The agreements, both of which are preliminary, show China's desire to become a big exporter and licensor of bullet trains traveling 215 miles an hour, an environmentally friendly technology in which China has raced past the United States in the last few years."[49]

China is not alone, but I use it as an example because it appears to be pulling ahead with the most direct government intervention. In 2009, as part of its stimulus package, China devoted $440 billion to renewables.[50] The United States also passed a major stimulus package that year. *U.S. News and World Report*, in a story on the $70 billion for clean energy included in the measure —about 16 percent of China's investment—concluded, "[Renewable] energy won big in the stimulus package."[51]

It's worth noting that U.S. conservatives fought tooth-and-nail against the stimulus, and many argued that longer-term investments contained in the package—such as the renewable energy dollars—were a waste of money because they wouldn't create jobs *quickly enough*.

The Corporate Right lauds the power of the market to solve all of our ills. They say that government meddling in the market's dynamism is inherently destructive, will retard growth, and will kill the U.S. economy. It would be a tragic irony if they continued to mouth those talking points while other governments pull ahead in creating a dynamic new green economy for the twenty-first century.

Why a Gallon of Gas Should Cost $10

We shouldn't talk only about the importance of clean air and water—or the fight against global warming—for our communities. Let's look at it in economic terms. Let's ask what a gallon of gas really costs our society.

We know it sells for an average price of $2.86 in the United States, as of this writing. But that's not its true market price.

In 1998, when the average price of gas was 99 cents per gallon, a study by the International Center for Technical Assessment (CTA) estimated that the real cost—to U.S. consumers and taxpayers—was more like ten bucks (the CTA's low estimate was $5.16 a gallon, and its high one came in at a whopping $15.14, or almost $4 per *quart*).[1]

The difference between what we pay for gas and what it costs represents the tax breaks and the tax-funded services that are provided to energy producers to get that gallon of gas into your tank, along with other "externalities": costs of a private transaction that are borne by a third party.

As we saw in chapter 10, environmental pollution—and the health issues that result—is a classic example of a negative externality. And according to the CTA's analysis, "Environmental, health and social costs represent the largest portion of the externalized price Americans pay" for their gas. The CTA estimated the total—which included not only human health costs, but also decreased agricultural yields and "damage to buildings and materials" from emissions—to be as high as $942 billion in 1998.

Energy producers and users routinely get a range of direct subsidies at the federal and local levels that in 1998 totaled $9 billion to $18 billion. (It's worth noting that according to *Forbes* magazine, ExxonMobil didn't pay a dollar in taxes to the U.S. government in 2009, despite earning record profits of nearly

$50 billion. The company used a series of offshore subsidiaries to shelter its windfall profits.)[2] Yet those direct subsidies were far lower in value than the indirect "program subsidies" energy producers received in the form of government-funded research and development, export promotion, infrastructure investment, environmental cleanup, and similar programs. The latter ran as high as $114 billion.

Now, as you may have already noticed, a lot of the energy we use comes from some unsavory neighborhoods. In 1998, long before we had tens of thousands of troops deployed in oil-rich Iraq, U.S. defense spending "allocated to safeguard the world's petroleum supplies" totaled $100 billion. Yet even that figure only scratched the surface. We provide military aid to energy exporters across the globe, in places as diverse as Latin America, the Caspian Sea region, the Middle East, and the Horn of Africa. And then there's the Strategic Petroleum Reserve, the Coast Guard and other maritime protection, and as much as $40 billion in "externalized police, fire, and emergency response expenditures" here at home.

Not all of these costs are easy to quantify, and the precise numbers are open to debate. When the CTA added them all up in 1998, it arrived at a figure as high as $1.69 *trillion* in "social costs and government 'welfare' for the gas industry."

Whatever the exact number may be, there's no question that those largely unseen costs represent a significant distortion in the market. We subsidize our car culture, and although that may be a perfectly valid public policy goal, when we pretend that it's all a function of some illusory "hidden hand," it keeps us from talking about it—from weighing the benefits of those subsidies against other priorities.

11

THE EUROPEANS ARE ALL RIGHT

Don't believe that more progressive governments are always on the brink of bankruptcy

> The difference between the Road Map and the Democrats'
> approach could not be more clear. From the enactment of a
> $1 trillion "stimulus" last February to the current pass-at-all-
> costs government takeover of health care, the Democratic
> leadership has followed a "progressive" strategy that will take
> us closer to a tipping point past which most Americans receive
> more in government benefits than they pay in taxes—a
> European-style welfare state where double-digit unemploy-
> ment becomes a way of life. Americans don't have to settle for
> this path of decline.
>
> —*Representative Paul Ryan (R-WI), pitching his slash-and-burn*
> *"road map" in the* Wall Street Journal[1]

If you're a regular consumer of the conservative media, you might
be surprised that Europe hasn't already collapsed, crushed under
the weight of its bloated welfare state, bedeviled by pointy-headed
"Eurocrats," and overrun by wild-eyed *jihadis*.

In 2010, *Detroit News* columnist Nolan Finley warned that the
Affordable Care Act would inevitably "turn the U.S. into Europe."
Calling Obama "an ardent Europhile," Finley wrote that we could
have universal health care, high-speed rail service, and cheap public

universities in this country, but only, he added ominously, "if we're willing to live a European lifestyle." He confidently predicted, "Most Americans will chafe at giving up their personal choices and elbow room to make Euro-socialism work here. The Nanny State is anathema to our natural individualism . . . once government takes over the care and feeding of its citizens, nothing is beyond its reach."[2]

A few months earlier, an essay by Manhattan Institute fellow Jim Manzi in the influential *National Journal* set off a nerd-fight among economic wonks. Manzi set out the central false dichotomy that underlies conservative criticism of European capitalism: social democracy versus economic "dynamism." The central data point around which Manzi constructed his argument was Europe's supposedly slower rate of economic growth:

> From 1980 through today, America's share of global output has been constant at about 21%. Europe's share, meanwhile, has been collapsing in the face of global competition—going from a little less than 40% of global production in the 1970s to about 25% today. Opting for social democracy instead of innovative capitalism, Europe has ceded this share to China (predominantly), India, and the rest of the developing world.[3]

A compelling case against social democracy, right? It would be if it were true. But Jonathan Chait of the *New Republic* smelled something fishy in Manzi's numbers and took a look himself. He noted that Manzi had compared Europe "since the 1970s," with the United States since 1980. Chait confirmed via e-mail that Manzi had used data since 1973 for Europe and since 1980 for the United States, effectively eliminating the shocks of the 1970s oil crisis from only one side of the ledger.[4]

Chait also teased out that Manzi's definition of "Europe" included the former Soviet republics. Given that their economies were decimated with the fall of communism, there was more than a bit of sleight of hand in their inclusion. Never mind the fact that that they *aren't social democracies*. (For the record, unless otherwise specified, "Europe" in this chapter refers to the advanced core countries known as the EU-15.)

Paul Krugman then went back to the source of Manzi's data and concluded, "It turns out that it's even worse than that." Using Manzi's broad definition of "Europe," which included the USSR, Krugman found that it did have 40 percent of world output in the early 1970s. That share hadn't fallen to 25 percent, however; it was still above 30 percent. "The only thing I can think is that Manzi compared Europe including the eastern bloc in 1970 with Europe not including the east today," he wrote.

Krugman concluded that Manzi's well-publicized oopsie probably wasn't a "deliberate case of data falsification." Rather, "Like so many conservatives, Manzi just knew that Europe is an economic disaster, glanced at some numbers, thought he saw his assumptions confirmed, and never checked." And that, according to Krugman, was "the real moral of the story: the image of Europe the economic failure is so ingrained on the right that it's never questioned, even though the facts beg to differ."[5]

It makes sense that the merits and demerits of the U.S. and European political economies would become a source of fierce ideological debate on both sides of "the pond." After all, we share very similar political cultures, eight in ten Americans are of European descent, and we all have advanced, mixed economies, with competitive capitalism the economic driver and a social safety net of some sort to smooth out the rough edges and guarantee that the "losers" don't starve to death in the streets. Indeed, the differences come down to a matter of public policy priorities. Those differences can have an enormous impact on an economy, but it's overstating the case to call them two distinct "models." There is, in fact, just a degree or two of separation.

Of course, progressives shouldn't idealize European capitalism any more than conservatives should demonize it. Europe faces the same problems that the rest of the developed world does: a long-term decline in growth rates since the heyday of the 1950s and the 1960s, an aging population, competition from the fast-growing Asian economies, job outsourcing, and the rest. As I write, Europe is in the midst of a debt crisis that resulted from shady dealings by their own bankers, not only Wall Street's.

European unification did create a new layer of bureaucracy in Brussels, and it has been a bumpy ride. After the fall of communism, the former Eastern Bloc countries were gradually incorporated into the union, as were poorer countries such as Portugal. But, as Steven Pearlstein noted in the *Washington Post*, "The fundamental problem is that even with a single currency and a unified political and bureaucratic structure, the arrangement is only a 'halfway house' on the way to genuine political and economic integration, and a rickety one at that. While capital and goods and tourists can move relatively freely across borders, workers and services cannot, and national governments continue to jealously protect their regulatory and fiscal prerogatives."[6]

These are serious issues but not subjects that interest the Corporate Right all that much. Their central argument—that social democracies are saddled with permanently high unemployment and sluggish growth because they do a bit more to protect their poorer citizens' well-being—simply doesn't reflect the facts.

The Facts Beg to Differ

Every year, like a kid on Christmas morning, I look forward to an annual report from a right-wing, corporate-funded think tank: the Heritage Foundation's *Economic Freedom Index*. It's a collection of various data that are basically tilted against social democracies—for example, the less bargaining power workers have, the "freer" the economy.

And year after year, it never disappoints. In 2010, the Heritage Foundation judged the United States to be the eighth freest country in the world. Now, the silliness of these indices is pretty clear, considering that the two "freest" countries in the world were Singapore—where one party has had a monopoly on power since independence, there are no jury trials, but there *are* severe restrictions on free speech—and Hong Kong, which is administered by China's "communist" government. Yet between numbers two and eight on the list are five supposedly bloated social democracies (Australia, New Zealand, Ireland, Switzerland, and Canada). According to Heritage, sixteen of the twenty-five most competitive economies belong to social democracies.[7]

The World Economic Forum, a think tank supported by the Swiss government, issues a similar index. In 2009–2010, eight of its ten "most competitive" economies were social democracies.[8] The Fraser Institute, Canada's answer to Heritage, also issues an *Economic Freedom of the World Report* annually. In its most recent rankings, "only" six of the ten most competitive economies in the world were social democracies.[9]

I mention these indices with tongue at least partly in cheek; they tend to cherry-pick data so that "freedom" means the ability of corporations to do whatever they want. This doesn't quite square with my definition of freedom. Yet the indices underscore the point that the cautionary tale of Europe—supposed proof that higher taxes on the wealthy and a more robust safety net are disincentives to hard work and lead to economic stagnation—is simply divorced from reality.

Let's take the claims on which the narrative is based, one by one, and see how they stack up. And unless otherwise specified, we'll leave out the former Eastern Bloc countries and compare apples with apples.

European Growth: Slow as Molasses on a Cold Day?

Over the last decade, gross domestic product (GDP) grew by about 1 percentage point more annually in the United States than in the EU-15. But when we talk about a rising GDP, we mean a growing population, as well as increasing productivity: more people making stuff means more total stuff. The differences in population growth between the United States and the EU are stark. Since 1980, the population of the United States has increased by more than a third, compared with 7 percent in the EU (as a whole).[10] Adding people, however, doesn't necessarily make countries more affluent. A better standard is the growth of GDP *per person*. As Paul Krugman pointed out, "Since 1980, per capita real G.D.P.—which is what matters for living standards—has risen at about the same rate in America and in the E.U. 15: 1.95 percent a year here; 1.83 percent there."[11] That's essentially a rounding error.

During this same thirty-year period, *total* income growth per person increased by 58 percent in the EU and 63 percent in the United States.[12] But that doesn't tell the whole story, either. Not if we're comparing similarly wealthy economies, anyway, because the EU doesn't include three of the richer European social democracies: Switzerland, Norway, and Iceland. As Jonathan Chait noted, "Those three countries had 71% growth in per capita GDP since 1980 . . . which, if added to the EU 15, would bring the growth record of the United States and the social democracies even closer to parity."[13]

There are also two major problems with looking at GDP in the first place. First, Europe does have higher rates of taxation, and this leads to more people working off the books—their output doesn't work its way into the statistics. And second, it's an average, meaning that the incomes of Bill Gates and the poorest person in the United States are both factored into the numbers. We have much higher levels of inequality than the Europeans tolerate. An economy with modestly lower income distributed more equally will have far less poverty than one that's larger overall but has its income skewed toward the top. The United States creates more millionaires than Europe does but also has a lot more people living in poverty, and poverty leads to all sorts of social ills: poor health, inadequate nutrition, drug use, incarceration—the works. In 2000, the average poverty rate for the EU-15 was around 8 percent. In the United States, it was almost twice as high: 15.9 percent.[14]

Nolan Finley offered up the spin for his *Detroit News* readers when he wrote that because they pay somewhat higher taxes,

"Europeans don't knock themselves out earning money. Productivity gains in Western Europe are half the U.S. average."[15]

On average, European productivity growth has been slower than that of the United States. But Finley used productivity growth per worker, not per working *hour*. And as we'll see shortly, Europeans don't bust their asses working megahours quite as enthusiastically as we tend to do. In his book *The European Dream: How Europe's Vision of the Future Is Quietly Eclipsing the American Dream*, Jeremy Rifkin wrote that the idea that any European country could eclipse U.S. productivity may be "unthinkable" for many but is nonetheless true when you look at productivity per hour:

> In 2002, the average worker in Norway produced $45.55 of output per hour, compared to $38.83 in the United States. Belgium, Ireland and the Netherlands also produced more output per hour than the U.S. Still, these are small countries. What about the majors, the countries that count? Well, Germany in 2002 enjoyed higher productivity per hour worked than America. . . . And the coup de grace? French workers produced $41.85 per hour—that's 7 percent more than Americans.[16]

"Europe" may have a common market, but it is not a single economy. And while all of the European economies have robust social safety nets and strong labor movements, several have experienced higher gains in productivity than the United States. Between 1979 and 2005, productivity growth in Germany, France, the Netherlands, Sweden, Italy, Spain, Belgium, and Sweden averaged 1.7 percent. The United States experienced productivity growth over that same period of . . . 1.7 percent—but Belgium, France, and Sweden topped us.[17]

They're Poor!

The *Wall Street Journal*'s editorial board got terribly excited when a study by a right-wing think tank in Sweden "found that if Europe were part of the U.S., only tiny Luxembourg could rival the richest of the 50 American states in gross domestic product per capita." A "rising tide still lifts all boats," the *Journal* reminded us, "and U.S. GDP per capita was a whopping 32% higher than the EU average in 2000, and the gap hasn't closed since."

As far as the raw data go, that's true. (But, again, several European states have GDP per capita that are either higher than, or comparable to, the United States').[18] The thing is, those data tell only part of the story about a country's economic health. We do have different priorities, and European workers expect six to eight weeks of vacation, paid sick days, and fewer hours of overtime— Europeans simply don't work themselves to the bone as we do. American men and women worked an average of forty-one hours per week in 2005, while European men averaged thirty-eight hours and European women only thirty. As the Organisation for Economic Co-operation and Development noted, "As for holiday and paid leave entitlements, the striking differences between Europe and the United States (including sickness and maternity) obviously explain some of the transatlantic gap in annual working hours."

When you factor in the difference in time spent on the job, the GDP gap essentially disappears.[19] Now, is this simply a matter of Americans' having a superior work ethic, unblunted by the perfidy of the nanny state? Well, no. Overworked Americans are *miserable*. According to research cited by Boston College's Sloan Work and Family Research Network, four in ten workers who work a lot of extra hours say they "feel very angry toward their employers," versus 1 percent who work only a few extra hours. Just 3 percent of two-income couples who work long hours said they were content with the effort, and nine out of ten U.S. workers said either, "My job requires that I work very hard," or "I never seem to have enough time to get everything done on my job."[20]

And What about Their Chronically High Unemployment?

Gary Becker, the University of Chicago economist whom George W. Bush honored with a 2007 Medal of Freedom, said that "Rigid labor markets and high social security and other taxes on employed workers explain Europe's excessive unemployment."[21]

Here again, we see that while all of the EU countries have "rigid labor markets and high social security and other taxes," not all have higher unemployment rates than the United States. As I write, our unemployment rate is one of the highest in the developed world, but this has a lot to do with the fact that it is harder to lay off European workers during a downturn. Looking at some numbers from before the recession hit, from 2001 to 2005, we see that the average unemployment rate in the EU-15 was 6.9 percent, compared to 5.5 percent on our side of the pond. During those years, however, six of the EU-15 had lower rates than the United States.[22]

Yet there's more to this story. As Paul Krugman wrote, "If your vision is of millions of prime-working-age adults sitting idle, living on the dole, think again." The reality is that Europeans enter the labor force later and retire earlier than their U.S. counterparts do. Retiring earlier is a choice, not the result of losing a job. So a better statistic is the share of working-age adults in their prime. Krugman looked at that group alone and wrote that in 2008, "80 percent of adults aged 25 to 54 in the E.U. 15 were employed (and 83 percent in France). That's about the same as in the United States."[23] Europeans are less likely than we are to work when they're young or old, but is that really such a terrible thing?

One thing that's true is that European countries tend to have much higher rates of *long-term* unemployment than the United States does. In chapter 1, I noted that conservatives who argue that extending unemployment benefits will keep people from seeking work are pretty ridiculous, given how limited those benefits are in the United States. This is not so in Europe, and research shows that very generous benefits without time limits does result in longer periods of joblessness. But here's the important thing to keep in mind: it's not a simple matter of people getting an unemployment check and then not trying to find work; the flip side of that is that workers can wait for a decent job to come along that fits their qualifications. The research shows that although generous unemployment benefits lead to more long-term joblessness, when those workers do return to the labor market, they do so at a higher average salary and with better benefits than people who have to take the first position that opens up. It's a trade-off.

They're Taxed to Death!

This one is at least true on its face, if quite misleading. As we saw in chapter 5, while the Right whines about a massive tax burden stifling our competitive edge, the United States has one of the lowest total tax rates in the wealthy world.

What conservatives never mention is that taxes are used to finance things we want and for which we'd otherwise pay out of pocket. For example, in 2006, Americans paid about 7 percent of their average income on health insurance and out-of-pocket expenses, and the unlucky ones paid much more.[24] Most Europeans don't pay a single euro for basic, high-quality care. In much of Europe, the cost of a college education is free. In the United Kingdom, tuition is capped by law at a bit more than $5,000. In the United States, a public four-year college charges more than $7,000 a year on average, and private university tuition runs more than $25,000 per year.[25] So, yes, the total tax burden in the EU-15 is around 12 percent higher. But when you factor in costs like health care and education—and job-training programs, public transportation, and on and on—it's a different picture. It is because these benefits are available to all that European inequality and poverty levels are so much lower than they are here. It also explains why many European economies offer more potential for upward mobility.

Anyone who travels to Europe will immediately note that their infrastructure is modern, their streets are clean, and their government agencies aren't reminiscent of third world countries. Paul Krugman posed the question: "For those Americans who have visited Paris: did it look poor and backward? What about Frankfurt or London? You should always bear in mind that when the question is which to believe—official economic statistics or your own lying eyes—the eyes have it."[26]

They Live in Shoe Boxes!

One of the most entertaining claims to U.S. superiority is this: we live in bigger homes. As the *Wall Street Journal* was happy to point out, "The average living space for poor American households is 1,200 square feet. In Europe, the average space for all households, not just the poor, is 1,000 square feet."[27] Case closed!

Well, not really. This is a simple matter of population density: in the EU-15, there are 120 people per square kilometer; in the United States, we only have 29 people per square kilometer.[28] And that average obviously includes large ranch homes in sparsely populated rural expanses. I live in a tightly packed U.S. city, and given that most middle-class people here can't dream of affording 1,200 square feet, I don't think our poor folks can, either. I'm a member of the American middle class, and I live in a studio that's maybe 375 square feet.

It Comes Down to Priorities: Guns or Butter?

Perhaps the greatest Atlantic divide lies in the area of military spending. Contrary to the views of many Americans, Europe's economy, not our own, is the largest in the world. Yet in 2008, the EU (all twenty-seven states, not the core fifteen), accounted for only 26 percent of the world's military spending. With an economy that's around 7 percent smaller, the United States accounted for 46 percent of global military spending.[29] Combine that with Europe's far more generous social welfare systems and modern infrastructure, and you end up with a *very* clear difference in priorities.

Interestingly, conservatives simultaneously argue that lavish U.S. military spending subsidizes Europe's social welfare programs by providing the Europeans with a common defense, and that we're the smarter party in this deal. Our kids get the wonderful opportunity to die in distant lands, while theirs are burdened with free college tuition and good health care. Max Boot, a prominent and utterly pathological neoconservative, lamented that we spend *too little* on the military these days, writing, "It's hard to remember now, but there was a time when the federal government spent most of its money on the armed forces. In 1962, the total federal budget was $106 billion of which $52 billion—almost half—went for defense. It wasn't until 1976 that entitlement spending exceeded defense spending." For Boot, however, the really frightening prospect is that we'll go the way of Europe. "Last year government spending in the 27 European Union nations hit 52% of GDP," he wrote. "But most of them struggle to devote even 2% of GDP to defense, compared to more than 4% in the U.S. When Europeans after World War II chose to skimp on defense and spend lavishly on social welfare, they abdicated their claims to great power status."[30]

Yet in a 2010 poll of citizens in twenty-seven countries, 53 percent of respondents said that the EU had a positive influence on the world, while 46 percent felt the same about the United States. Europe is unquestionably a global power.[31]

Boot asked, "What happens if the U.S. switches spending from defense to social welfare? Who will protect what used to be known as the "Free World"? Who will police the sea lanes, stop the proliferation of weapons of mass destruction, combat terrorism, respond to genocide and other unconscionable human rights violations, and deter rogue states from aggression?"[32] What he doesn't say is that the American Right has long opposed the kind of international security cooperation that might shift some of the cost of policing the world to other states. If we didn't insist on doing it ourselves, perhaps we wouldn't have to.

But I suppose that when Americans are waiting in line for food stamps—or waiting to pay their respects to a soldier who died in some God-forsaken country thousands of miles away—they can take an abstract pride in being the world's only superpower. Boot's argument has always seemed to me like the biggest loser in Las Vegas saying *the house is a sucker*.

Keeping Score: Europe vs. the United States

So, let's summarize. European social democracies aren't saddled with sluggish growth compared to the United States. "Double-digit unemployment" is not "a way of life" for Europeans. Most European countries do have slightly lower average incomes, but they all have much less poverty (and far fewer of the social ills that accompany it). They pay higher taxes but get free health care, deeply subsidized higher education, and a modern infrastructure to show for it. They throw a tiny fraction of their citizens into jail compared to the United States.

They don't spend a fortune on the military—we do. And among the twenty most developed countries in the world, the United States is now dead last in life expectancy at birth but leads the pack in infant mortality—40 percent higher than the runner-up—and in the percentage of the population who will die before reaching age sixty.[33] Half of our kids need food stamps at some point during their childhoods.[34]

So take pride in American power, and remember that it comes at a very high price.

The Incredible Shrinking Americans

When we examined the messy debate over the relative superiority of the American or European economic model, we saw that there are fundamental differences in priorities across the Atlantic divide. We make different choices, and those choices have consequences.

In 2007, Benjamin Lauderdale of Princeton University and John Komlos of the University of Munich identified a fascinating development. They found that since World War II, white and black Americans have been shrinking, *dramatically*, relative to their European counterparts.

According to the researchers, a population's average height is a "mirror" reflecting the socioeconomic health of a society. They speculated that Americans' worship of "market-based" social policies may explain why we're now looking up to the Germans and the Swedes.[1]

The researchers had unearthed a dramatic reversal of long-standing trends. Americans had always been giants, with the tallest men in the world, going back as far as the data exist (at least to the mid-nineteenth century). During World War I, American GIs still towered over the Europeans they helped liberate. But for three decades following the end of World War II, Americans' average height stagnated, while Western Europeans continued the growth spurt that one would expect during a period of relative peace and rising incomes.[2]

Now, with an average height of 5'10", American men are significantly shorter than men from countries like Denmark (6-footers) and the Netherlands (6'1"). In fact, Americans—men and women—are now shorter, on average, than the citizens of *every single country in Western and Northern Europe*.[3]

And our vertical challenge is continuing to increase; U.S. whites born between 1975 and 1983 started to grow again, but still not as quickly as Western Europeans who were born in the same period. Meanwhile, the average height of U.S. blacks in that age group remained unchanged.[4]

The study avoided capturing the effect that immigrants coming from less developed (and presumably shorter) countries might have by looking only at non-Hispanic whites and blacks in the United States. The researchers also compared people born during the same period, in order to avoid the effect that aging has on height. The data were actual measurements, rather than the heights that people reported to researchers, as some earlier studies had used.

How can one explain this reversal—one that the study's authors called "remarkable"? The researchers speculated that it's a result of "differences in the socioeconomic institutions" of Europe and the United States. "We conjecture that the U.S. healthcare system, as well as the relatively weak welfare safety net, might be why human growth in the United States has not performed as well in relative terms," they wrote.[5]

Scientists have a good understanding of the factors that determine height. Genetic variations are key to individuals' heights but aren't a significant factor in the average height of a population. This has to do with health and nutrition, especially during childhood, from prenatal health through adolescence. The authors of the study note that in the scientific community, "There is widespread agreement that nutritional intake, the incidence of diseases and the availability of medical services have a major impact on human size."[6]

More research is needed to fully understand why Americans are shrinking relative to the Europeans, but some differences between the two cultures—and their political economies—stand out.

Health care is one. It's not only that Europeans are universally covered, while one out of seven Americans is uninsured. As we saw in chapter 8, public-sector health care also places greater emphasis on prevention, while our for-profit, insurance-based system creates incentives to treat illness, rather than prevent it. This likely plays a role in our declining (relative) stature.

The United States also has far more concentrated wealth than any of its European allies, which means that although we are, on average, one of the wealthiest countries in the world, we also lead all of the advanced economies in poverty. Poverty limits access to both health care and good nutrition.[7]

A more important factor, in terms of average height, is childhood poverty. Here, the United States stands alone among the advanced economies with a stunning figure: 19 percent of U.S. children—almost one in five—live in poverty. No other industrialized country comes close; it's about five times the child poverty rate in Northern Europe. Again, nutrition and access to health care both vary with family income for children, just as they do for adults.[8] A study by sociologists Mark Plank at Washington University and Cornell's Thomas Hirschl found that 49 percent—half—of all children in the United States require food stamps at some point before age twenty. That's true for *nine out of ten* black children.[9]

Nutrition is a key determinant of height. According to the study, "U.S. children consume more meals prepared outside the home, more fast food rich in fat, high in energy density, and low in essential micronutrients, than do European children." That is ultimately a cultural issue—a result of a fast-food lifestyle that may have long-term consequences for growing bones.[10]

We saw in chapter 7 how our uniquely inflexible workplaces make it difficult for many Americans to effectively balance work and family life. This, in turn, means eating more fast food on the run and spending less time taking care of sick kids—both of which are factors that constrain average height. The potential impact might be greater still before children are born; research shows that every week of paid maternity leave significantly reduces infant mortality rates, which are an important indicator of prenatal health.

In Europe, the market drives inequality, just as in the United States. The Europeans address this problem better than we do with a stronger social safety net. At least partly as a result of that, Europeans have grown in height as much as the rise in their average incomes during the twentieth century would predict; Americans have not.

12

"ILLEGAL" IMMIGRATION ISN'T HURTING YOUR PROSPECTS

Don't believe that a border-crossing Mexican stole your job

We're not just talking about the number of jobs that we may be losing, or the number of kids that are in our schools and impacting our school system, or the number of people that are abusing our hospital system and taking advantage of the welfare system in this country—we're not just talking about that. We're talking about something that goes to the very heart of this nation—whether or not we will actually survive as a nation.

—Former representative Tom Tancredo (R-CO)[1]

During George W. Bush's second term, Congress twice came close to passing a sweeping package of immigration reforms. On both occasions, decidedly centrist measures to address an immigration system that everyone agrees is broken—if for very different reasons—were defeated under the weight of some of the most egregious spin, dodgy claims, and outright lies in memory, whoppers often colored by no small degree of truly virulent xenophobia.

Immigration is an issue that doesn't cleave neatly along ideological lines. It divides the Right. On one hand, Republican leaders warily eyeing the fast-growing Latino and Asian American votes—voters who are not exactly pleased with the heat of conservatives' rhetoric—express great concern over their party's electoral chances in the future. On the other is the hard-Right base whose passions have been inflamed by immigration as a social issue and whose members want nothing short of mass deportations.

In the spring of 2010, former Republican House majority leader Dick Armey, the chairman of the corporate-funded front-group FreedomWorks and a key organizer in the angry and ostensibly "grass-roots" Tea Party movement, denounced the politics embraced by the Tom Tancredo wing of his party, asking, "Who in the Republican Party was the genius that said that now that we have identified the fastest-growing voting demographic in America, let's go out and alienate them?" He added, "When I was the majority leader, I saw to it that Tom Tancredo did not get on the stage because I saw how destructive he was."[2]

Armey represents the business elites whose interests the GOP has traditionally defended, and corporate America sees immigration as key to maintaining a vibrant and often low paid workforce as the native-born population ages. Big Ag needs pickers, Silicon Valley wants more computer geeks who will accept lower wages, and a variety of industries—textiles, construction, even oil extraction—have come to rely on foreign-born workers (legal or otherwise). In 2008, immigrants represented more than 15 percent of the U.S. workforce, according to the Census Bureau.[3] (Unauthorized immigrants made up around 5 percent of the workforce.)[4]

Those practical concerns matter little to the true immigration hard-liners. For them, immigration represents a battle for nothing less than the soul of the nation. Fox News host Bill O'Reilly expressed the fears that animate many of them when he said, "The bottom line is . . . there is a movement in this country to wipe out 'white privilege' and to have the browning of America."[5]

From this wide divide on the Right, a number of different and often contradictory narratives have emerged. Much of the conservative base blames "illegal immigrants" for any number of social ills: for taking Americans' jobs and keeping down natives' wages, for spreading disease and crime and pestilence, and for supposedly sucking thirstily from the public teat. The Corporate Right, on the other hand, claims that immigrants only do the work that Americans refuse to do. And many conservatives believe that large numbers of unauthorized immigrants would simply disappear if only the government would "enforce the law."

All of these narratives are, on closer inspection, grossly inaccurate.

They're Taking Our Jobs!

The idea that immigrants, especially undocumented immigrants, take jobs from the native-born and keep wages low and taxes high is so deeply embedded in our discourse that even many progressive-minded people have come to believe it. And it's no surprise—with virtually no mainstream debate about how so-called free trade affects working people, how easy it is to break unions, or how debased corporate America's ethical culture has become, people believe immigration plays a much greater role in the plight of many U.S. workers than it actually does. Immigrants are visible in a way that those other factors are not.

Yet a belief commonly held is not necessarily true. Here is the reality: new immigrants (legal or not) have a negative short-term impact on local governments' fiscal situation, but over the long haul, they contribute more in taxes than they take in services. Immigrant labor may have a negative effect on wages for a small group of Americans, but that's anything but established, and the positive contributions—including their contributions to native workers' wages —are enjoyed by a much, much larger group of Americans. All of these factors are very small in relation to the economy as a whole, and almost none of the rhetoric about how immigration hurts working people is justified by the data.

The myth arises in part from the belief that there is one U.S. "labor market" that adheres strictly to the laws of supply and demand. As the liberal historian Thom Hartmann put it, "Working

Americans have always known this simple equation: More workers, lower wages. Fewer workers, higher wages." Yet that kind of simplistic view is dangerously inaccurate. Immigrants certainly do supply labor, but they also buy goods and services that in turn stimulate more *demand* for labor. The suggestion that an expanding workforce increases labor supply but not labor demand defies common sense—working people have to eat, clothe themselves, and have shelter.

The bottom line in terms of the economic impact is that study after credible study shows that the influx of immigrant labor has almost no impact on employment or wages for natives overall. The classic proof is Berkeley economist David Card's study of the Miami labor market after the Mariel boatlift dumped 125,000 new arrivals into it, increasing the local workforce overnight by almost 10 percent. He found that it had "virtually no effect" on either wages or employment opportunities.[6] That work was confirmed by Harvard's George Borjas (who favors more restrictions on immigrants—more on him later) in his 1994 follow-up study.

Reviewing a broad swath of academic literature, economists Jennifer Hunt of Yale and Brown's Rachel Friedberg concluded,

> Empirical estimates in a variety of settings and using a variety of approaches have shown that the effect of immigration on natives is small. There is no evidence of economically significant reductions in native employment. Even those natives who should be the closest substitutes with immigrant labor have not been found to suffer significantly as a result of increased immigration.[7]

What's more, a 2007 study conducted by the Public Policy Institute of California found that immigrants who arrived in that state between 1990 and 2004 actually *increased* wages for native workers by an average of 4 percent. Author Giovanni Peri, an economist at UC Davis, told the *Los Angeles Times* that the benefits were shared by all native-born workers, including high school dropouts.

(As immigrants fill lower-skilled jobs, they push even unskilled natives up into better jobs.) "The big message is that there is no big loss from immigration," Peri said. "There are gains, and these are enjoyed by a much bigger share of the population than is commonly believed."[8]

Howard Chang, an expert in immigration at the University of Pennsylvania who reviewed a wide range of economic studies, added that the "evidence indicates a weak relationship between native wages and immigration across all types of native workers, white or black, skilled or unskilled, male or female."

The United States Commission on Immigration Reform (CIR) conducted the most comprehensive and sophisticated study of the economic impact of immigration in the late 1990s, when Senator Alan Simpson (R-WY) and Representative Lamar Smith (R-TX) launched a crusade against the foreign invasion of the day. The CIR found that competition with immigrant labor mostly hurts earlier immigrants. "The data suggest that the jobs of immigrant and native workers are different," they concluded. The CIR also noted that immigrants contribute as much as $10 billion to the U.S. economy, adding, "Not many changes in policies would produce benefits as large as" liberalizing immigration.[9]

Most of these studies looked at legal, as well as illegal, immigration, but, economically, the only difference is that immigrants who are legal far exceed the number who lack proper papers—"illegal" immigrants' impact is basically the same but smaller (unauthorized immigrants use fewer social services but require more spending on law enforcement).

They're Draining Public Services!

The conventional wisdom—that immigrants suck up more in services than they pay in taxes—is also unsupported by the data. To understand why, you have to look at the entirety of what immigrants pay into the system and what they take out of it, and you have to distinguish between the short and the long term.

The kernel of truth to the anti-immigrant claims is that recently arrived illegal immigrants do take more in public services and law enforcement than they pay in taxes. But looking ahead to the next generation, this deficit reverses quite dramatically. There are a number of studies biased toward finding higher costs by including the cost of educating immigrant children without considering the taxes those children will pay when they reach maturity. Yet it's a mistake to view education as a "sunk cost," rather than as an investment in future workers whose higher earnings and greater tax payments will more than repay their education costs over the course of their careers. The authors of the CIR study noted that only by looking at the big picture, which includes the returns on the investment of education, can the true budgetary effect of immigration be considered.

The CIR found that when you look at that picture, the average immigrant and his or her offspring will *contribute $80,000 more in taxes than they take in services*. The economists found that even immigrants with less than a high school education contributed positively to the budget when the second generation was included.

Demographics are another issue we have to consider. We hear a lot about the pending Social Security "crisis" and the graying of the population. Our economy needs immigrants because native-born fertility rates continue to hover just at the replacement level. It's a law of economics that growth is made up of population growth plus increases in productivity. The only way the pie gets bigger is through more workers and/or more productive workers. Most of our population growth today comes from immigration.

According to the Census Bureau, "Compared to the native-born, a significantly higher percentage of immigrants are of [prime] working age (between 28 and 54 years of age)."[10] The Social Security Administration estimates that three out of four illegal immigrants pay Social Security and other payroll taxes but can't claim the benefits, amounting to an "illegal surplus" of billions of dollars per year—enough to erase 15 percent of the program's projected long-term budget shortfalls.[11] According to the CIR study, "[D]ue to contributions by immigrants, the total net benefit to the Social Security System will be nearly $500 billion."

When you look at the totality of the data, it's hard to escape the conclusion that immigrants are a vital part of our economic mix. As the University of Pennsylvania's Howard Chang noted, "A fair reading of the economic literature on immigration presents little justification for more restrictive immigration laws. Contrary to popular belief, economic considerations point toward liberaliz[ation.]"

The Fallacies of Anti-Immigrant Data: "Hate Research" and the Borjas Exception

Although credible studies using real-world economic data suggest that immigrant labor—legal or otherwise—has no significant impact on the fortunes of the native-born, it remains a persistent belief among many Americans and certainly goes a long way toward shaping the debate.

Part of the reason for the disconnect between popular opinion and the economic research is simple: while it's always easy to distort statistics, there's no area of public policy with more ideologically informed junk research than immigration. There are any number of ways to bias a study, but with immigration research, the most common is fairly straightforward: Count only one side of the ledger or look at a very narrow set of data. Count the costs in services used by unauthorized immigrants but not the taxes they pay. Look at any native-born workers who are displaced by migrants, but ignore the much larger number who gain from foreign-born labor.

The most prolific manufacturer of anti-immigrant "data" is the Center for Immigration Studies (CIS). Billing itself as a "nonpartisan think tank," the CIS publishes dozens and dozens of reports about the horrific "costs" of immigration. The CIS may be nonpartisan, but it's highly ideological. Funded heavily by the Scaife and Olin foundations, the CIS was spun off from the Federation for American Immigration Reform (FAIR) after the latter became associated with white supremacist views (it's listed as a hate group by the Southern

Poverty Law Center). The Institute for Policy Studies notes that FAIR's "policy rhetoric is often inflammatory, clearly anti-immigrant, and partisan."[12] FAIR was started by John Tanton, a leader in the English First movement who fell from grace after a newspaper printed a memo that he wrote questioning the "educability" of Latinos. In 2010, the CIS tried to walk back a report it released that referred to immigrants as "Third World golddiggers."[13] The CIS and a handful of similarly hard-line groups churn out an almost endless stream of dubious "research," which, tragically for our national discourse, is often cited as credible information by the corporate media.

A more serious argument that immigration harms some native workers comes from Harvard economists George Borjas, Richard Freeman, and Lawrence Katz. In a much-discussed 1996 study, they estimated that 44 percent of the decline in high school drop-outs' wages between 1980 and 1995 was a result of immigration.[14] Extending that work, Arthur Sakamoto and Changhwan Kim of the University of Texas got similar results in a more recent study. These findings have become known among economists as the "Borjas exception." Unlike the pabulum that CIS puts out, these statistical results are the work of serious economists and can't be dismissed out of hand.

The reason they need to be taken with a hefty grain of salt, however, is that they're based on computer models—economic simulations—that are at odds with the large body of research look-ing at real labor markets and real live immigrants. Borjas and his colleagues base these models on a somewhat dubious claim: that workers are highly mobile and move quickly to wherever there are jobs at a given time. According to Borjas, when an influx of immi-grant labor hits a town, as it hit Miami with the arrival of those Cuban refugees, natives move to other labor markets, and the economic results of their competition with newer workers don't end up reflected in the data from the areas they fled.

But, as economist Doug Henwood wrote, "There appears to be no evidence that natives actually migrate in the ways that would be required by Borjas' assumptions."[15] David Card said that studies like Borjas's are based on "the belief that labor market competition posed by immigration has to affect native opportunities, so if we don't find an impact, the research design must be flawed."[16]

Howard Chang noted that Borjas, Freeman, and Katz themselves have conceded that their model "will likely overstate the economic effects of immigration." If the real-world data did correspond with their models, then progressive reformers would have to take the findings quite seriously, but as it stands, the preponderance of evidence shows that fears of unauthorized immigrants leading us to economic ruin are unfounded.

They Just Need to Enforce the Laws!

In the spring of 2010, the Obama administration announced that it would halt funding of a high-tech "virtual fence" along the U.S.-Mexican border. The project had been a centerpiece of George W. Bush's efforts to control illegal immigration, but the construction of the barrier, which had been opposed by many people living near the border, had become a disastrous boondoggle. The defense contractor Boeing had made grand promises at the inception of the project, but despite massive cost overruns and significant delays in the scheduled completion of the fence, the thing simply didn't work. Boeing built a 28-mile test section in the Southern Arizona desert that, according to a National Public Radio report, "utterly failed to meet performance expectations. . . . The entire border was supposed to be covered a year ago, but after three years—and $1.4 billion—the system is still full of bugs." And, according to a report by the Government Accountability Office obtained by NPR, "The bugs are coming faster than the fixes."[17]

The security fence was merely the latest failure of the "enforcement-only" approach favored by hard-liners to control unauthorized immigration. The last ten years have shown us that pumping billions of dollars into beefing up patrols and installing all manner of shiny new gizmos along our two thousand–mile southern border only results in an increase in arrests and detentions and a nice, fat profit for Department of Homeland Security contractors. It has just about zero effect on the number of immigrants residing in the country illegally.

Consider some numbers. According to a study by the Pew Hispanic Center, "The number of migrants coming to the United States each year, legally and illegally, grew very rapidly starting in the mid-1990s, hit a peak at the end of the decade, and then declined substantially after 2001."[18] During that very same time period—starting in Bill Clinton's first term with his "prevention through deterrence" immigration strategy—spending on border enforcement *skyrocketed*. In 1994, the government spent around $550 million on border security and about $350 million on inspections at entry points. Clinton increased the budget for border enforcement every year—spending almost quadrupled during his presidency—and the immigrants flowed right in.[19] And under Bush's watch, it quadrupled again; in 2008, we spent a total of $9.7 billion on enforcement. All in all, dollars for immigration enforcement increased more than *tenfold*, even as the number of unauthorized immigrants living in the United States increased dramatically.

Despite those efforts, in a wildly successful disinformation campaign, anti-immigration hard-liners have convinced many Americans that the United States is not serious about enforcing its immigration laws. It's a narrative that plays to people's distrust of government and anxieties about losing sovereignty in the era of globalization. With a focus on immigration, that narrative also allows conservative lawmakers to advance a larger domestic agenda, justifying calls for an expanded security state with more surveillance, increased police actions, and an almost endless series of increases in Homeland Security spending. In reality, though, it's a Big Lie, and it's hard to overstate just how big it is. Not only does the United States attempt to enforce its immigration laws, it does so with an almost authoritarian zeal that one would expect to find in a police state.

Immigration and Customs Enforcement (ICE) is the second-largest police agency in the country. According to official figures analyzed by the Detention Watch Network, ICE rounds up hundreds of thousands of people each year, but only half of them are ever charged with a crime.[20] (Being in this country without papers is a civil violation; it's the only civil offense for which people are regularly jailed.) In 2009, almost 400,000 immigrants were "removed."[21] With more than 1.5 million people in immigration proceedings, a *Washington Post* analysis found that ICE "holds more detainees a night than Clarion Hotels have guests, operates nearly as many vehicles as Greyhound has buses and flies more people each day than do many small U.S. airlines."[22]

According to a suit filed by the American Civil Liberties Union (ACLU), children as young as three years old have been detained along with their parents in prisons leased by Homeland Security. Before the lawsuit was settled by the government, children were dressed in prison garb, and guards disciplined them by "threatening to separate them from their parents."[23] According to Amnesty International, "Children are subjected to pepper spray, placed in solitary confinement, and routinely restrained in violation of international standards."[24] ICE runs two "family detention centers," and the *Los Angeles Times* reported that the agency is building three new ones.[25]

Homeland Security is one of the largest jailers in the world, "but it behaves like a lawless local sheriff," Paromita Shah, an immigration expert with the National Lawyers Guild, told the *New York Times*.[26] The 280,000 people detained by ICE each year, mostly poorer workers, have limited access to legal help – there are no public defenders in our immigration courts. According to the *Minnesota Star-Tribune*, three out of four are left to navigate a bewildering legal system on their own, like characters in a Kafka novel.[27]

In addition to its own detention facilities, ICE leases thousands of beds in 312 local prisons, where a majority of immigrant detainees are held. They include dozens of private, for-profit prison facilities. The immigration detention system has proved to be a cash cow for companies such as Halliburton, Corrections Corporation of America (CCA), and the GEO Group. "Housing federal detainees typically brings in more per 'man-day' . . . than they can get from state prison systems," wrote Leslie Berestein in the *San Diego Union-Tribune*.[28]

Michele Deitch, an expert on prison privatization at the University of Texas in Austin, told the *Union-Tribune* that "The private prison industry was on the verge of bankruptcy in the late 1990s, until the feds bailed them out with the immigration-detention contracts."[29]

The Utter Futility of "Enforcement Only"

The reason these efforts don't work—can't work—is threefold. First, there are the structural realities: the United States and Mexico share not only one of the longest borders in the world, but also one that separates people with one of the greatest differentials in wealth. Second, the legal immigration system is virtually closed to people without means—to low-skilled workers from Mexico, for example. And, finally, Americans want to live in a more-or-less free society, without being asked to show cops their papers all the time. "Enforcement only" could certainly work if we wanted to live in a very different kind of country.

More important, the policy does nothing to address the underlying supply of willing foreign workers or the demand for exploitable migrant labor here at home. Just as Prohibition was ineffective and the "war on drugs" has raged on for two decades without much impact, attempts to crack down on the black market in workers without addressing the economic factors that drive that market simply *can't* work. In such cases, "enforcement only" has a proven track record—it's perfectly ineffective. Prohibition, after all, didn't keep Americans from boozing.

Finally, it's essential to understand how trade and immigration are related. Since the mid-1990s, we've seen a large but finite surge in immigration, much of it from Mexico and in large part in response to the effects of trade deals that the United States and Mexico signed in the 1980s and the 1990s. According to a study by the Pew organization, Mexican immigration "grew very rapidly starting in the mid-1990s, hit a peak at the end of the decade, and then declined substantially after 2001. By 2004, the annual inflow of foreign-born persons was down 24 percent from its all-time high in 2000."[30]

This time line corresponds perfectly with the damage wrought in Mexican labor markets by the North American Free Trade Agreement. NAFTA led to a flood of subsidized corn into Mexico. Employment in Mexico's agricultural sector dropped by 13 percent between 1993, the year before the deal went into effect, and 2002.[31]

Service sector employment in Mexico was stable; it didn't absorb many of those workers. And although manufacturing increased in the *maquiladoras*—lightly regulated "free-trade zones" located conveniently near the U.S. border—between 1994 and 2000 (when it peaked with about 800,000 jobs), the *maquiladora* zone then shed 250,000 of those same jobs during the three years that followed, most of them outsourced to China. Make capital mobile, make goods mobile, and people will have no choice but to mobilize themselves to follow the jobs.[32] Unemployed Mexican agricultural workers had no place to go for work but north.

Mexico was promised millions of new jobs under NAFTA, but the promise proved false. The country had a mini baby boom in the early 1980s, and its economy hasn't been able to absorb those babies as they've come of age and entered the workforce. Mexico doesn't have unemployment insurance.

Immigrants Take Jobs Americans Won't Do!

The Corporate Right, which has made strange bedfellows with immigrants' rights activists in recent years, has pushed a narrative that's very different from the one embraced by the nativists. Corporate America argues that newly arrived workers take jobs that Americans won't do. Yet that's only partially true; many unauthorized immigrants fill nonunion jobs that are impossibly crappy, pay poverty wages, and are rife with workplace violations, and they work those jobs side by side with millions of natives and legal residents. The reality is that there are *not enough* Americans who are willing or able to tolerate poverty wages and other workplace abuses.

At the same time that spending on immigration enforcement was going through the roof, the resources allocated to enforcing over-time, minimum wage, workplace safety, and other protections for workers were cut and cut again. According to research conducted by NYU's Brennan Center for Justice, the number of workplaces that fell within the jurisdiction of the Department of Labor's wage and hour division more than doubled between 1975 and 2004, and the number of workers in those establishments increased by 55 percent. Yet during that period, the number of inspectors available to enforce basic labor standards declined by 14 percent, and the number of "compliance actions" the agency completed plummeted by more than a third.[33]

Those who advocate more law enforcement to tackle the immigration issue often invoke images of the United States descending into anarchy—of a nation losing control of its borders and therefore its sovereignty. There is anarchy in America, there is lawlessness, but you'll find a lot more of it in the kitchen of your favorite diner than along the Rio Grande.

Unfortunately, there's not much in the way of nationwide data on workplace violations, but we do have a large body of local and state studies, and all point to the same conclusion: they are simply *rampant* at the lower end of the economy and among vulnerable populations.

Consider the findings of just a few of those studies, as compiled by the Brennan Center:

- A 2004 study of two hundred workers conducted at multiple sites in Fairfax County, Virginia, found that
  - 54.6 percent were paid less than agreed on.
  - 53.1 percent reported nonpayment for work done.
  - 35.6 percent said they'd been victims of racial discrimination.

- 25.8 percent had been given bad checks.
- 16 percent reported that they'd been subject to violence on the job.
- 14.9 percent said they'd received threats from employers.
- A 2002 study of chicken processors found that six in ten plants failed to pay workers overtime.
- In a 1998 study of restaurant workers in Los Angeles, only two out of forty-three establishments complied with basic labor laws.
- A 2005 study of grape pickers in California's Central Valley found that half of all workers reported pay stubs that reflected less than the total number of hours worked, and half reported that they had not received all of the overtime pay they were owed.
- A 1998 study looking at workers in the restaurant, garment, hotel, and motel industries—all occupations with large numbers of unauthorized workers—found that only one in twenty restaurants complied with minimum wage laws and only a third of hotels and motels were in compliance, as were only four of ten shops in the garment industry.

Study after study reported similar findings. And it bears repeating: although these illegal jobs are clustered in industries in which many unauthorized workers toil, millions of legal immigrants and U.S. citizens *work those same jobs* and are also victims of widespread employer abuses. According to one 2003 study, the percentage of workers being ripped off via minimum wage violations is not that much lower for natives than it is for immigrants— 13 percent versus 9 percent among women and 9 percent versus 6 percent among men.[34]

Most of the focus of the immigration debate in this country has been on the immigrants themselves, especially unauthorized immigrants. But very little attention is paid to the other side of the transaction: the incentives that U.S. companies and households have to hire an unauthorized worker over a citizen.

For one thing, enforcement efforts rarely target employers. As the *Washington Post* noted, while "federal immigration authorities arrested nearly four times as many people at workplaces in 2007 as they did in 2005 . . . only 92 owners, supervisors or hiring officials were arrested in an economy that includes 6 million companies that employ more than 7 million unauthorized workers. Only 17 firms faced criminal fines or other forfeitures."[35] Those raids devastate workers' families, but they represent little more than an inconvenience to employers, who have little reason to improve working conditions when they can hire new employees who are just as easy to exploit.

Illegal immigrants sell their labor on a black market that's similar in many ways to those for other illicit goods and services, such as the drug trade. The sellers' incentives are well understood: the lion's share of those who have moved to the United States in the last decade are economic refugees, fleeing home countries where they can't eke out a dignified life. Human traffickers, who can realize enormous profits from shipping people across national boundaries, provide for the market their incentives, again, are well understood.

The buyers, of course, are Americans—and not only corporate America. Middle-class households and many small firms use illegal labor, but their side of the transaction goes largely undiscussed. Without looking at both sides of the coin—demand, as well as supply—it's impossible to arrive at a reform agenda that can result in an effective, humane, and sustainable system of immigration control.

Illegal Immigrants or Illegal Jobs?

An unregulated sector of the economy, rife with illegal jobs, is the largely unexamined "pull factor" for much of the (low-skilled) immigration to the United States. Most recent immigrants work at jobs that fall somewhere between what's available in their native countries and the kind of jobs one would expect to find in a highly advanced economy. They also tend to be jobs that can't be easily outsourced to countries with an abundance of cheap labor.

A good example of these kinds of jobs can be found in New York City, where the cost of living is among the highest in the country. A report in *Crain's New York Business News* found that in underregulated New York restaurants, greengrocers, retail corner laundries, and private households, "Typically, workers will be quoted a flat weekly salary of $300 and then have to work 60 hours a week, receiving an effective wage of $5 an hour with no provision for overtime."[36] New York State's minimum wage was $7.15 per hour, and federal and state laws require overtime pay for any hours worked over forty per week.

In order to create a sustainable model for immigration control, we need to look at decreasing the demand for workers who are willing to fill those jobs. This means breaking Americans' addiction to exploitable labor. As long as there are $5-per-hour jobs in New York City that few natives can afford to work, and millions of workers who don't have jobs that pay that much in poorer countries, we'll have a large number of people who want to migrate to our shores. As long as our immigration system doesn't permit enough of them to migrate legally, we'll have an "illegal immigration problem." It's simply the law of supply and demand at work.

Yet it's not true that all unauthorized immigrants work those kinds of jobs. There's no question that employers are sometimes legitimately unable to find citizens or legal residents to fill even decent jobs. That's especially true in rural communities, where young people tend to take off for the big city and the population is aging and in decline. In 2007, I spoke with Oklahoma state senator Harry Coates soon after his state passed one of the most restrictive immigration laws in the nation. Employers in Oklahoma weren't only having problems filling low-paying "McJobs," he told me. "In the oil fields, they're paying $18 to $20 per hour to start," he said, "but they can't find enough willing workers to fill the jobs. We've told our young people to work with their minds, not with their hands." Coates added, "We've shot ourselves in the foot by running off willing workers for willing employers."

Deflecting Illegal Immigration

Progressive immigration and workplace reform would focus our enforcement resources on cleaning up the bottom end of the labor market: on the jobs that bring people to our shores, rather than on the immigrants who work them. Guaranteeing workers—immigrant and native alike—the right to organize and enforcing wage and overtime laws would equalize the price of hiring unauthorized and legal workers and would go a long way toward addressing the demand for illegal labor without the ugliness of raids and deportations.

Once the goal of eliminating substandard and often illegal jobs—un-American jobs—from the U.S. workplace is accomplished, there would be far less resistance to new workers coming in to fill jobs that can't be staffed by Americans. Public opinion research shows that when people perceive the economy to be functioning well for them, much of the anxiety over immigration disappears.

That approach, which doesn't separate families or result in tens of thousands of people being detained without trial, is known as "deflection," and it's proved to be successful. During the 1980s and the early 1990s, California saw an explosion of new arrivals, mostly from Mexico and many without proper papers. But beginning in the mid-1990s, Los Angeles successfully "deflected" an estimated one million new Mexican immigrants to other locales by cleaning up the largely unregulated shadow economy that provides the jobs many people come to the United States to work (similar to the approach I advocate on the national level).

In part, the deflection resulted from the local labor market becoming saturated. Yet there was also a significant policy component—California raised the minimum wage several times during the 1980s, and by 1990, it was 12 percent higher than the national minimum. Beginning in the middle of the decade, Los Angeles then cracked down on employers who ripped off their employees or otherwise violated California's stringent workplace laws.[37]

UCLA sociologist Ivan Light, the author of *Deflecting Immigration: Networks, Markets, and Regulation in Los Angeles*, explained how the use of wage and other workforce enforcement measures played a vital role in the effort:

> Slums and sweatshops had long been illegal in Los Angeles, but the enforcement of anti-slum and anti-sweatshop ordinances, as well as the enforcement of minimum wage laws, had been lax.
>
> To combat immigrant poverty, high-profile law enforcement of these ordinances sharply increased beginning in the late 1980s and continued through the 1990s. Although enforcement of ordinances and wage laws did not eliminate sweatshops and slums, enforcement did slow their growth below the rate of immigrant influx.
>
> In effect, the enforcement of anti-slum and anti-sweatshop laws helped push, or deflect, Mexican immigrants from Los Angeles to other parts of the United States.[38]

Light neglected to state the obvious: the effort also raised the living standards of U.S. citizens and legal permanent residents who were working in the same previously unregulated "Wild West" economy.

It's the way to build a humane and self-regulating system. Immigration researchers talk about the effect of "transnational social networks" on migration, which is a fancy way to describe communities that spill across international borders. Such networks exist between the United States and the countries that account for the lion's share of new immigration, and researchers have found that they are highly effective mechanisms for communicating information about job markets, legal environments, and other factors that people weigh when deciding whether (and to where) they might emigrate.

Every policy creates some winners and losers, and many come with unintended consequences. L.A.'s crackdown on workplace violations caused some minimum-wage employers to leave the state (or the country) for friendlier climes, and Light noted that while "a higher minimum wage can drive away jobs for low-wage immigrants," it can "also drive away low-wage jobs that native-born teenagers and minorities rely upon." There are additional labor costs, of course, which must be shared by employers and consumers.

The net result, however, was that Los Angeles shifted the incentives that had drawn millions of new immigrants to its environs, and it did so with a policy mix that was far more comprehensive than simply locking up or deporting a lot of otherwise innocent working people.

As a local approach, the effort did nothing to alter the immigration picture at the national level—those one million immigrants who were deflected from Los Angeles simply chose other destinations. But if it were enacted on a national level and paired with other measures, such as reducing the long backlog of applications for legal residence, we could deflect a large share of new immigrants who are considering making the move to the United States before they actually make it.

The Real Costs of Stupid Immigration Laws

In April 2010, Arizona governor Jan Brewer, whom we last encountered in chapter 1 balancing her budget by cutting off health care for tens of thousands of low-income children, signed SB 1070 into law. To say the very least, the bill was controversial.

Despite the fact that the federal government has exclusive domain over regulating immigration, Arizona's law made being in the country illegally a state crime (it was only a civil offense on the federal statutes). It made transporting an unauthorized immigrant a crime. And it empowered police to detain anyone they *suspect* of committing those crimes.

This is a book about economics, so I'll leave the legal issues aside. I'll only say that when reactionary xenophobia and economic reality clash, the latter always wins.

Reaction to the bill was swift. Within weeks of the law's passage, two of Arizona's largest cities, Flagstaff and Tucson, announced that they were suing to block the law.[1] A boycott of Arizona goods and services was called. The Boston, Los Angeles, and Oakland city councils stopped doing business in the state, and, as of this writing, New York and Washington, D.C., were considering following suit.[2] San Francisco and Boulder, Colorado, suspended all official travel to the Copper State.[3] According to the Arizona Hotel and Lodging Association, nineteen conferences were canceled just in the first week after the bill was signed.[4]

According to an analysis by the Immigration Policy Center, "If significant numbers of immigrants and Latinos are actually persuaded to leave the state because of this new law, they will take their tax dollars, businesses, and purchasing power with them."

The University of Arizona's Udall Center for Studies in Public Policy estimates that the total economic output attributable to Arizona's immigrant workers was $44 billion in 2004, which sustained roughly 400,000 full-time jobs. Furthermore, over 35,000 businesses in Arizona are Latino-owned and had sales and receipts of $4.3 billion and employed 39,363 people in 2002, the last year for which data is available. The Perryman Group estimates that if all unauthorized immigrants were removed from Arizona, the state would lose $26.4 billion in economic activity, $11.7 billion in gross state product, and approximately 140,324 jobs, even accounting for adequate market adjustment time.[5]

Again, the federal government has exclusive domain over regulating immigration to the United States, so Arizona's law is unlikely to withstand legal challenges. But if it does, what follows would be utterly predictable: the state not only will lose out on tourism and international business travel, but a huge share of its workforce, both legal and otherwise, will also seek less nasty climes. Arizona will face enormous litigation costs, and local police agencies will start to complain that they don't have the resources to enforce other laws. Brand Arizona will continue to take a pummeling, companies will face a whole new set of hiring challenges, and the state's business community will start to complain. Eventually, the very same lawmakers who pushed the new law will admit that it didn't work out as they'd intended.

I say this with the confidence born of past experience. In 2007, Arizona passed another tough "enforcement only" immigration law, which mandated the use of an (unreliable) electronic verification system and subjected employers to the loss of their business licenses for hiring the wrong people. It turned out to be a disaster that might rank up there with the Edsel or New Coke in the pantheon of boneheaded ideas.

The state had a very low unemployment rate when the law was passed—it was, at least in part, a "solution" to a problem that Arizona didn't have. Unemployment was at 4.1 percent when the law went into effect in early 2008 and had been at 3.7 percent when a judge upheld the measure a year earlier.[6] By the middle of 2008, lawmakers were scrambling to undo the shock they'd inflicted on the state, as up to 8 percent of the population—according to one estimate—decided to hightail it out of Arizona en masse.[7] The state faced new labor shortages, as well as a loss in demand from all of those worker-consumers. Eventually, the law was amended, in part due to pressure from Arizona businesses.

The people of Arizona learned the hard way that immigrants not only supply labor, but also demand goods and services in turn. In addition, they learned that newer immigrant communities have a mix of people with different legal statuses all jumbled together, and that when there's a widespread perception that politicians (and citizens) are attacking immigrants, it doesn't much matter that some people differentiate between those who are "legal" and "illegal"—Arizona lost plenty of citizens and lawful permanent residents with that drop in population.

A University of Arizona study concluded that economic output in Arizona would drop 8.2 percent annually if foreign-born workers left the state's labor force. "Getting rid of these workers means we are deciding as a matter of policy to shrink our economy," Judith Gans, an immigration scholar at the university's Udall Center, told the *Wall Street Journal*. "They're filling vital gaps in our labor force."[8]

Arizona's experience isn't unique. In 2006, the town of Riverside, New Jersey, passed a strict immigration ordinance. A year later, the *New York Times* reported, "With the departure of so many people, the local economy suffered. Hair salons, restaurants and corner shops that catered to the immigrants saw business plummet; several closed. Once-boarded-up storefronts downtown were boarded up again." The town was also hit with serious legal bills defending against several lawsuits. According to the *Times*, "The legal battle forced the town to delay road paving projects, the purchase of a dump truck and repairs to town hall." The law was repealed a little more than a year after it went into effect.[9]

Hazleton, Pennsylvania's ordinance was blocked before being implemented—but not before the municipality had spent $2.4

million in court costs. The town's insurance carrier refused to cover the costs.[10]

When Oklahoma passed a draconian immigration law, the *Chicago Tribune* reported, "Construction companies that relied upon undocumented laborers are having trouble completing jobs. . . . And business is down sharply at the stores, groceries and restaurants that serve a Hispanic clientele." Republican state senator Harry Coates told the *Trib*: "You really have to work hard at it to destroy our state's economy, but we found a way. . . . We ran off the work force."[11]

With Washington paralyzed on the issue, these local ordinances, despite being ineffective and coming with great economic costs, are politically popular. But as we saw in chapter 12, there's a much better way.

13

BLACKS STILL KEPT BACK

Don't believe the U.S. economy is a postracial meritocracy

The mess in the black community is proof of the utter failure of democrat enforced liberalism and not holding people
accountable. Blacks must be challenged to take responsibility for their lives. For crying out loud, this is America. A
high school education is free. There is no reason other than
a moral and parental breakdown for blacks not to graduate
high school.

—Lloyd Marcus, prominent black Tea Partier[1]

In 2010, the conservative *National Review* held one of those
wonky panel discussions to which Washingtonians are so often
drawn. The title: "Really a Racial Recession?: Discrimination Is
an Insufficient Explanation for Black Unemployment." According
to *Salon*'s Gabriel Winant, the dominant theme of the six panelists
seemed to be "What's the matter with black people?"[2]

You'd think that one group might have some insights on this subject—African Americans—but the *National Review* didn't bother to
invite any (or if they did, none chose to show up). Winant called it
"*National Review*'s White People Summit on the Problems of Black
America." Perhaps this shouldn't have come as a surprise. The conservative movement has developed a decidedly simplistic narrative
about the persistent social ills that plague many African American

families. Rather than the robust and often nuanced debate within the black community itself over exactly how race, class, and culture interact, conservatives have decided that in the post–civil rights era, it's a "culture of poverty" (or a "culture of dependency") that lies at the heart of the matter.

The Manhattan Institute's Myron Magnet, writing in the *Wall Street Journal*, laid out the basic argument in an op-ed subtly titled "Freedom vs. Dependency":

Even as the opportunity opened by the Civil Rights Act resulted in such dramatic gains for the vast majority of black Americans, the condition of a minority of blacks, perhaps one in 10, markedly worsened in the years after 1964, so much so that a recognizable underclass—defined by the self-defeating behavior that kept it mired in intergenerational poverty—became entrenched in the nation's cities.

What's clear in retrospect is that racism can't be to blame, since just at the moment that the underclass came into existence the Civil Rights Act was permitting blacks to flood into the mainstream.

Blame instead the enormous changes unfolding in American culture in exactly those years: the sexual revolution, the counterculture's contempt for the "system," the celebration of drugs, dropping out, and rebellion. When this change in our nation's most fundamental values and beliefs filtered down from the elites who started it to those at the very bottom of the social ladder, the consequences were catastrophic. The new culture devalued virtues that the poor need to succeed and celebrated behavior almost guaranteed to keep them out of the mainstream.[3]

In other words, when blacks adopted the culture and values of white hippies, they lost the get-up-and-go to get ahead. I'll leave a discussion of African American culture in all of its depth to others, except to say that the data don't back up the Right's central claims. As we'll see, racism does exist and its effects are not inconsequential. But racism alone doesn't explain the breadth or the persistence of the gap between blacks and whites today. What Magnet doesn't consider is the *lingering and purely economic legacy* of the time when widespread institutional racism *was* the norm in this country.

The Culture of Poverty

The term "culture of poverty" was first coined in Oscar Lewis's 1961 book *The Children of Sanchez*. Lewis, who had studied poverty in small Mexican communities, asserted that they shared common cultural attributes. Then, although he had only studied small samples, he concluded that the same attributes were *universal* among poor people.[4]

In 2006, the culture of poverty debate was put front and center when Bill Cosby gave a fiery speech decrying blacks' cultural deficits. Algernon Austin and economist Jared Bernstein (who would go on to serve as chief economic adviser to Vice President Joe Biden), wrote in response to Cosby's analysis:

> Key to the success of the cultural argument is the omission of inconvenient facts about social and economic trends. . . . For example, people arguing that African-Americans are suffering from a culture of poverty stress that blacks are much more likely to be poor than whites. True, but this fact misses the most important development about black poverty in recent years: its steep decline during the 1990s.[5]

They noted, as I did earlier, that black poverty had fallen dramatically during the Clinton administration, only to rise again during the Bush years. "The 'culture of poverty' argument cannot explain these trends," they wrote. "Poor black people did not develop a 'culture of success' in 1993 and then abandon it for a 'culture of failure' in 2001."

Education scholar Paul Gorski noted that after the publication of Oscar Lewis's book, "Researchers around the world tested the culture of poverty concept empirically." Fifty years of studies have revealed a number of observations about the causes of poverty, but, as Gorski noted, "On this they all agree: There is no such thing as a culture of poverty. Differences in values and behaviors among poor people are just as great as those between" the rich and poor. "The culture of poverty concept," he added, "is constructed from a collection of smaller stereotypes which, however false, seem to have crept into mainstream thinking as unquestioned fact."[6]

Gorski did an exhaustive literature review on the culture of poverty meme. Are poor people lazier than their wealthier counterparts? Do they have a poor work ethic that keeps them from pulling themselves up by their bootstraps? Quite the opposite is true. A 2002 study by the Economic Policy Institute found that among working adults, poorer people actually put in more hours than wealthier ones did. In 2004, 83 percent of children from low-income families had at least one employed parent, according to the National Center for Children in Poverty. Gorski added, "The severe shortage of living-wage jobs means that many poor adults must work two, three, or four jobs."[7]

There is quite a bit of data to suggest that kids whose parents are heavily involved in their schooling do better than kids whose parents aren't. But are poor people less interested in participating in their kids' schooling, as the culture of poverty folks suggest? No—several studies have found that rich and poor parents have the same *attitudes* about education. Poor parents do indeed spend less time going to school events and volunteering to spend time in their children's classrooms, but that's not a matter of culture. As Gorski wrote, it's because "they are more likely to work multiple jobs, to work evenings, to have jobs without paid leave, and to be unable to afford child care and public transportation."[8]

Are poor people more likely to use drugs and alcohol? Gorski noted that the research shows that drug use in the United States "is equally distributed across poor, middle class, and wealthy communities," but that "alcohol abuse is far more prevalent among wealthy people than among poor people."[9]

Perhaps the most pervasive narrative is that poor people, and black people especially, don't cherish traditional institutions such as marriage. It's self-evident that having one breadwinner instead of two (or one breadwinner and one parent to raise the kids) is an economic disadvantage, and any number of studies have found that single-parent households (especially single-mother families) are more likely to be poor. But the "culture of poverty" narrative confuses correlation with causation. When middle-class women head a household, studies have found that they don't lose economic status at all—they maintain their position.

It's also worth noting that we tend to see wealthier single mothers as strong and heroic, juggling work and kids. As Jean Hardisty, the author of *Marriage as a Cure for Poverty: A Bogus Formula for Women*, notes, it's a different story for those without means. "Single mothers who are low-income, especially those receiving welfare benefits, are constantly criticized by the general public," she wrote, "and are held accountable for their single status rather than praised for finding self-fulfillment in motherhood. They are usually judged to be irresponsible, or simply unable to meet the child's needs, including the supposed need for a father or father figure."[10]

Hardisty notes that poor people of color also face tangible barriers to setting up and maintaining a stable, two-parent home:

> Race accounts for several barriers to marriage in low-income communities of color. The disparate incarceration of men of color, job discrimination, and police harassment are three barriers that are race-specific. Other barriers are universally present for low-income people: low-quality and unsafe housing, a decrepit and underfunded educational system; joblessness; poor health care; and flat-funded day care . . . are some of the challenges faced by low-income women and men. These burdens make it difficult to set up stable, economically viable households, and also put stresses on couples that do marry.[11]

In 1998, the Fragile Families Study looked at 3,700 low-income unmarried couples in twenty U.S. cities. The authors found that nine in ten of the couples living together wanted to tie the knot, but only 15 percent had actually done so by the end of the one-year study period.[12]

Yet here's a key finding: for every dollar that a man's hourly wages increased, the odds that he'd get hitched by the end of the year rose by 5 percent. Men earning more than $25,000 during the year had twice the marriage rates of those making less than $25,000. Writing up the findings for the *Nation*, Sharon Lerner noted that poverty "also seems to make people feel less entitled to marry."

> As one father in the survey put it, marriage means "not living from check to check." Thus, since he was still scraping bottom, he wasn't ready for it. "There's an identity associated with marriage that they don't feel they can achieve," [Princeton sociology professor Sara] McLanahan says of her interviewees. (Ironically, romantic ideas about weddings— the limos, cakes and gowns of bridal magazines—seem to stand in the way of marriage in this context. Many in the study said they were holding off until they could afford a big wedding bash.)[13]

And just as people with little money hold the same attitudes about education as those with big bucks do, Hardisty cited studies showing that "a large percentage of single low-income mothers would like to be married at some time. They seek marriages that are financially stable, with a loving, supportive husband." The dream of many poor women is the same as everyone else's: they "often aspire to a romantic notion of marriage and family that features a white picket fence in the suburbs."[14] Low economic status leads to fewer marriages, not the other way around.

You might notice that the data in the preceding section cover both African Americans and low-income people. That's because class, race, and culture aren't easily separable. But the culture of poverty meme attempts to do that: to ignore the structural economic inequalities that perpetuate poverty and to ignore racism. Replacing all of that is the simplistic notion that poverty is a *natural* extension of poor families' own profound human flaws. It's an ideological belief divorced from decades of research on what really causes poverty to persist.

Racism Still Exists

I'm sure that all of the *National Review*'s pasty experts on the African American experience would agree that, sure, racism still exists—kinda-sorta, and on the margins. But because blacks have enjoyed the full rights of citizenship since the mid-1960s, if you argue that maybe racism has something to do with their lower average economic status, you're just "playing the race card" or embracing an "ideology of victimhood." It's a pretty offensive assertion. given that there is plenty of data to suggest that racism is alive and well in the United States and very much plays a role in African American lives.

In 2003, Northwestern University sociologist Devah Prager conducted a study in which she sent pairs of volunteers to apply for entry-level jobs advertised in local newspapers. The white "applicants" admitted to their prospective employers that they'd served eighteen months in prison for possession of cocaine with intent to distribute. The black volunteers offered the same level of education and experience but presented clean criminal records. Prager was surprised when more white "criminals" were offered jobs than African American men who'd stayed on the straight and narrow. "I thought the effect of a criminal record would swamp other effects," Pager said. "That assumption was clearly wrong. It really suggests that stereotypes and assumptions about black males are very much a factor in hiring decisions."[15]

Some people questioned Prager's findings because it was possible that the volunteers' performances weren't consistent. Perhaps the white volunteers simply happened to be more charismatic.

Another study, by the University of Chicago's Marianne Bertrand and MIT's Sendhil Mullainathan, took the human factor out of the equation entirely. The researchers gathered hundreds of real résumés that were comparable in terms of experience, education, and the quality of the résumés themselves. They then replaced the names with monikers that were picked to "sound white" or "sound black," and used the résumés to respond to thirteen hundred job ads in the *Boston Globe* and the *Chicago Tribune*. Bertrand and Mullainathan found that the "white" names got about one callback per ten résumés, while "black" names got one per fifteen.[16]

They then tried sending résumés with different levels of education and experience. The CVs of more experienced "applicants" who sounded white were 30 percent more likely to elicit a callback, but those whose names sounded black were only 9 percent more likely to get a response.[17]

In 2001, a class action lawsuit against Nissan prompted an analysis of 300,000 auto loans the company had made in thirty-three states between 1993 and 2000 and found that African Americans "consistently paid more than white customers, regardless of their credit histories."[18]

Another study, conducted by NYU's Furman Center for Real Estate and Urban Policy, found that "even when median income levels were comparable, home buyers in minority neighborhoods were more likely to get a loan from a subprime lender." These tended to come with "higher interest rates, fees and penalties."[19]

The Lingering Effects of Institutionalized Racism

We hear a lot about the gaps between blacks and whites in terms of income, health and well-being, educational attainment, and other variables. These statistics tell us a lot, but looking only at these data misses a crucial part of the story. The differences in *accumulated* wealth—in net worth—are far greater than the differences in income, and that impacts black families' prospects of moving up in a big way.

According to the *Washington Post*, white families, on average, have *ten times* the accumulated wealth of black families who earn the exact same income.[20] NYU's Dalton Conley found a similar divide in 2004 and noted that the trend remained true even when adjusting for education levels and savings rates.

Recall the importance of "intergenerational assistance" discussed in chapter 2—how one's chances to advance economically are drastically affected by whether the family can help start a young person on a solid path to a middle-class life. Remember Conley's hypothetical college graduates—one from a family with some money who enters the workforce debt free and the other saddled with $50,000 in debt, and what a huge difference that can make in terms of their long-term prospects. Think of the difference it makes when a young couple's parents can give them a down payment on their first home—that couple starts building equity right out of the starting gate, instead of throwing away money on rent. Small businesses don't begin with a good idea; they begin with an idea and start-up capital. If you're already established, you can get that start-up money from a bank or find an investor. Before then, your best chance is to hit up your family for a loan.

Now consider again that fifty years after achieving legal equality, a black family has only a tenth of the accumulated wealth of a white family that earns the exact same income today and saves the exact same amount of money for a rainy day. The difference in wealth is, as Conley told me, "the legacy of racial inequality from generations past."[21]

America's limited and fraying social safety net also means that occurrences such as temporary job loss, illness, or pregnancy can lead to drops in income—opportunities to fall down the ladder—that working people in other advanced countries don't face. This is a far greater threat for families without some accumulated wealth to cushion the blow.

Education also plays a crucial role in reproducing African Americans' lower economic status in their kids. Schools are primarily funded through state and local taxes, which leads to dramatic differences in the education that is available to kids in wealthier and poorer communities. That goes a long way in explaining a phenomenon long observed in American education: black children excel until the middle grades, then their achievement levels begin to decline. At younger ages, large numbers of African American kids are enrolled in early childhood programs such as Head Start. By the middle grades, the picture changes.

In 2010, almost fifty years after the passage of the Civil Rights Act, the *Washington Post* reported that a federal judge had ruled that one Mississippi county had created "racially identifiable" schools in violation of a 1970 federal desegregation order. The problem is much bigger than a single Southern school district. "Although minority students have the legal right to attend any school," the *Post*'s Stephanie McCrummen reported, "federal officials are questioning whether in practice many receive less access than white students to the best teachers, college prep courses and other resources. Department of Education lawyers also are investigating whether minority students are being separated into special education classes without justification, whether they are being disciplined more harshly and whether districts are failing to provide adequate English language programs for students who are not fluent, among other issues."[22]

According to the Urban Institute's annual report, *The State of Black America*, African American children got an average of 82 cents on the white education dollar in 2008. You get what you pay for, and twice as many black children as whites are taught by instructors with fewer than three years of experience.[23]

The wealth gap in the United States is not simply a product of bigotry today; it is also the accumulated legacy of generations of institutional racism at work. Black kids are starting from behind and simply aren't afforded much chance to catch up.

The African American Economy, Before and After the Crash

Although the Great Recession obviously hit *everyone* hard, it didn't cause everyone equal pain. In 2007, the gap between white and black unemployment rates fell to the lowest point in years: just 3 percentage points. Yet as the economy fell into recession, it quickly grew again, and by April 2009 it had doubled, reaching a thirteen-year high.[1] As the economy began to turn around in 2009, African Americans didn't see much recovery; median household income rose 7 percent for white families and only 1 percent for blacks.[2] In early 2010, when the national unemployment rate dipped below 10 percent, black joblessness spiked at more than 16 percent.[3]

Yet there's more to this story. It's a little-known fact that even before the crash, blacks had already taken a *huge* step back economically during the 2000s. Over the course of the previous decade, millions of African Americans had joined the middle class. With a booming economy and Clintonian policies like the Earned Income Tax Credit, which pulled millions of families out of desperation, the poverty rate among African Americans hit its lowest point in U.S. history in 2000. Black poverty had fallen by more than 10 percentage points since 1993, and poverty among African American children had dropped by an unprecedented 10.7 percentage points in five years (from 41.9 percent in 1995 to 31.2 percent in 2000).[4] By 2007, however, before the collapse of Lehman Brothers and the subsequent global economic meltdown, African Americans had already lost *all of* those gains. That year, sociologist Algernon Austin wrote, "On all major economic indicators—income, wages, employment, and poverty—African Americans were worse off in 2007 than they were in 2000."[5]

Even that doesn't tell the whole story, though, because, as we saw in chapter 2, it's not only a matter of where you are, but to what degree you can move up the ladder. We know that America's vaunted upward mobility is largely a myth. Among all Americans, the likelihood of moving down is equal to the chance of getting ahead. Yet some fifty years after the civil rights era, middle-class African American families face a reality that's even more grim: their kids *are far more likely* to experience downward than upward mobility in today's economy.

A 2007 study by the Brookings Institution's Julia Isaacs painted a dark picture for black families and especially for the large group of African Americans who moved up and into the middle class following the hard-fought gains of the 1950s and the 1960s. Isaacs looked at a unique set of data, one that allowed her to compare the incomes of people in their thirties in 2004 with their parents' generation in the mid-1970s (this gave her a chance to compare people at the same general stage in their careers—apples and apples).[6]

While white men's incomes have been stagnant for the last three decades, the current generation of thirty-something black men actually earn, on average, *12 percent less than* their fathers did in the mid-1970s (when adjusted for inflation). That downward mobility has an enormous impact on the black middle class. While children of middle-class whites tend to do better than their parents did at the same age, a majority of middle-class African American children do worse than theirs, both in income and in terms of their position on the nation's economic ladder. According to Isaacs, "Only 31 percent of black children born to parents in the middle of the income distribution have family income greater than their parents, compared to 68 percent of white children from the same income bracket."

The key findings from the study were truly eye-opening:

- Almost half (45 percent) of black children whose parents were solidly middle class end up falling to the bottom of the income distribution, compared to only 16 percent of white children.
- Achieving middle-income status does not protect black children from future economic adversity in the same way that it protects white children.

- Black children from poor families have poorer prospects than do poor white children. More than half (54 percent) of black children born to parents in the bottom fifth of the pile stay there, compared to 31 percent of white children.

Given these dynamics, it should come as no surprise that the black-white income gap has risen, not fallen, in the decades since legal, institutional racism ended in the United States. In 1974, black families earned, on average, almost two-thirds of what whites did; by 2004, that number had fallen to 58 percent.[7]

Although these findings are shocking, the fact that African Americans have long lagged behind their neighbors of European descent is apparent to most people. Yet one of the hottest and longest running debates in this country is over what, exactly, might be responsible for African Americans' persistently poorer outcomes. Is it their laziness, lack of innate intelligence, and "culture of dependency," as many conservatives believe, or is something else going on?

14

UNIONS STILL MATTER

Don't believe organized labor is corrupt, lazy, and an artifact of a different age

We need to preserve free-market enterprise. Businesses around the country need the flexibility to grow and change with their markets, and employees need the freedom to negotiate their hours and salaries with their employers. This bill would harm workers and businesses by changing the unionization process so drastically that the only ones who would benefit are the labor bosses.

—*Representative Peter Roskam (R-IL), announcing his opposition to the Employee Free Choice Act*

Conservatives argue that the number of Americans working in unions has plummeted because organized labor is anachronistic—ghosts of industries past, relics of the Golden Age of manufacturing. Yet the truth is that labor's decline is the result of a sophisticated, decades-long assault on workers' right—and practical ability—to organize and on the legitimacy of labor unions more generally.

The motive is obvious: there's nothing more terrifying to corporate America than the prospect of dealing with its workforce on an even playing field, and nothing more alarming for its allies on the Right than people who vote their own economic interests. Labor unions help accomplish both of those things.

The benefits that workers get from organizing go way beyond the union wage premium (but who among us couldn't stand 11 percent more in our paychecks?). Union workers are also more likely to get retirement benefits, decent health care, and family leave and are less likely to work in unsafe conditions or otherwise get screwed over by their employers than are their nonunion counterparts. According to economists Lawrence Mishel and Matthew Walters, union members make almost *30 percent more* when the wages and the value of benefits are combined.[1]

Those are the tangibles, but there are intangibles as well. When enough workers are organized and can speak with one voice, they represent a powerful influence on the political establishment—one that's largely missing in the United States today. Inequality, stagnant wages, out-of-reach health-care costs, bad trade policy that hurts the middle class, dwindling opportunities to get an affordable high-quality education, and a host of other issues that have a real impact on most American families—they're all problems that a healthy labor movement can force politicians to address.

Union members are more likely to vote their economic interests than be blinded by culture war issues. In 2004, although George Bush won the votes of white working-class men by 25 percent over John Kerry, blue-collar white guys who belonged to unions broke for Kerry by 21 percent.[2] Charles Noble, a political scientist at UC Long Beach, commented, "Clearly, union members had a different perspective on the election, most likely provided by the unions themselves, which poured millions into educating and mobilizing union households."[3] In 2008, John McCain beat Obama by 25 percent among all gun owners, but Obama won over union members who pack heat by a 12 percent margin. Guy Molyneux, a partner with Hart Research, which conducted exit polls for the AFL-CIO, told the *New York Times* that white male union members "supported Mr. Obama over Mr. McCain by a margin of 18 percentage points, while for all white men, exit polls found they backed Mr. McCain by a 16 percent margin."[4]

There's a substantial body of research that shows a crystal-clear relationship between falling unionization rates, stagnating wages, and increases in inequality and poverty. That's true in all countries; data from the Organisation for Economic Co-operation and Development (OECD) show that "countries with high levels of union density or collective bargaining coverage are much more equal than countries with low union density, but perform no worse in terms of creating jobs."

Gaps between higher-paid and lower-paid workers are lowest where union density is high, and bargaining is either centralized or closely coordinated. For example, the top 10% of male full-time workers earn at least 4.6 times as much as the bottom 10% in the U.S., compared to 3.7 times as much in Canada, 2.9 times as much in Germany, and just 2.3 times as much in Sweden. High union density also narrows pay gaps between women and men, and between younger and older workers. By narrowing pay gaps, unions counter poverty and make family incomes much more equal than would otherwise be the case.[5]

Although that relationship holds true everywhere, no country has seen such a precipitous decline in its labor movement as the United States has during the last three decades. We now have the lowest

Union Coverage Rate in the United States, 1977–2005*

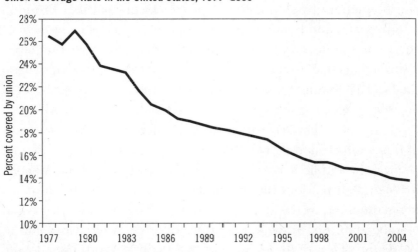

*Covered by a collective bargaining agreement.
Source: Hirch and Macpherson (1997) and BLS.

rate of workers covered by collective bargaining anywhere in the industrial world, and, as we saw in the introduction to this book, the decline has correlated with painful economic stagnation for all but the top of the economic food chain. Consider the graph on page 231, which comes from the Economic Policy Institute. (Those rates include government employees; the private-sector numbers are lower.)

As economists Lawrence Mishel and Ross Eisenbrey wrote, "Wage inequality began to grow at the same time" that the decline in unionization gathered steam in the late 1970s.[6]

Who Needs Unions?: The Artful Spin of the Right's Propaganda Machine

In 2005, Harvard economist Richard Freeman found that more U.S. workers wanted to join a union than ever before—53 percent. It's their right, guaranteed by the U.S. Constitution, but even as the number of wage earners who want to bargain collectively with their bosses has increased, the labor movement's steep decline has continued apace.

Corporate America has been fighting labor through lobbying and regulation, by shipping a disproportionate number of union jobs overseas and by dumping union positions in a steady wave of corporate mergers. Perhaps most important, they've also achieved it through a concerted campaign to convince America that despite the fact that joining a union results in an almost 30 percent boost in one's wages and benefits, unions are in fact harmful to workers.

Companies that rely on cheap labor finance a broad network of innocuous-sounding front-groups such as the Capital Research Center, the Public Service Research Foundation, and the Alliance for Worker Freedom that advocate for workers' "right" to labor unencumbered by the extra pay and benefits that come with union membership. According to the pro-labor group American Rights at Work, the oldest of these, the National Right to Work Foundation, "employs over 200 staff to lobby, fundraise, distribute propaganda, and interfere with workers' union organizing efforts, and the National Right to Work Legal Defense Foundation employs nearly 50 staff for its litigation efforts."[7]

Arguably the most active of these propaganda shops, the Center for Union Facts, is a newcomer established in 2006 by lobbyist Richard Berman. Berman, who is reportedly proud of his nickname, "Doctor Death," is an infamous right-wing corporate frontman with a long career muddying the waters of our public discourse for the sake of his well-heeled clientele. According to the watchdog group Citizens for Responsibility and Ethics in Washington, "Using his lobbying and consulting firm, Berman and Company, as a revenue vehicle for his activities, Berman runs at least 23 industry-funded projects," such as the Employment Policy Institute, the Center for Consumer Freedom, the American Beverage Institute, and the Employee Freedom Action Committee. Through these, Berman, a veteran of the tobacco wars—he was funded by Philip Morris in the 1990s—fought against drunken driving laws on behalf of the alcoholic beverage industry, against consumer and health protections on behalf of the food industry, and even against efforts to raise awareness of the dangers of mercury for the fishing industry.

The Center for Union Facts is positively Orwellian in its spin. In one instance, Berman cited a Department of Labor report to claim that unions had racked up "$400 million in labor racketeering fines and civil restitution in the last five years." Nate Newman, an expert on labor relations, dug into the report, only to find that "almost all of the big money associated with the $400 million figure in labor racketeering was committed by private industry *against unions*, not by union officials."[8]

Newman added, "But that's how you lie with statistics."

Throw around a word like "labor racketeering" while only talking about union officials and leave the impression that the crime only involves acts by unions, not acts where unions and their members are the victims.

That is the central message coming from the Corporate Right: unions are corrupt, perhaps even mobbed up, and their work helps only union bosses and their political patrons, while screwing over workers. The overarching strategic goal is to shift working America's focus from what unions *do*—negotiate with management on behalf of their dues-paying workers and advocate for stronger labor protections in Washington—to the most dubious negative stereotypes about who labor activists are.

The reality, of course, is that the labor movement is not untarnished; it has its share of real-world problems. But while there was a time when corrupt organizers could easily get fat off workers' dues, today's union activities are *very* closely regulated by the government. The thirty-year trend of loosening oversight of corporate America has been turned on end in the labor movement.

In 2005, the *Financial Times* reported that because union-sponsored campaigns against firms such as Wal-Mart were "a thorn in the side of big business," George W. Bush's Department of Labor was "turning the tables on these critics, using little-known powers to act as a regulator for the union movement." Labor unions began to face "greater scrutiny of spending and hiring practices," and audits of individual unions "increase[d] sharply." According to the *Hartford Courant*, "virtually every dollar spent" by labor unions "and the time allocated by much of the staff, must find its way onto an expanded U.S. Department of Labor form—and it must be placed in a category according to what type of activity it represents."[9] Union organizers told the *Times* that the efforts were "motivated by pressure from Corporate America to weaken the lobbying influence and financial power of organized labor."[10]

The justification for these onerous rules was corruption. The Right had seized on the story of a union-owned insurer, Ullico, that got caught in a stock-trading scandal that netted a few of its executives $6 million. Conservatives compared the scandal to the $60 billion that Enron stole through market manipulation, but as Nathan Newman told journalist David Sirota, "Out of the hundreds of billions of dollars invested by various union officials in different funds all over the country," the best that conservatives could come up with were a couple of small but much-hyped scandals. "If anything," he added, "the fact that [a few officials at] Ullico couldn't even get away with stealing these relatively petty amounts speaks pretty well to union corporate accountability controls, controls obviously far better than the corporations plunged into bankruptcy because of money gone and unrecoverable."[11]

The Union Busters: Corporate America's Weapon against Organized Labor

Rick Berman and his ilk set the public stage for the Corporate Right's war on organized labor, but comprehensive, company-by-company union busting is what ultimately keeps many U.S. workplaces union-free, despite the fact that a majority of working people want to join up.

Having lobbied hard for sweeping changes in U.S. labor law—and the enforcement of those laws—corporate America has raised union busting to a high art form in the United States. Companies no longer need thugs and gun-toting Pinkertons to keep workers from exercising their legal right to organize; now they have high-priced, Armani-wearing lawyers to do the job.

According to American Rights at Work, the majority of companies that face a union vote hire a "union avoidance firm" to fight for a "no" vote, but most workers don't know it, because modern union busters prefer to operate under the radar.

> Unionbusters often provide material and instructions behind the scenes while the employer's management and middle-management/supervisory staff carry out the actual communications with workers. In this way, the unionbuster does not deal directly with employees and, as a result, may avoid having to disclose financial reports about such activity to the U.S. Department of Labor. The unionbuster's name or firm is not used or referenced in the anti-union materials distributed to

employees, further masking the unionbuster's involvement in orchestrating the anti-organizing campaign. More importantly, the anti-union company is rarely called on to divulge that it hired a unionbuster or reveal the specifics of such expenditures. Therefore, without a paper trail, unionbusters are hard to detect, underreported, and not in the public eye.[12]

According to journalist Art Levine, union busting has "become a multibillion-dollar industry encompassing more than 2,500 lawyers and consultants offering their services." Levine went undercover to attend a seminar conducted by one of the leaders in the field, the Jackson Lewis law firm, where two attorneys warned prospective clients that organized labor would "attempt to destroy you, no matter how good you are." Levine recalled some of the questions the attendees posed to the union busters:

> What if we simply wanted to fire union organizers? That was possible to do, said [Michael] Stief, as long as you were careful to do so for other reasons. "Union sympathizers aren't entitled to any more protection than other workers," he explained. But the firing could not be linked to their union activity.
>   What if we felt like saying a lot of anti-union stuff to our workers? [Michael] Lotito introduced a segment called "You Can Say It." Could we tell our workers, for instance, that a union had held a strike at a nearby facility only to find that all the strikers had been replaced—and that the same could happen to the employees here? Sure, said Lotito. "It's lawful." He added, "What happens if this statement is a lie? They didn't have another strike, there were no replacements? It's still lawful: The labor board doesn't really care if people are lying."[13]

The tactics they employ are as pervasive as they are insidious. A study by Cornell University labor scholar Kate Bronfenbrenner found that nine in ten employers facing a union campaign force employees to attend closed-door meetings to hear antiunion propaganda; 80 percent train supervisors on how to attack unions and require them to deliver antiunion messages to workers they oversee; half of employers threaten to shut down the plant if workers organize; and three out of four hire outside consultants to run antiunion campaigns, "often based on mass psychology and distorting the law."[14]

Increasingly, cunning forms of intimidation are enough to produce a "no" vote. If organizers manage to win a vote among workers, management can dispute the results, a process that can drag on for years. While it's pending, pro-union workers lose their jobs; a study published by economists John Schmitt and Ben Zipperer found that "almost one in five union organizers or activists can expect to be fired as a result of their activities in a union election campaign."[15]

That's illegal, but since the Reagan administration, U.S. labor protections have been thoroughly gutted, and companies that cross the line pay only modest penalties that can be written off as part of the cost of remaining union-free.

Organized Workers Balance Corporate Power and Strengthen Our Labor Markets

About one in four Americans has at least a four-year college degree, and many of those degrees are even worth something in the labor market (sorry, art history majors). Other people—Bill Gates, a gifted artist, or a writer who can turn a decent phrase—have specialized skills that allow them to command an income as high as the market for their scarce talents will bear. There are also people with more common skills who have the cash (and/or connections) and the fortitude to establish their own businesses—think George W. Bush or a mechanic who owns his or her own shop.

That leaves a lot of people (about 80 percent of working Americans) who are hourly workers, "wage slaves" in the traditional sense. There's no doubt that their salaries are heavily *influenced* by the laws of supply and demand. We saw this clearly in the latter half of the 1990s, when, under Bill Clinton, the Fed allowed the economy to grow at a fast clip, unemployment dropped below 4 percent, and, for a brief period, a three-decade spiral in inequality was reversed as incomes grew for people in every bracket.

A common fallacy, however, is that wages are *determined* by market forces. They're not, for a variety of reasons. Let's just focus on two key ones: what economists call "information asymmetries," and coercion. Both are anathema to a functional free market, and both exist today, in abundance, in the U.S. workplace.

Remember the basic economic theory from chapter 3: in order for a free-market transaction to work, both the buyer and the seller need to have a good grasp of what the product being sold—in this case, people's sweat—is worth elsewhere, who else is buying and selling, and so on. In other words, they have to have more or less equal access to information. There can be no misrepresentation by either the buyer or the seller in a free-market transaction. And both parties have to enter into the transaction freely; neither side can exercise power or undue influence over the other, whether implicitly or explicitly, through threats or other means.

Now let's look at how that theoretical construct plays out in the real world of the U.S. workplace. When an individual worker nego- tiates a price for his or her time, effort, and dedication with any business bigger than a mom-and-pop operation, there's quite a bit of explicit coercion (much of it in violation of our labor laws). But there's *always* an element of *inherent* coercion when an individual negotiates with a company alone as a result of the power differ- ential: a firm that's shorthanded by one person will continue to function, while a person without a job is up a creek with no paddle, unable to put a roof over his or her head or food on the table.

The "information asymmetries" in such a negotiation are immense—they're actually more like process asymmetries. Companies spend millions of dollars on human resource experts, consultants, labor lawyers, and so forth, and they know both the conditions of the market and the ins and outs of the labor laws in intimate detail. Although working people with rare skills are often members of professional associations, read trade journals, and have a pretty good sense of what the market will bear, many low- and semiskilled workers don't know their rights under the labor laws, don't know how to assert them, and (rightfully) fear reprisals when they do. They often have little knowledge of the financial health—or illness, as the case may be—of the company to which they're applying for a job, how profitable it is, how much similar workers in other regions or firms earn, and so on.

That's where collective bargaining comes in: when workers bargain as a group, they do so on a level playing field with employers, and the resulting wages (and benefits) are as high as the market can bear, but no higher.

Unions, like corporations, have a great deal of information about the market. They know how a firm is doing, how profitable it is, and where it is relative to the larger industry in which it operates. They know what deals workers at other plants have negotiated. They have attorneys who are just as familiar with labor laws as their counterparts in management. And although an individual has very little leverage in negotiations—again, most companies can do with one less worker—collectively, an entire workforce has the ability to shut down or at least slow down a company's operations if management chooses not to negotiate in good faith (as is often the case).

When workers without a lot of education or special skills don't bargain collectively, the results are especially bad. The wages of the "working poor" represent a clear "market failure." In economic theory, it's a given that a producer can't sell his or her wares below the cost of production. In terms of human sweat, the equivalent is the cost of covering a person's basic necessities: nutritious food, safe housing, and decent medical care. These are out of reach for millions of Americans who work full time and live below the poverty level.

Will the Right Kill Labor's Signature Legislation?

Even the most devout of free-marketeers—economists such as Alan Greenspan and the late Milton Friedman—agree that it's appropriate and necessary for government to intervene in the case of market failures (they believe it's the only time that such "meddling" is appropriate). But the Corporate Right, which claims to have an almost religious reverence for the power of "free" and functional markets, has gotten fat off the failure in the U.S. labor market, and it's dead-set on continuing to game the system for the enrichment of its executives and shareholders.

Since 2006, organized labor has been pushing the Employee Free Choice Act (EFCA), a bill that would go some way toward restoring U.S. workers' ability to organize effectively. The measure is simple: it beefs up penalties for employers who violate workers' rights under the law, creates a mediation and arbitration system for disputes, and allows workers to form a union if a majority simply sign a card saying that they want representation, a process known as "card check" union elections.

The bill passed the House in 2007 but died in the Senate under a veto threat by George W. Bush. After the Democrats were swept into power in 2008, it was reintroduced in both chambers of Congress, but as of the summer of 2010, it faces stiff resistance from the "Money Party," and appears unlikely to pass without being significantly watered down. Key conservative Democrats in the Senate—Ben Nelson (Nebraska), Blanche Lincoln (Arkansas), and Thomas Carper (Delaware)—have signaled that they would join a unified Republican caucus in opposing the measure if the "card check" provision remains in the bill. Their objections are the result of a multimillion-dollar disinformation campaign with which the Corporate Right has done a yeoman's job of demonizing the proposal. America's union busters seized on a compelling talking point that was tailored to suit our political culture, namely that the "card check" provision of the EFCA does away with "secret ballots," something that Americans have come to expect when casting a vote.

In the context of union elections, however, it's a *blatant* lie. There has never been a "right" to a secret ballot for labor organizing; in fact, most union organizing in recent decades has been done via card check. The issue is this: it's currently up to employers to decide whether their workers organize via majority sign-up—"card check"—or through a National Labor Relations Board election. Under EFCA, workers themselves, not their bosses, would get to make that call.

To help make their case, the business community commissioned a Zogby poll that came dangerously close to the dishonest "push-polls" of political campaign infamy. The questions were remarkably biased, and the results were what the pollsters and their clients were looking for:

> Please tell me whether you agree or disagree with the following statement: "Every worker should continue to have the right to a federally supervised secret ballot election when deciding whether to organize a union."[16]

Nine out of ten respondents agreed, including 87 percent of Democrats. That's to be expected; the strategy is to depict management's assault on the ability to organize as protecting "workers' rights." Seven out of ten respondents said that they'd be less likely to vote for a member of Congress "who voted in favor of taking away a worker's right to have a federally supervised secret ballot election to decide whether to organize a union." Again, this "right" doesn't exist in the American workplace.

The Right's noise machine, armed with its push-poll, has been disciplined and on message since 2006: Big Labor wants to do away with secret ballots, and it's pulling the Democrats' strings to make it happen.

But as Stalin said, "It's not the people who vote that count. It's the people who count the votes." More important, it's how the votes are counted and whether voters are being coerced. The secret-ballot election process is almost impossible in today's anti-union environment, with a National Labor Relations Board— the body that's supposed to protect workers' rights—stacked with antiunion appointees. (In April 2010, Barack Obama used recess appointments to install two new members who are more sympathetic to workers, overcoming Republican blocks in the Senate.)

As journalist Jordan Barab noted, the elections process is so heavily stacked in management's favor that "card-check campaigns—instead of secret ballot elections—have become labor's main tool for organizing the unorganized." According to AFL-CIO statistics cited by Barab, card checks were used to "sign up roughly 70 percent of the private-sector workers who joined unions (in 2006), compared with less than 5 percent two decades ago."[17]

With or without the card check, the Employee Free Choice Act wouldn't be a magic bullet for the labor movement. It's a modest proposal, anything but the pernicious play to crush workers' rights under the heel of organized labor that its well-financed opponents make it out to be.

Given that seven out of ten Democratic voters told Zogby that they favor "a new law that would make it easier for labor unions to organize workers," the fact that almost nine out of ten believe that the central provision of labor's key legislation is "antiworker" stands as a sobering testament to corporate America's ability to influence our national discourse.

Whither the $20-an-Hour Wage?

In 2008, the *New York Times* reported that the number of Americans making $20 per hour or more, or its equivalent when adjusted for inflation, has declined dramatically since the 1970s.

> The $20 hourly wage, introduced on a huge scale in the middle of the last century, allowed masses of Americans with no more than a high school education to rise to the middle class. It was a marker, of sorts, but it is becoming extinct.
>
> Americans greeted the loss with anger and protest when it first began to happen in big numbers in the late 1970s, particularly in the steel industry in western Pennsylvania. But as layoffs persisted, in Pennsylvania and across the country, through the '80s and '90s and right up to today, the protests subsided and acquiescence set in.[1]

The equivalent of a $20-plus wage in today's dollars reached around a quarter of the nonmanagerial workforce in 1979. Since then, however, "the percentage of people earning at least $20 an hour has eroded in every sector of the economy," falling last year to 18 percent of all hourly workers. The *Times* called it "a gradual unwinding of the post–World War II gains."[2]

The trend corresponds with the decline of union membership among private-sector workers. During World War II, more than a third of U.S. wage earners belonged to labor unions. By 1973, that number had gradually declined to 24 percent. The percentage hovered in the 20s until 1980, when Ronald Reagan came to office and brought about an unprecedented shift in U.S. labor relations. As Viveca Novak, writing in *Common Cause* magazine a decade later, would put it:

> When President Ronald Reagan fired the federal air traffic controllers en masse in 1981, he rewrote the rules governing

acceptable employer conduct. Previously companies had considered public opinion in deciding how far to push the weak labor law; now that was less of an obstacle. Reagan's appointments to the NLRB [National Labor Relations Board] sent another signal, challenging a tradition of long-serving, usually non-ideological members. The board took on a distinctly anti-union aura and let cases sit for years without decisions.[3]

What followed was a rapid decline in the share of unionized workers in the United States. By the end of Reagan's first term in office, the unionization rate in the private sector had fallen to 15 percent; by the end of his second, it had fallen to about 12 percent; and by 2009, only 7.2 percent of private-sector workers belonged to a union.[4]

Membership in a labor union carries with it what economists refer to as a "union wage premium": the persistent gap between what union and nonunion workers earn at the same job. Organized workers make 11.3 percent more than those who aren't in a union[5] (and it was much higher when labor had more clout; economist George Johnson estimated that union workers in the 1930s earned 38 *percent* more, on average, than their nonunion counterparts).[6]

The $20 wage, or its equivalent at the time, "blossomed first in the auto industry in 1948 and served, in effect, as a banner in the ideological struggle with the Soviet Union," according to the *Times*. "As the news media frequently noted, salt-of-the-earth American workers were earning enough to pay for comforts that their counterparts behind the Iron Curtain could not afford."[7]

Skip forward to today, and it's pretty clear that the decline is continuing. In 2007, the Big Three automakers bought out eighty-thousand employees earning more than $20 an hour, "replacing many with new hires tied to a 'second tier' wage scale that never quite reaches $20." A year later, they bought out another twenty-five thousand.[8]

As we saw in chapter 14, only organized workers negotiating from strength can bring a decent, livable wage back for the majority of Americans who lack a college degree.

<u>15</u>

THERE'S NOTHING FREE
ABOUT FREE TRADE

Don't believe that corporations want fewer
rules and everyone else is an isolationist Luddite

It goes back to my education in college; and that is, the notion of the United States of America playing a leading role in global economic growth so that we can increase the number of good American jobs. That means good jobs right here in the United States of America. I believe that trade is key to that. Trade, global trade, is going to play a big role in creating jobs, jobs, jobs.

—Representative Peter Dreier (R-CA), during a January 2009
speech on the House floor

D reier gave that speech during the most severe unemployment crisis the United States had faced since the 1930s. It's a stunningly counterintuitive assertion, because trade agreements facilitate the offshoring of jobs to countries with lower labor costs, which in turn beefs up companies' profits. That dynamic is evident in executive pay—a 2004 study by the Institute for Policy Studies found that "CEOs at companies that outsource the most U.S. jobs are rewarded with bigger paychecks." The authors found that "Average CEO compensation at the 50 firms outsourcing the most service jobs increased by 46 percent in 2003, compared to a 9 percent average increase for all CEOs at the 365 large companies surveyed by *BusinessWeek*."[1]

As Dean Baker put it, "The truth is, we carefully structured these trade agreements—we put great effort into it—to put our manufacturing workers into competition with manufacturing workers in developing nations."

> That meant going to these places and asking: What kind of problems does General Motors face if they want to set up a manufacturing plant in Mexico or Malaysia or China? What can we do to make it as easy as possible? That means that they know they can set up their factory and not have it national-ized, not have restrictions on repatriating profits, etc. Then they need to be able to import the goods back into the United States, and that means not only making sure there are no tar-iffs or quotas, but also that there's no safety or environmental restrictions that might keep the goods out.[2]

The offshoring trend can only get worse as long as we stay the present course on trade. Alan Blinder, a conservative economist at Princeton University, estimated that as many as 29 percent of U.S. jobs are offshorable.[3]

And it's not simply a matter of jobs sent overseas. In a 2007 study analyzing fifty years of research, economist Josh Bivens argued that the current (and largely bipartisan) trade regime adds some bucks to the paychecks of America's highest earners but keeps wages down for 70 percent of the U.S. workforce, even adjusting for the greater purchasing power they might enjoy because of cheap imports flooding the shelves of Wal-Mart. He found that corporate-driven "free-trade" agreements not only increase the gap between richer and poorer countries, but also add to inequality among citizens of wealthy states such as the United States. Bivens estimated the direct cost of "free trade" deals to families in the middle of the economic pile to be $2,135 per year. That's about 50 percent more than the same family pays in federal income taxes annually ($1,495).[4]

"Free Trade" Is a Corporate Power Grab

It's tempting to focus only on the economic impacts of trade deals such as NAFTA, but it's just as important to dig deeper into the antidemocratic nature of the "free trade" orthodoxy pushed by Big Business. All too often, progressives tie themselves up in knots discussing trade because they argue the issue on corporate America's terms, instead of going to the root of the matter: "free trade" isn't free, and it often has nothing to do with what most people would consider "trade."

If the central question we're asking is "Free trade or protectionism?" the debate is already lost. That's how the corporate globalizers have presented it and that's how the media—which clearly have a horse in the race—report it. And that's why the so-called free traders have been able to keep the upper hand.

Here's the truth about "free trade" agreements. When you talk about trade policy, you're really talking about the enormous influence of corporate power over democratic governance. Senator Sherrod Brown (D-OH), the gutsy leader of the fair-trade caucus, explained the close connection during the lead-up to the vote on the Central American Free Trade Agreement (CAFTA) in 2005. "Our political system is now up for the highest bidder," Brown told me at the time. "Energy bills are written by oil companies and environmental bills are written by the chemical companies."

> Similarly, this trade agreement—CAFTA—but other trade agreements, too, have been written by a select few for a select few—and that select few is typically the drug industry, the insurance and financial institutions, and the energy companies, and the largest multinational corporations. It's the same old song, whether it's international or it's domestic.[5]

In his book *The Myths of Free Trade*, Brown described thousands of corporate jets stacked up over D.C. as the vote neared, carrying industry execs eager to descend on the city to lobby for the agreement. Trade policy is clearly an insider's game.

In their book *Whose Trade Organization?* Lori Wallach and Patrick Woodall found that among the hundreds of "experts" who sat on the advisory boards that hammered out the thousands of pages of WTO and NAFTA rules, there were only a handful of representatives of labor.[6] The rest were multinational execs and various lawyers, lobbyists, and sundry industry experts. There was *almost* zero input from human rights groups, environmentalists, or the rest of society. It's not only that the treaties we've signed are flawed, but the process by which they're created makes it all but impossible that they would benefit working people or protect our commons. These are simply not corporate America's priorities (nor those of its counterparts in Japan or the EU).

What Is a Trade Barrier?

Most people still believe that discussions of "free trade" are about ships full of bananas or ball bearings or whatever, crisscrossing the high seas. Understanding why that's just a small part of the issue is key to grasping the difference between "free trade" and what these deals we've been signing for the last thirty years are really about: a corporate power grab.

Prior to World War II, trade wars were common, and they often led to shooting wars. In the mid-1940s, the General Agreement on Tariffs and Trade (GATT) was created to avoid those conflicts and foster world peace. Many of its authors were FDR liberals. They had high ideals.

Between 1944 and the mid-1990s, trade negotiations were conducted by dull, (mostly) white guys in business suits, and nobody really gave a damn. Poor countries griped about agricultural subsidies and the rich countries' protectionism, but they were free to try various development strategies, including those that didn't adhere to the dictates of "the market" (a big subject itself, but one for another day).

During the first decades of the GATT, which governed trade between 1947 and 1995, the United States and "old" Europe had economies based heavily on manufacturing. Today, however, almost all advanced economies share a very similar distribution: about 1 to 2 percent in agriculture, maybe 20 or so percent in manufacturing, and around 80 percent in services.

For approximately the first forty years of the GATT's existence, its members negotiated reductions in tariffs, quotas, and other traditional forms of market protectionism. They were the manufacturers, and those deals were for the most part negotiated on a level playing field between the world's advanced economies—what they call "North-North" negotiations in trade lingo.

People who brand opponents of today's trade deals "protectionists" might ask themselves why nobody resisted the GATT during those years of slashing tariffs and quotas and the like. The reason is that reducing tariffs is what most people think of when they hear about "opening markets" and freeing up international trade. The controversy began only as "free trade" was gradually redefined to include all manner of domestic policies.

Beginning in the 1970s, two things happened—or, I should say, two things aside from the oil shock of '73. In 1979, during the Tokyo round of the GATT, negotiators began to look at "nontariff barriers." These included onerous customs procedures, mountains of paperwork required to import goods, subsidies for domestic industry, and so on. That shift to "nontariff barriers" coincided with the emergence of the new conservative movement, with its think tanks and front-groups, and the elections of Reagan and Thatcher to head the Western world's leading political and economic powers.

Now, once they started to look at nontariff barriers, it was inevitable that somewhere along the line, someone in those think tanks would say, "We can call all of those environmental laws and food-safety regulations nontariff barriers, too!"

With that mind-set, in 1994, after years of negotiations, the GATT culminated in the creation of the WTO, which had enforcement powers unlike any other multilateral organization. Its rules hadn't been written by FDR liberals, but by the Reagan-Thatcher Big Business conservatives in the corporate jets circling Washington.

For too many of them, the new "free trade" framework provided a back door through which they could advance a broader agenda. They could push a set of treaties that pressured—and, in many instances, legally compelled—domestic legislatures to conform to the prevailing economic theories known as the "Washington Consensus" (whenever anyone calls something a "consensus," it probably isn't even close). And the definition of "nontariff barrier" continued to expand.

(In the meantime, since the early days of the GATT, dozens of countries, many of them newly liberated from the clutches of European colonialism, had been added—and most were poor and had inadequate infrastructure and very different economic distributions. Many relied on agriculture not only for food, but also as a significant source of employment. Early on, the developed countries promised to start cutting agricultural subsidies and giving those developing countries a level playing field for agriculture, but so far they just haven't gotten around to it yet.)

In addition, they began to look not only at the flow of goods across borders, but also at services. This brings us to a really key point: there's a massive pile of cash just sitting out there in the functions that governments commonly perform: from education to sanitation and everything in between. According to Tony Clarke of the Polaris Institute, a Canadian NGO, the total estimated value of the world's service sector, including public services, is between $15 trillion and $20 trillion. That's a honeypot.[7]

By the time we arrived at the "Singapore Round" in 1996, there was an aggressive push to (1) enact a broad set of "investor protections" that made a variety of laws—some protecting the public interest—subject to the WTO's dispute-resolution process and (2) allow countries (or even private companies) to exert pressure on other governments to privatize their public services.

Organized labor, community activists, environmentalists, food security specialists, farmers, and many other groups started to see these rules as a significant threat to their work. They gathered to greet the ministers a few years later in Seattle—the famous "teamsters and turtles" coalition—which led to the infamous "Battle in

Seattle" (actually a brutal police riot). Since that time, the fight has really been about how deep into the realm of domestic policy various trade agreements should reach.

Democracy vs. "Free Trade"

Pressuring countries to adhere to the economic policies of the "Washington Consensus," whether they're popular or not, is job number one for the big multinationals, because a majority of governments on the planet today are, to varying degrees, democratic. And democracy is a huge challenge to many of the big multinationals' interests. Workers' movements, environmentalists, pesky public interest groups, and, above all, voters exert various degrees of influence on those elected representatives.

Trade treaties constrain legislatures to remain true to the prevailing economic orthodoxy. Most folks don't know this, but when state lawmakers draw up new legislation, they often drop a line to the office of the U.S. Trade Representative to make sure their bills comply with our trade commitments.

Other countries acting on behalf of their biggest corporations can challenge laws that aren't "WTO legal." These aren't about widgets being shipped from here to there; the range of what falls under the catchall "free trade" is astounding. A few of the more notorious decisions include:

- A Massachusetts law preventing state and local governments from doing business with the brutal dictatorship in Burma was overturned by domestic courts after a WTO challenge.
- An EU policy that gave preferential tariffs to small banana exporters in Europe's former colonies was successfully challenged by the United States after lobbying by the Chiquita banana company.
- Venezuela, backed by Brazil, successfully challenged provisions of the United States' Clean Air Act that kept fuels with higher levels of pollutants out of the market.

The WTO has an enforceable arbitration process, but it isn't always necessary to lodge a formal grievance. Because the vast majority of challenges to various domestic laws have been upheld, merely the threat of bringing a case is usually enough to make governments rethink their legislation. This is common when it comes to health, environmental, and food safety laws. In the first ten years of WTO arbitration panels' operation, all but two such challenges brought before them prevailed.[8]

In NAFTA and in regional deals such as CAFTA and the proposed Free Trade Area of the Americas (FTAA), the business community managed to get what it had tried and failed to achieve in the WTO: the ability of multinationals to cut out the middle man and sue governments directly for the loss of profits resulting from a regulation or a law they consider too "burdensome." Under those rules, "signatory governments are required to provide extensive rights and privileges to foreign investors," who are then "empowered to privately enforce these new rights by demanding cash payment from governments" that don't give them what they want, according to a report by Public Citizen.[9]

The cases are decided behind closed doors in "private tribunals operating outside the nations' domestic court system":

> The track record of cases demonstrate[s] an array of attacks on public policies and normal governmental activity at all levels of government—federal, state and local. Even though these NAFTA cases implicate commonplace public policies, the investor-state system is a closed and unaccountable one. Citizens whose policies are being attacked have no avenue of meaningful participation and neither do the state and local officials they elected to represent them. [Domestic] court decisions can be challenged and jury decisions undermined, yet no judge or jury has standing to participate in the private NAFTA tribunals.[10]

These rules shift significant amounts of risk from investors to governments. At the same time, they sharply limit what governments can ask for in return.

The common response to this critique is pretty straightforward: most of the parties to international trade deals such as the WTO are democratic states. Their legislators are elected by the people, and when they enter into a treaty, they're doing it on behalf of those who put them in office. Hence, democracy is safe, even if democratic governments don't always have the freedom—the "policy space"—to advance their constituents' interests.

But we have to remember those private jets stacked up over Washington during the run-up to the vote on CAFTA. That trade deal faced stiff public resistance—one poll taken in the weeks before Congress voted found that three out of four Americans opposed trade agreements that resulted in job losses at home, even if they resulted in cheaper goods and services. And cheaper goods were a central selling point for the deal.[11]

As the vote neared, it looked as if George Bush might have become the first president to fail to get a trade agreement through Congress in forty years. But all of the lobbying might of various business groups came to bear on members of Congress. As the *Washington Post* reported, "A prominent business leader recently laid it on the line: Business groups are prepared to cut off campaign contributions to House members who oppose the pact. 'If you [lawmakers] are going to vote against it, it's going to cost you,' Thomas J. Donohue, president and CEO of the U.S. Chamber of Commerce, warned recently during a meeting on Capitol Hill."[12] Several years later, months before the 2008 presidential elections, Donohue would announce a $60 million war chest dedicated to punishing those whom the *Los Angeles Times* described as "candidates who target business interests with their rhetoric or policy proposals, including congressional and state-level candidates." "We plan to build a grass-roots business organization so strong that when it bites you in the butt, you bleed," Donohue said.[13]

On the eve of the vote, the Bush administration started to cut deals with members of its own party who were resisting the pact. The *Los Angeles Times* reported, "For more than an hour, lawmakers milled about the House floor and gazed at the electronic scoreboard displaying the vote tally, which showed CAFTA several votes short of the mark." Nancy Pelosi, then the House minority leader, told the *Times*, "Right there in front of us, for the world to see, they were twisting arms, making deals, changing votes." Finally, when the count reached 217 to 215, the vote was gaveled to a close, and the deal had scraped through by a hair.[14]

Yet if the pressure on lawmakers here in the United States was great, it paled in comparison with that brought to bear on leaders of smaller, poorer states such as Costa Rica. Lori Wallach, the director of Public Citizen, noted that "The U.S. ambassador to Costa Rica, Mark Langdale, was slammed with a rare formal denunciation before Costa Rica's Supreme Electoral Tribunal in August after he waged a lengthy campaign to influence the vote on CAFTA. As part of that [campaign], Langdale employed misleading threats and suggested there would be economic reprisals if CAFTA were rejected." The Bush administration repeatedly threatened to remove Costa Rica's trade preferences—which waived some duties on products it exports to the United States—if the Costa Rican people rejected CAFTA in a referendum.[15]

This kind of geopolitical arm-twisting is par for the course in venues like the WTO. In 2001, immediately after the attacks of 9/11, U.S. trade representative Robert Zoellick made the case that advancing the Anglo-U.S. model of corporate "free" trade was key to winning the "War on Terror." At the time, author Naomi Klein wrote, "Zoellick explained that 'by promoting the WTO's agenda, these 142 nations can counter the revulsive destructionism of terrorism.' Open markets, he said, are 'an antidote' to the terrorists' 'violent rejectionism.'"[16]

The United States has become infamous among trade observers for using that kind of rhetorical "linkage" to advance its agenda, but it's far from unique in that regard. These kinds of power plays are especially evident in negotiations between wealthy states and the developing world, so-called North-South negotiations.

As Aileen Kwa, who analyzed the backroom deals in which trade agreements are formed in great detail, wrote, "In comparison to the United States, the EU is usually more sophisticated in the rhetoric it adopts . . . it promotes its agenda at the WTO as being 'in the interests of developing countries.' This is ironic since developing countries' assessment[s] of their own interests are the complete opposite."[17]

The highly developed states use economic blackmail—threatening poorer countries' trade preferences and foreign aid accounts—and blatantly undemocratic methods to overcome the developing world's concerns about these deals and get them to sign on the bottom line.

In their seminal book *Behind the Scenes at the WTO*, Kwa and coauthor Fatoumata Jawara cast a bright light on the murky world of international trade negotiations. "Any country whose political system operated as the WTO . . . [does]—where . . . rules were routinely ignored, and people or interested groups routinely used bribery and blackmail to achieve their political ends—would not only be rightly condemned by the international community as undemocratic and corrupt, it would also face a real and constant threat of revolution," they wrote.

> Crucial meetings are held behind closed doors, excluding participants with critical interests at stake, with no formal record of the discussion. When delegates are, in principle, entitled to attend meetings, they are not informed when or where they are to be held. Meetings are held without translation into the languages of many participants, to discuss documents which are only available in English, and which have been issued only hours before, or even at the meeting itself. Those most familiar with issues (Ambassadors) are sometimes discouraged or prevented from speaking in discussions about them at Ministerial meetings. "Consultations" with Members on key decisions are held one-to-one, in private, with no written record, and the interpretation left to an individual who has a stake in the outcome. Protestations that inconvenient views have been ignored in this process fall on deaf ears. Chairs of

committees and facilitators are selected by a small clique, and often have an interest in the issues for which the committee is responsible. The established principle of decision-making by consensus is routinely overridden, and the views of decision-makers are "interpreted" rather than a formal vote being taken. . . . Rules are ignored when they are inconvenient, and a blind eye is turned to blackmail and inducements. The list is endless.

A free-market transaction, remember, has to be free of coercion. All parties have to have access to the same information. By these standards alone, "free trade" is anything but.

The Hypocrisy of Free Traders

Just because politicians *say* they believe in open markets and free trade between nations doesn't make it true. In reality, they believe in "free trade" until someone else gets a comparative advantage, and then their hypocrisy emerges and they become fierce protectionists.

Here's my favorite "free trade" story. It occurred in 2004, when the free-trading, market-worshipping Bush administration approved duties that ranged from 4 to 113 percent on shrimp from China and Vietnam. *Forbes* called it "a blatant display of protectionism."[18] Vietnam may have been a trade rival at the time, but beginning in the late 1980s, there had been a big bipartisan push—led by Republican John McCain and Democrat John Kerry—to introduce a free market system to our former enemies in Hanoi. The hope was that we could accomplish with aid and technical assistance what we failed to do with guns and napalm forty years earlier.

Two areas that USAID officials identified for development were shrimp and catfish farming in the lush, nutrient-rich Mekong Delta. With its inexpensive labor and good climate, Vietnam had excellent prospects for developing its seafood exports. USAID and international development banks started to pump seed money into fish-farming projects. Their optimism proved well founded. According to the *New York Times*, "Within a few years, an estimated half-million Vietnamese were living off a catfish trade nurtured by private entrepreneurs. Vietnam captured 20 percent of the frozen catfish-fillet market in the United States." By 2002, shrimp was Vietnam's largest seafood export, and, according to Agence France-Presse, the United States—at $467 million—was its biggest buyer.[19]

Rural poverty rates in Vietnam dropped from 70 percent to 30 percent during the 1990s, according to the *Times*. But prices also dropped, and catfish producers in Mississippi, Louisiana, Alabama, and Arkansas, and shrimpers from eight coastal states began to feel the pinch. So, in 2002, the Mississippi Delta Catfish Farmers—an industry lobby—reached out to Trent Lott (R-MS), then the Senate majority leader.[20]

Lott amended an appropriations bill with a little rider that declared that out of two thousand types of catfish, only the American family—Ictaluridae—could be labeled "catfish," according to the *New York Times*. As a result, the Vietnamese could sell their fish in the States only under the Vietnamese words "basa" and "tra." Needless to say, sales dropped dramatically. A "fried basa po-boy" just doesn't have the same down-home feel. But that wasn't enough; the same group then initiated an "antidumping" measure against Vietnam. With the help of Lott and Arkansas Democrat Marion Berry—who, with typical congressional tact, reminded worried consumers that we dumped quite a bit of Agent Orange in the Mekong Delta—the Commerce Department imposed tariffs of 64 percent on Vietnamese catfish.[21]

A foreign industry is said to be "dumping" when it sells its goods at prices below the cost of production to drive out local competition. At a fair trade conference, a member of a Vietnamese delegation told me that the rural catfish farmers are simply too poor to "dump" their products on the U.S. market, even if they wanted to. "There aren't big agribusinesses in the Mekong Delta," she said. "If these people sell below cost, their families won't eat."[22]

The Southern Shrimp Alliance, another industry political action committee, was impressed by Lott's moves. It hired a couple of mega-law firms and lobbyists to follow the catfish model. According to *Forbes*, the Southern Shrimp Alliance was going up against twenty firms retained by Brazil, Ecuador, India, Thailand, China, Vietnam, and the American Seafood Distributors Association (the latter being quite happy with cheaper imports). The shrimpers, however, hired heavy legal and lobbying talent. They were highly effective, but the dumping charge was as bogus for shrimp as it had been for catfish. U.S. shrimpers catch their fare in the open ocean, while most Asian shrimp are raised with cheap labor in efficient fishponds.

As a result of all of this chicanery, shrimp exports to the United States declined by 34 percent in the first half of 2004, according to the *Voice of Vietnam*. Rural poverty rates, too, began to rebound.[23] And for his maneuvering, Lott went on to win the 2003 "Spirit of Enterprise" award from the U.S. Chamber of Commerce for his dedication to free-market ideals. Keep that in mind the next time you hear a member of Congress blathering on about the importance of "free trade."

Now, I'm happy to call Trent Lott, George Bush, and Co. a bunch of hypocrites, but I won't judge them for trying to save their jobs, just as I won't condemn a vulnerable steelworker who does the same. Free trade sounds great to a lot of people until their livelihood is at stake. That's just as true for Trent Lott when he protects his corporate patrons as it is for those struggling to eke out a living in fish ponds and rice paddies in the developing world. The only difference is rhetorical.

In the introduction to this book, I argued that conservatives claim that they're willing to take chances in the free market, when in reality they're rigging the rules to their advantage. The notion of "free markets" then allows them to sit back and argue that these are unbendable and organic economic laws that aren't subject to debate. The same principle applies to the global marketplace; we conclude where we began.

A CLOSER
LOOK

Corporate America Says
You Can't Have a Green Economy

Transforming the U.S. economy into a twenty-first-century engine of "green-collar" job creation is a signature progressive idea. Yet few of its advocates mention that the bulk of what they envision would come into conflict with our commitments under the international "free trade" regime.

As we saw in chapter 15, that's what "free trade" deals are about: limiting by treaty the policy space in which lawmakers can operate. Nowhere is the conflict between domestic policy and those treaty obligations so stark as with proposals to create lots of domestic green-collar jobs.

During the 2008 presidential campaign, candidate Barack Obama offered an ambitious plan called "New Energy for America." He promised that it would "create five million new green jobs, good jobs that cannot be outsourced."[1] But most green jobs can be. Although installing new solar panels would have to be done by local workers, they could be built anywhere. When it comes to the government, "Buy American" is itself WTO illegal. According to an analysis by the watchdog group Public Citizen, the World Trade Organization's Agreement on Subsidies and Countervailing Measures deems any government contribution to the private sector that would give a preference to "domestic over imported goods," either by law "or in fact," to be a no-no. Article 5 of that agreement allows a WTO challenge to "any subsidy (tax credit, funding for R&D, and other" provisions) that "prejudices" against the goods or the services provided by another country. There was an exception for "environmental upgrades" when the deal was first struck, but it expired in 2000.[2]

Candidate Obama promised to "help nurture America's success in clean technology manufacturing by establishing a federal investment program to help manufacturing centers modernize" by using tax dollars for the "critical up-front capital" needed to modernize "manufacturing facilities to produce new advanced clean technologies." It probably wouldn't stand a chance if challenged.[3]

Even installing those solar panels is tricky. Under the Agreement on Government Procurement, public funds can only be used to purchase goods and services on the open market (aside from weapons and other defense spending and a few other exceptions). Although U.S. workers might do the work, any foreign country can win the contract—there's no way to assure that the profits from that work would remain in the U.S. economy. And while Big Oil made sure that energy production wasn't included in the list of services the United States threw open to foreign competition under the General Agreement on Trade in Services, energy *transmission* was included, limiting the government's ability to set high environmental standards in both transmission and "related products and services."[4]

Obama promised to "increase fuel economy standards 4 percent per year while protecting the financial future of domestic automakers." This is a nice thought, but it would most likely be subject to challenge: in 1994, U.S. gas efficiency standards were successfully contested by the EU (under the auspices of the WTO's predecessor, the General Agreement on Tariffs and Trade [GATT]). According to Public Citizen,

> The GATT panel found that the U.S. policy, which was facially neutral—meaning there was one rule for both imports and exports—had the effect of putting a larger burden on some foreign automakers. The (panel) ruled that the U.S. method of calculating fleetwide efficiency standards advantaged U.S. automakers in practice.[5]

To address pollution, Obama promised to implement an "economy-wide" cap-and-trade program that would use "market mechanisms" to decrease greenhouse gas emissions. He proposed auctioning off emissions permits to polluters and using the money to help pay for investments in renewable energy (which, again, he can't make without inviting a challenge under the WTO's rules).

Yet the obvious problem—one of many potential problems—is the concept, central to the ideology of "free trade," of "most favored nation" status. In a nutshell, this simply means that a member of the WTO, such as the United States, has to treat all other members the same way. Which means that goods imported from countries with weaker emissions standards have to be treated exactly the same as domestic products. And that, in turn, means that firms, domestic or foreign, can simply move their dirty industries abroad, to countries without tight greenhouse gas standards, and import the products back to the United States. Obviously, that would keep our consumer culture's massive carbon footprint intact. Any firm that didn't do so would find itself at a competitive disadvantage in the marketplace.

Even a policy as simple and seemingly domestic as banning the sale of incandescent bulbs and encouraging the use of more efficient alternatives would be subject to challenge under the terms of the Agreement on Technical Barriers to Trade. This limits the government's ability to impose energy-efficiency requirements "with a view to or *with the effect* of creating unnecessary obstacles to international trade [emphasis added]." In other words, if a country that has a thriving incandescent lightbulb industry loses market share, the rules would be on shaky ground.[6]

These are only a few of many examples, all premised on the idea that the economic health of multinationals' bottom lines is more important than public health, the health of the planet, or other social goods. And it's not only energy—these rules impact progressive proposals on health care, education, the financial sector, and just about everything else (except military spending).

In 2008, I asked Van Jones, the founder of Green For All and the author of *The Green Collar Economy*, about this issue, and he responded with defiance (Jones later joined the Obama administration, before being forced to resign under the weight of a dubious scandal pimped by Fox News). "I want the WTO to tell us we can't do this," he said, "because then we won't have a WTO. I want the free traders to stand up in front of the world and explain to Americans why some people are going to tell you that you can't have clean energy and you can't have your home retrofitted [with American-made products] because it is more efficient for it to be made in Asia or Germany, that you can't bring Detroit back to build wind turbines. I want the free traders to defend having an overseas body to declare this agenda illegal. I want that fight."[7]

Notes

Introduction. How Our Conventional Wisdom Fails Us

1. Joshua Holland, "Town Hall Lunacy Includes Outraged Calls to 'Keep Government out of Medicare!'" AlterNet.org, August 27, 2009.
2. Timothy Noah, "The Medicare-Isn't-Government Meme," Slate.com, August 5, 2009.
3. "The 'Liberal Media' Hearts the Teabaggers," NoMoreMisterNiceBlog, February 2, 2010.
4. Phillip Rucker, "Former Militiaman Unapologetic for Calls to Vandalize Offices over Health Care," *Washington Post*, March 25, 2010.
5. Holly Bailey, Richard Wolffe, and Tamara Lipper, "Tricks of the Trade," *Newsweek*, March 14, 2005.
6. Kenneth Vogel, "GOP Operatives Crash the Tea Party," *Politico*, April 14, 2010.
7. American Bankers Association press release, "Take Action to Oppose Dodd Regulatory Restructuring Proposal," November 11, 2009.
8. "The Big Bank Bailout Bill?" Factcheck.org, February 3, 2010.
9. Rob Blackwell, "Bair Says Reform Bill Will Make Bailouts 'Impossible,'" *American Banker*, April 15, 2010.
10. Lee Fang, "Wall St. Consultant Frank Luntz Pens Memo on How to Channel Economic Anxiety into Protecting Wall St. Abuses," Think Progress, February 1, 2010.
11. Kevin Drum, "How the Game Is Played, Part 576," *Mother Jones*, February 12, 2010.
12. William T. Dickens and Jonathan S. Leonard. "Accounting for the Decline in Union Membership, 1950–1980," *Industrial and Labor Relations Review* 38, no. 3 (April 1985).
13. Emmanuel Saez and Thomas Piketty, "Income Inequality in the United States, 1913–1998," *Quarterly Journal of Economics* 118, no. 1 (2003): 1–39. (Tables and figures updated to 2007 by Saez in Excel format, August 2009 [accessed online March 17, 2010]).
14. Ibid.
15. U.S. Dept of Commerce: BEA, "GDP-Real (Adjusted) United States," updated January 2010.

16. Saez and Piketty, "Income Inequality in the United States, 1913–1998."

17. Ibid.

18. Quote by Doug Henwood from the film *The American Ruling Class* (2007).

19. Ibid.

20. Bureau of Labor Statistics, January 22, 2010.

21. Labor productivity increased by an average of 2.8 percent per year between 1959 and 1973 but slowed to 1.5 percent annually in the period between 1973 and 1995.

22. Cited in Mark Engler's *How to Rule the World* (New York: Nationbooks, 2008).

23. Bureau of Labor Statistics, "Around the World in Eight Charts," March 2008.

24. Nina Munk, "Don't Blink. You'll Miss the 258th-Richest American," *New York Times*, September 25, 2005.

25. "Forbes 400: Poor Billionaires," *Forbes Magazine*, September 30, 2009.

26. Steven Greenhouse and David Leonhart, "Real Wages Fail to Match a Rise in Productivity," *New York Times*, August 28, 2006.

27. John Irons, "Corporate Tax Declines and U.S. Inequality," EPI Snapshot, April 9, 2008.

28. Emily Brandon, "Decline in Traditional Pensions Hits New Low," *US News and World Report*, May 13, 2009.

29. EPI, *State of Working America*, 2008.

30. Greg Winter, "Public University Tuition Rises Sharply Again for '04," *New York Times*, October 20, 2004.

31. Adrian Michaels, "Europe's Winter of Discontent," *Telegraph*, January 27, 2009.

32. Ian Traynor, "Governments across Europe Tremble as Angry People Take to the Streets," *Guardian*, January 31, 2009.

33. Kristie M. Engemann, "Social Changes Lead Married Women into the Workforce," *Regional Economist*, April 1, 2006.

34. St. Louis Federal Reserve Bank, "Personal Saving Rate," updated March 1, 2010.

35. See Jules Archer, *The Plot to Seize the White House* (New York: Skyhorse Publishing, 2007; originally published by Hawthorn Books in 1973).

36. Frank Ahrens, "Moon Speech Raises Old Ghosts as the *Times* Turns 20," *Washington Post*, May 23, 2002.

37. Jason Deparle, "Goals Reached, Donor on Right Closes Up Shop," *New York Times*, May 29, 2005.

38. Kathleen Hall and Joseph N. Cappella, "How the Conservative Media Harm Democracy," *Washington Post*, February 18, 2010.

39. Glenn Greenwald, "The Scope—and Dangers—of GE's Control of NBC and MSNBC," Salon.com, August 3, 2009.

40. Glenn Greenwald, "GE's Silencing of Olbermann and MSNBC's Sleazy Use of Richard Wolffe," Salon.com, August 1, 2009.

41. "Scarborough Shills GE Stock on GE-Owned MSNBC," Media Matters for America, March 24, 2009.

42. "Parents and Physicians Outraged over Comments from NBC's Dr. Snyderman on Autism Omnibus Hearings, Vaccines," *Nashville Examiner*, June 19, 2007.

43. Ibid.

44. Sebastian Jones, "The Media-Lobbying Complex," *The Nation*, March 1, 2010.

1. Conservatives Don't Want Good Government

1. Tony Blankley, "Sunday's Socialist Triumph," *National Review*, March 24, 2010.
2. Steve Benen, "They're Really Losing It," *Washington Monthly*, March 24, 2010.
3. Heidi Przybyla, "Tea Party Advocates Who Scorn Socialism Want a Government Job Share Business," Bloomberg News, March 26, 2010.
4. Craig Gilbert, "Ryan Shines as GOP Seeks Vision," *Milwaukee Journal-Sentinel*, April 25, 2009.
5. Brian Beutler and Christina Bellantoni, "Boehner Distances Republicans from Ryan Budget . . . but He Can't Name a Single Objection," Talking Points Memo, February 4, 2010.
6. Alex Altman, "Paul Ryan: The GOP's Answer to the 'Party of No,'" *Time*, February 17, 2010.
7. Joseph Rosenberg, "Preliminary Revenue Estimate and Distributional Analysis of the Tax Provisions in 'A Roadmap for America's Future' Act of 2010," Tax Policy Center, March 2010.
8. Steven Johnson, "Are Seven Percent Returns Realistic?" SimCivic.org, revised 2005.
9. Dean Baker, "Economic Stimulus on the Cheap," *Guardian*, February 9, 2009.
10. Victoria Colliver, "Health-Insurance Premiums Outpacing Wages, Inflation," *San Francisco Chronicle*, September 16, 2009.
11. Paul Van de Water, "The Ryan Budget's Radical Priorities," Center on Budget and Policy Priorities, March 10, 2010.
12. Ibid.
13. Gilbert, "Ryan Shines as GOP Seeks Vision."
14. Mark Ames, "Ayn Rand, Hugely Popular Author and Inspiration to Right-Wing Leaders, Was a Big Admirer of Serial Killer," February 26, 2010.
15. Ibid.
16. "Zogby Poll: *Atlas Shrugged* by Ayn Rand Read by 8.1 Percent," PRWeb, October 17, 2007.
17. Ames, "Ayn Rand, Hugely Popular Author and Inspiration to Right-Wing Leaders, Was a Big Admirer of Serial Killer."
18. Jeremy Duda, "Goddard: No Prop 100 Support without Brewer Veto of Tax Cuts," *Arizona Capital Times*, March 18, 2010.
19. Ray Boshara, "The $6,000 Solution," *Atlantic Monthly*, January–February 2003.

A Closer Look: Is Big Business Passing Itself Off as "Small Business"?

1. "A Poll on Trust: What's Good for General Motors," *Economist*, February 25, 2010.
2. Jan Norman, "Americans Trust Small Business Most, Big Companies Least," *Orange County Register*, August 27, 2009.
3. Frank Newport, "Socialism Viewed Positively by 36% of Americans," Gallup Organization, February 4, 2010.
4. Edmund Andrews, "Tax Cuts Offer Most for Very Rich, Study Says," *New York Times*, January 8, 2007.
5. William Ahern, "Comparing the Kennedy, Reagan and Bush Tax Cuts," Fiscal Facts, August 24, 2004.
6. "Puncturing a Republican Tax Fable," Fact-check.org, December 19, 2003.
7. Ibid.

8. "Table of Small Business Size Standards," United States Small Business Administration, 2007.

9. "Small and Medium-Sized Enterprise Definition," European Commission, May 6, 2003.

10. Steven Pearlstein, "Small Business, Big Fable," *Washington Post*, July 8, 2009.

2. It's Not Your Fault There Aren't Enough Good Jobs

1. Michael A. Fletcher and Dana Hedgpeth, "Are Unemployment Benefits No Longer Temporary?" *Washington Post*, March 9, 2010.

2. OECD data cited by Matt Yglesias, "U.S. Unemployment Benefits in International Context," Think Progress, July 16, 2009.

3. Jonah Goldberg, "Tough Love the Only Long-Term Cure for Haiti," Townhall.com, January 20, 2010.

4. David Stout, "Bush Vetoes Children's Health Bill," *New York Times*, October 30, 2007.

5. Jeanne Sahadi, "Top 10 Millionaire Counties," CNN, March 29, 2006.

6. David Moore, "Half of Young People Expect to Strike It Rich," Gallup, March 11, 2003.

7. Jeffrey Jones, "Most Americans Do Not Have a Strong Desire to Be Rich," Gallup, December 11, 2006.

8. "The Uninsured: A Primer," Kaiser Family Foundation, October 2009.

9. The 2009 MetLife Study of the American Dream.

10. Isabel Sawhill and John Morton, "Economic Mobility: Is the American Dream Alive and Well?" Economic Mobility Project, May 2007.

11. Ibid.

12. Ibid.

13. Julia Isaacs, "Reaching for the Prize: The Limits on Economic Mobility," Brookings Institution, October 24, 2008.

14. Julia Isaacs, Isabel Sawhill, and Ron Haskins, "Getting Ahead or Losing Ground? Economic Mobility in America," Brookings Institution, February 2008.

15. Author interview, May 2006.

16. Author interview, May 2006.

17. The College Board.

18. Isabel Sawhill, "Opportunity in America: The Role of Education," Princeton-Brookings Policy Brief, Fall 2006.

A Closer Look: Is the Value of Education Declining?

1. Michael Abramowitz and Lori Montgomery, "Bush Addresses Income Inequality," *Washington Post*, February 1, 2007.

2. R. B. Freeman, "The Decline in the Economic Rewards to College Education," *Review of Economics and Statistics* 59, no. 1 (February 1977): 18–29.

3. Greg Ip, "The Declining Value of Your College Degree," *Wall Street Journal*, July 17, 2008.

4. Laurence Veysey, *The Emergence of the American University* (Chicago: University of Chicago Press, 1965).

5. Morton Winsberg, "Social Sciences in the United States 1948 to 1975," *Geographical Review* 67, no. 3 (July 1977): 335–343.

6. Richard Fry, "College Enrollment Hits All-Time High, Fueled by Community College Surge," Pew Research Center, October 29, 2009.

7. James Heckman and Paul LaFontaine, "The Declining American High School Graduation Rate: Evidence, Sources, and Consequences," *NBER Reporter*, March 22, 2008.

8. "Colleges Spend Billions on Remedial Classes to Prep Freshmen," *USA Today*, September 19, 2008.

9. "Education and Skills: Adult Literacy Rate—High-Level Skills," Conference Board of Canada, January 2010.

10. "Education and Skills: Students with High-Level Reading Skills," Conference Board of Canada, January 2010.

11. "Highlights from TIMSS 2007: Mathematics and Science Achievement of U.S. Fourth- and Eighth-Grade Students in an International Context," National Center for Education Statistics, January 2009.

12. "Education at a Glance 2007: OECD Indicators," Organisation for Economic Co-operation and Development.

13. Virginia E. Garland and Sara E. Wotton, "Bridging the Digital Divide in Public Schools," *Journal of Educational Technology Systems* 30, no. 2 (2001–2002): 115–123.

14. For an excellent discussion of the history of social reproduction theory, see James Collins, "Social Reproduction in Classrooms and Schools," *Annual Review of Anthropology* 38 (October 2009): 33–48.

15. David Berliner, "Rational Responses to High-Stakes Testing and the Special Case of Narrowing the Curriculum," Paper presented at the International Conference on Redesigning Pedagogy, National Institute of Education, Nanyang Technological University, Singapore, June 1, 2009.

3. There Is No Free Market

1. Author interview, October 2008.

2. Michael Kinsley, "Libertarians' Likeable Lunacy," *Los Angeles Times*, January 12, 2008.

3. Center for Responsive Politics, accessed January 9, 2010.

4. Dean Baker, "Professional Protectionists: The Gains from Free Trade in Highly Paid Professional Services," *CEPR*, September 2003.

5. Mark Pittman, "Paulson Bank Bailout in 'Great Stress' Misses Terms Buffett Won," Bloomberg News, January 10, 2009.

6. Dana Hedgpeth, "Wall Street Decamps to K Street for Work on Bailout," *Washington Post*, November 8, 2008.

7. Elana Shore, "Are Bailed Out Banks Really Lobbying More?" *Washington Independent*, April 22, 2009.

8. Public Citizen, "Bailed-Out Banks' PACs, Lobbyists Have Sponsored 70 Fundraisers for Congress, Donated $6 Million since Election," August 26, 2009.

9. Christopher Condon and Jody Shenn, "No Good Deed Goes Unpunished as Banks Seek Profits," Bloomberg News, January 4, 2010.

10. Ibid.

11. Peter Whoriskey, "How Free-Marketers Crafted Bank Program," *Washington Post*, November 8, 2008.

4. How Could Anyone Believe the Big Banks Are Victims?

1. John Carney, "How the Government Caused the Mortgage Crisis," *Business Insider*, October 16, 2009.
2. Jeb Hensarling, "The True Cause of the Housing Crisis," Politico, April 29, 2009.
3. AEI Scholar's bio, accessed online February 5, 2010.
4. Peter Wallison, "Barney Frank: Predatory Lender," *Wall Street Journal*, October 15, 2009.
5. Federal Reserve Board, "Community Reinvestment Act," fact sheet.
6. Remarks by FDIC chairman Sheila Bair to the New America Foundation Conference: "Did Low-Income Homeownership Go Too Far?" December 17, 2008.
7. Mary Kane, "Low-Income Borrowers Blamed in Bailout Crisis," *Washington Independent*, September 30, 2008.
8. Michael S. Barr, Prepared testimony before the House Committee on Financial Services, February 13, 2008.
9. George Bush, "President Hosts Conference on Minority Homeownership, George Washington University," October 15, 2002.
10. Andrew Leonard, "Panic on Wall Street," *Salon*, August 17, 2007.
11. Ian Katz and Robert Schmidt, "Gensler Turns Back on Wall Street to Push Derivatives Overhaul," Bloomberg News, February 12, 2010.
12. Margareta Pagano and Simon Evans, "A £516 Trillion Derivatives 'Time-Bomb,'" *The Independent* (UK), October 12, 2008.
13. Jim Puzzanghera and E. Scott Reckard, "Washington Mutual Created 'Mortgage Time Bomb,' Senate Panel Says," *Los Angeles Times*, April 13, 2010.
14. Amir Efrati, Susan Pulliam, Serena Ng, and Aaron Lucchetti, "U.S. Probes Morgan Stanley," *Wall Street Journal,* May 11, 2010.
15. "SEC Charges Goldman Sachs with Fraud in Structuring and Marketing of CDO Tied to Subprime Mortgages," SEC press release, April 16, 2010.
16. Kevin G. Hall and Chris Adams, "Senate Panel: Ratings Agencies Rolled Over for Wall Street," McClatchy Newspapers, April 22, 2010.
17. Joseph Stiglitz, "Nobel Laureate: How to Get Out of the Financial Crisis," *Time*, October 17, 2008.
18. Gillian Tett, "Derivative Thinking," *Financial Times*, May 30, 2008.
19. Ibid.
20. Alexander Ineichen and Bykurt Silberstein, "AIMA's Roadmap to Hedge Funds," Alternative Investment Management Association, November 2008.
21. Nouriel Roubini, "Current Market Turmoil: Non-Priceable Knightian 'Uncertainty' Rather Than Priceable Market 'Risk,'" Roubini Global Economics, August 15, 2007.

A Closer Look: Were the Titans of Finance Really Too Big to Fail?

1. V. V. Chari, Lawrence Christiano, and Patrick Kehoe, "Facts and Myths about the Financial Crisis of 2008," Minnesota Federal Reserve Working Paper 666, October 2008.
2. Brian Love, "Credit Crunch? What Credit Crunch?" Reuters, December 11, 2008.
3. "Wall Street Firms Shed Thousands of Jobs in Historically Drastic Downsizing," Associated Press, December 8, 2008.
4. Bureau of Labor Statistics.

5. Stevenson Jacobs, "Layoffs Expected to Decimate Wall Street Ranks," Associated Press, December 7, 2008.
6. United States Treasury, Office of the Currency Controller, "OCC's Quarterly Report on Bank Derivatives Activities," Third Quarter, 2007.
7. United States Treasury, Office of the Currency Controller, "OCC's Quarterly Report on Bank Derivatives Activities," First Quarter, 2001.
8. Paul Krugman, "Look Who's Talking," *New York Times*, July 29, 2008.
9. Sydelle Moore, "The Big Question: Will a New Bank Fee Help?" *The Hill*, January 12, 2010.
10. Edward Wolff, "Recent Trends in Household Wealth in the U.S., Update to 2007: Rising Debt and the Middle Class Squeeze," Working Paper no. 589, Levy Economics Institute of Bard College, March 2010.
11. Lawrence Mitchell, *The Speculation Economy: How Finance Triumphed Over Industry* (San Francisco: Berrett-Koehler, 2007).

5. Tax Cuts Aren't a Solution to Every Problem

1. Rush Limbaugh, "The Top 50% pay 96.54% of All Income Taxes," Rushlimbaugh. com, October 4, 2005.
2. "Historical Effective Federal Tax Rates: 1979 to 2005," Congressional Budget Office, December 2007.
3. Ibid.
4. "Historical Effective Federal Tax Rates: 1979 to 2006," Congressional Budget Office, December 2007.
5. Robert McIntyre et al. "Who Pays? A Distributional Analysis of the Tax Systems in All 50 States," Institute on Taxation and Economic Policy, December 2003.
6. Ibid.
7. Ibid.
8. Scott Burns, "Your Real Tax Rate: 40%," *MSN Money*, February 21, 2007.
9. Chuck Collins, Alison Goldberg, and Sam Pizzigati, "Shifting Responsibility: How 50 Years of Tax Cuts Benefited the Wealthiest Americans," Wealth for the Common Good, April 12, 2010.
10. Jamison Foser, "The Media's Tax Fraud," Mediamatters for America, March 6, 2009.
11. 2008 Republican Platform: Economy," GOP.com, accessed April 6, 2010.
12. "Tax Burdens Falling in OECD Economies as Crisis Takes Its Toll," Organisation for Economic Co-operation and Development, November 24, 2009.
13. "Table: Taxation of Corporate and Capital Income (2009)," OECD Tax Database, accessed April 22, 2010.
14. "Table 15.3—Total Government Expenditures as Percentages of GDP: 1948–2008," Federal Budget of the United States, 2010.
15. "Table 15.1—Total Government Receipts in Absolute Amounts and as Percentages of GDP: 1948–2008," Federal Budget of the United States, 2010.
16. Justin Fox, "Tax Cuts Don't Boost Revenues," *Time*, December 6, 2007.
17. Andrew Samwick, "A New Year's Plea," Vox Baby, January 3, 2007.
18. Megan McCardle, "I Take It All Back," *The Atlantic Online*, October 16, 2007.
19. Paul Krugman, "The Tax Cut Con," *New York Times*, September 14, 2003.
20. David Leonhardt, "The Perils of Pay Less, Get More," *New York Times*, March 16, 2010.

21. Catherine Rampell, "Federal Revenue at Lowest Share of G.D.P. since 1950," *New York Times*, October 20, 2009.

22. Doyle McManus, "Deficit Reduction through Tax Reform," *Los Angeles Times*, April 15, 2010.

23. Anita Wadhwani, "Tennessee Removes about 100,000 People from Medicaid Rolls," *Kaiser Health News*, April 8, 2010.

24. Lawrence Schumacher, "DFL Budget Cuts Hurt Working Poor, Elderly, Students, Renters, Disabled," *Twin Cities Daily Planet*, March 31, 2010.

25. Richard Fausset, "Clayton County Loses Vital Bus Service, Link to Atlanta," *Los Angeles Times*, April 1, 2010.

26. Jeff Maynor, "Ashtabula County: Judge Tells Residents to 'Arm Themselves,'" WKYC.com, April 9, 2010.

27. Jennifer Steinhauer, "California Budget Deal Closes $26 Billion Gap," *New York Times*, July 24, 2009.

28. Kevin O'Leary, "Tuition Hikes: Protests in California and Elsewhere," *Los Angeles Times*, November 21, 2009.

29. George Will, "Thanks to Crushing Liberalism, California's No Longer Golden," *Washington Post*, January 10, 2010.

30. Paul Krugman, "State of Paralysis," *New York Times*, May 24, 2009.

31. Charles Duhigg, "Saving U.S. Water and Sewer Systems Would Be Costly," *New York Times*, March 14, 2010.

32. Dan Brown, "Collapsed I-35 Bridge Rated Deficient Years Ago, Mirrors National Problem," *Minnesota Star-Tribune*, August 2, 2007.

33. "Over 100 State Bridges Rated Worse Than 35W," *St. Paul Pioneer Press*, August 5, 2007.

34. "Inspections, Reports Raise Questions about Bridge's Safety," *St. Paul Pioneer Press*, August 2, 2007.

35. "Transportation—New Laws 2007," Minnesota House of Representatives Public Information Services, 2007.

36. James Barron, "Steam Blast Jolts Midtown, Killing One," *New York Times*, July 19, 2007.

37. Eric J. Lerner, "What's Wrong with the Electric Grid?" *Industrial Physicist*, August 13, 2003.

38. Michael J. Copps, "America's Internet Disconnect," *Washington Post*, November 8, 2006.

39. "Report Card for America's Infrastructure," American Society of Structural Engineers, 2009.

40. Francisco Rodríguez, "Have Collapses in Infrastructure Spending Led to Cross-Country Divergence in per Capita GDP?" Wesleyan Economic Working Papers, April 2006.

A Closer Look: No, Tax Cuts Don't Always Generate Jobs and Prosperity

1. Howard Kurtz, online discussion: "Howard Kurtz on Obama's Media Blitz and the Fox News Snub," WashingtonPost.com, September 21, 2009.

2. Author interview, December 2005.

3. Larry Beinhart, "Tax Cuts: The B.S. and the Facts," AlterNet.org, November 11, 2008.

4. Ibid.

6. Republicans Have Never Cared about the Deficit

1. Congressional Budget Office, www.gpoaccess.gov/usbudget/fy09/pdf/budget/defense.pdf.
2. Robert Higgs, "The Trillion-Dollar Defense Budget Is Already Here," *Independent Review*, March 15, 2007.
3. Hale Stewart, "A Refutation of Republican Economic Talking Points," DailyKos.com, July 24, 2005.
4. "Historical Debt Outstanding—Annual 2000–2009," United States Treasury Department.
5. Stephen Dinan, "Obama Wins More Spending Cuts Than Bush," *Washington Times*, January 14, 2010.
6. Sam Stein, "Tax Day Fact Check: Most Americans Got a Tax Cut This Year," Huffington Post, April 15, 2010.
7. Kathy Rufing and Paul Van de Water, "What the 2009 Trustees' Report Shows about Social Security," Center on Budget and Policy Priorities, May 18, 2009.
8. Ibid.
9. Ibid.
10. Dean Baker, "Bush's Numbers Racket," *American Prospect*, February 2005.
11. Doug Henwood, "Antisocial Security," *Left Business Observer*, no. 87, December 1998.
12. "U.S. Health Costs: Background Brief," Kaiser Foundation, July 2009.
13. "Health-Care Costs 101," California Healthcare Foundation, 2007.
14. Ibid.
15. "Medicare Chart Book," Kaiser Family Foundation, 2005.
16. Paul Krugman, "Administrative Costs," NewYorkTimes.com, July 6, 2009.
17. Alison Acosta Fraser, "Why Our Domestic Entitlements Could Doom Our Children," Heritage Foundation Commentary, February 22, 2007.
18. Henwood, "Antisocial Security."
19. Acosta Fraser, "Why Our Domestic Entitlements Could Doom Our Children."
20. John S. Irons, Testimony before the Senate Special Committee on Aging, June 17 2009.
21. Ibid.
22. Sam Pizzigati, "Over-Taxed? Not by the Numbers," *People's World*, May 20, 2010.
23. David Cay Johnston, Interviewed by Brian Lamb, *Booknotes*, C-SPAN, April 18, 2004.
24. David Cay Johnston, "Fiscal Therapy," *Mother Jones*, January/February 2009.
25. Dean Baker, "Stop Baby Boomer Bashing: Protect Social Security and Medicare," *Truthout*, February 16, 2009.
26. "The Nation's Long-Term Fiscal Outlook," Government Accountability Office, September 2006.
27. Jeremy Grant, "Learn from the Fall of Rome, US Warned," *Financial Times*, August 14, 2007.
28. "*Wash. Post* Turns News Pages over to Conservative Billionaire Peterson's News Service," Media Matters for America, January 3, 2010.
29. Jeannette Catsoulis, "Review: I.O.U.S.A. (2008)," *New York Times*, August 22, 2008.

30. Jamison Foster, "Coverage of Economy Repeats Iraq Mistakes," Media Matters for America, January 16, 2009.
31. Ibid.
32. Robert Kuttner, "Obama vs. the Fiscal Fear Mongers," *American Prospect*, August 19, 2008.

A Closer Look: How More Government (of One Sort) Brings Greater Individual Liberty and Personal Choice

1. The Pew Research Center for the People and the Press, "Distrust, Discontent, Anger and Partisan Rancor," April 18, 2010.

7. America Has No Respect for Family Values

1. Arrah Nielsen, "Gender Wage Gap Is Feminist Fiction," IWF, April 15, 2005.
2. "Wage Gap by the Numbers," Center for American Progress, January 6, 2009.
3. Ibid.
4. David Green, "The Gender Pay Gap Does Not Exist," *Telegraph* (UK), April 30, 2009.
5. Remco Oostendorp, "Globalization and the Gender Wage Gap," World Bank Policy Research Working Paper 3256, April 2004.
6. Francine Blau and Lawrence Kahn, "Understanding International Differences in the Gender Pay Gap," *Journal of Labor Economics* 21, no. 1 (2003).
7. Joshua Holland, "Womenomics 101," AlterNet.org, March 16, 2006.
8. Doug Henwood, "The New Economy and After," *Left Business Observer*, no. 106, January 2004.
9. Richard B. Freeman, "The US Economic Model at Y2K: Lodestar for Advanced Capitalism?" NBER Working Paper no. 7757, June 2000.
10. Jody Heyman et al., "The Work, Family and Equity Index: How Does the United States Measure Up?" Institute for Health and Social Policy, 2007.
11. Ibid.
12. Kari Lydersen, "Family Medical Leave Act under Attack," *New Standard*, July 8, 2005.
13. Marilyn Waring, "What Really Counts," Columbia University Teachers College, March 1, 1999.
14. Eduardo Porter, "Women in Workplace—Trend Is Reversing / Study: They May Be Unable to Fit More In," *New York Times*, March 2, 2006.
15. Laura D'Andrea Tyson, "New Clues to the Pay and Leadership Gap," *Business-Week*, October 27, 2003.
16. Karen Kornbluh, "The Mommy Tax," *Washington Post*, January 5, 2001.
17. Lydersen, "Family Medical Leave Act under Attack."
18. Gene Sperling, *The Pro-Growth Progressive* (New York: Simon & Schuster, 2005).
19. Employee Benefits Research Institute, "Pension, Annuity Income: Differences between Men and Women," Fast Facts from EBRI, March 22, 2007.
20. Karen Kornbluh, "A Real Mother's Day Gift: Flexibility, Economic Security and a Good Night's Sleep," Center for American Progress, May 7, 2004.
21. Employee Benefits Research Institute, "Income Statistics of the Population Aged 55 and Over," Table 6.1, updated September 2009.

22. Sperling, *The Pro-Growth Progressive*.
23. Ibid

A Closer Look: The Myth of the Pipeline

1. David R. Francis, "Why Do Women Outnumber Men in College?" *National Bureau of Economic Research Digest*, April 2007.
2. Nancy Carter and Christine Silva, "Pipeline's Broken Promise." *Catalyst Research Reports*, February 2010.
3. Betsy Stark, "The Myth of the Pipeline: Inequality Still Plagues Working Women, Study Finds." ABC News, February 18, 2010.

8. Our Health-Care System Is a Huge Rip-Off

1. "Obama Exaggerating the Numbers on Uninsured Americans, Says GOP'er Foxx," Talk Radio News Service, July 24, 2009.
2. Melinda Beeuwkes Buntin and David Cutler, "The Two Trillion Dollar Solution: Saving Money by Modernizing the Health Care System," Center for American Progress, June 2009.
3. John Barrasso, Remarks at Bipartisan Meeting on Health Care Reform, Blair House, Washington, D.C., February 25, 2010.
4. "How House Bill Runs over Grandma," *Investors' Business Daily*, July 31, 2009.
5. Damien McElroy, "Stephen Hawking: I Would Not Be Alive without the NHS," *Telegraph* (UK), August 12, 2009.
6. "Number of Underinsured U.S. Adults Increased by 60% between 2003 and 2007, Study Finds," *Kaiser Daily Health Policy Report*, June 10, 2008.
7. Mark Pearson, "Written Statement to Senate Special Committee on Aging," September 30, 2009.
8. Russell Jaffe, MD, PhD, "*SICKO*, America's Healthcare System Found 'Critically Ill,'" ScienceBlogMD, July 4, 2007.
9. *The World Health Report 2000*, World Health Organization, June 21, 2000.
10. "Trends in Health-Care Costs and Spending," Kaiser Family Foundation, March 2009.
11. Ibid.
12. Gregory Mankiw, "Measuring Wages," Greg Mankiw's blog, July 20, 2006.
13. Sylvia Allegretto and Jared Bernstein, "The Wage Squeeze and Higher Health Care Costs," Economic Policy Institute, January 26, 2006.
14. "Survey of Employer Health Benefits, 2006," Kaiser Family Foundation, September 26, 2006.
15. Mark Merlis, Douglas Gould, and Bisundev Mahato, "Rising Out-of-Pocket Spending for Medical Care: A Growing Strain on Family Budgets," Commonwealth Fund, February 1, 2006.
16. "Health Care in America 2006 Survey," ABC News/Kaiser Family Foundation/ *USA Today*, October 2006.
17. David Himmelstein, Elizabeth Warren, Deborah Thorne, and Steffie Woolhandler, "Illness and Injury as Contributors to Bankruptcy," *Health Affairs* (February 2, 2005).
18. "Hidden Health Tax: Americans Pay a Premium," Families USA, May 2009.

19. Russell Jaffe et al., "An Equation of Health: Role of Transparency and Opacity in Developing Healthcare Efficacy Measures and Metrics," *Journal of Management Development* 26, no. 5 (2007).

20. Josh Bivens, "Seeing the Big Picture on Health Reform and Cost Containment," Economic Policy Institute, July 27, 2009.

21. Steffie Woolhandler et al., "Costs of Health Care Administration in the United States and Canada," *New England Journal of Medicine* 349, no. 8 (August 21, 2003): 768–775.

A Closer Look: The Health-Care Economy

1. David Leonhardt, "Boom in Jobs, Not Just Houses, as Real Estate Drives Economy," *New York Times*, July 9, 2005.

2. Michael Mandel, "What's Really Propping Up the Economy," *Businessweek*, September 25, 2006.

3. Ibid.

9. Obama Is Not a Socialist

1. Liz Halloran, "Top Republicans: Yeah, We're Calling Obama Socialist," National Public Radio, March 5, 2010.

2. Norman Ornstein, "Obama: A Pragmatic Moderate Faces the 'Socialist' Smear," *Washington Post*, April 14, 2010.

3. Ibid.

4. Tom Hamburger, "Chamber of Commerce Vows to Punish Anti-Business Candidates," *Los Angeles Times*, January 8, 2008.

5. Cecilia Kang, "Undercover Persuasion by Tech Industry Lobbyists," *Washington Post*, April 24, 2010.

6. Frank Ahrens, "Waxman Gains House Energy Committee, Auto Stocks Drop," WashingtonPost.com, November 20, 2008.

7. Raymond Fishman and Edward Miguel, "How Economics Can Defeat Corruption," *Foreign Policy Magazine*, August 13, 2008.

8. Ibid.

9. Ibid.

10. Ibid.

11. Jeffrey Birnbaum, "34,000 Lobbyists Swarm Congress," *Washington Post*, June 22, 2005.

12. Andy Kroll, "8 Health Lobbyists Per Lawmaker," MotherJones.com, February 24, 2010.

13. Annalyn Censky, "Record $3.5 Billion Spent on Lobbying in 2009," CNN, February 12, 2010.

14. "Revolving Door" Center for Public Integrity, accessed March 31, 2010.

15. Stuart Pfeifer, "Toyotas' Sudden Acceleration Blamed for More Deaths," *Los Angeles Times*, March 26, 2010.

16. "Regulators Hired by Toyota Helped Halt Acceleration Probes," Bloomberg News, February 13, 2010.

17. "Mine Owner Ran Up Serious Violations," Associated Press, April 6, 2010.

18. Kimberly Kindy and Dan Eggen, "Critics: Government, Business Links Tilt Regulation toward Coal Firm Interests," *Washington Post*, April 18, 2010.

19. Ken Ward Jr., "Media Reports: Federal Criminal Probe Underway in Wake of Massey's Upper Big Branch Mine Disaster," *Charleston Gazette*, April 30, 2010.
20. Laurence H. Tribe, "What Should Congress Do about Citizens United?" Scotusblog .com, January 24, 2010.
21. Michael Waldman, "Bigger Than *Bush v. Gore*," NewYorkTimes.com, January 22, 2010.
22. Interview: "Is Wal-Mart a Person? Thom Hartmann Tells Why It Is—Kind of— But Not Really," Buzzflash.com, January 28, 2005.
23. Joel Friedman, "The Decline of Corporate Income Tax Revenues," Center on Budget and Policy Priorities, October 24, 2003.

10. Green Jobs Are a Great Idea

1. Senate Floor Statement by U.S. Senator James M. Inhofe (R-OK), January 4, 2005.
2. Alan Boraas, "Alaska's Don Young's Histrionics Have Locked ANWR," Alaska Wildlife Alliance, April 12, 2008.
3. Jeffrey Kuhner, "A Convenient Lie," *Washington Times*, December 13, 2009.
4. "Economic Analysis of Environmental Externalities," World Bank Group, July 1998.
5. Ibid.
6. Brian Skoloff and John Flesher, "Gulf Spill Taints 'Mediterranean of the Americas,'" Associated Press, May 3, 2010.
7. Amanda Terkel, "The BP Oil Spill's Toll on Gulf Coast Wildlife: 'All Bets Are Off,'" Think Progress, May 8, 2010.
8. Ann Taylor, "Oil Spill Approaches Louisiana Coast," *Boston Globe*, April 30, 2010.
9. Mark Safenfield, "Current Timeline to Shut Down Gulf of Mexico Oil Spill: Three Months," *Christian Science Monitor*, May 2, 2010.
10. Patrick Johnson, "C'mon, How Big Is the Gulf of Mexico Oil Spill, Really?" *Christian Science Monitor*, May 1, 2010.
11. Joe Weisenthal, "David Kotok: $12.5 Billion Is Just the Start of the Oil Cleanup Costs, and a Double-Dip Is Now Way More Likely," *Business Insider*, May 2, 2010.
12. Ibid.
13. "Cost of Oil Spill Could Exceed $14 Billion," Reuters, May 2, 2010.
14. "BP Forges Ahead with Gulf of Mexico Oil Spill Response," British Petroleum press release, April 25, 2010.
15. Tom Bonnett, "BP Says Oil Spill Is 'Drop in the Ocean,'" Sky News Online, May 14, 2010.
16. Chad Bower, "BP Official: 'Apollo 13' Effort in Capping Oil Spill under Water," WWLTV News (Louisiana), May 2, 2010.
17. Joel Achenbach and Anne Kornblut, "Gulf Coast Oil Spill May Take Months to Contain, Officials Say," *Washington Post*, May 3, 2010.
18. Eric Lipton and John Broder, "Regulator Deferred to Oil Industry on Rig Safety," *New York Times*, May 7, 2010.
19. Russell Gold, Ben Casselman, and Guy Chazan, "Oil Well Lacked Safety Device," *Wall Street Journal*, April 29, 2010.

20. Ibid.

21. Gold, Casselman, and Chazan, "Oil Well Lacked Safety Device."

22. Matthew Mosk, Brian Ross, and Rhonda Schwartz, "BP Fought Safety Measures at Deepwater Oil Rigs," ABC News, April 30, 2010.

23. Ibid.

24 Lipton and Broder, "Regulator Deferred to Oil Industry on Rig Safety."

25 Ian Urbina, "Documents Show Early Worries about Safety of Rig," *New York Times*, May 29, 2010.

26. Gold, Casselman, and Chazan, "Oil Well Lacked Safety Device."

27. Abraham Lustgarten, "How the Disaster in the Gulf Could Have Been Prevented: BP's Terrible Record on Environmental and Human Health," ProPublica, April 30, 2010.

28. "Oil Price Surge Boosts BP Profits," BBC News, February 7, 2006.

29. Juliet Eilperin, "Substantial Safety Concerns Raised about the Atlantis, Another BP Oil Rig," *Washington Post*, May 15, 2010.

30. Sheila Tefft and Siddharth Dube, "Settlement Is Reached on Bhopal; Union Carbide to Pay India $470 Million for Gas-Leak Victims," *Washington Post*, February 15, 1989.

31. Michael Wald, "Tax on Oil May Help Pay for Cleanup," *New York Times*, May 1, 2010.

32. Michael Muskal, "Gulf Oil Spill: Senators Seek to Raise Liability Cap," Los Angeles Times.com, May 3, 2010.

33. Zachary Roth, "AG: BP Trying to Get Alabamians to Give up Right to Sue over Spill," Talking Points Memo, May 3, 2010.

34. "Trying to Shirk Responsibility for Oil Disaster, BP CEO Predicts 'Lots of Illegitimate' Lawsuits because 'This Is America,'" Climate Progress, May 6, 2010.

35. Suzanne Goldenberg, "Deepwater Horizon Survivor Describes Horrors of Blast and Escape from Rig," *The Guardian*, May 20, 2010.

36. Danny Fortson, "Rig Firm's $270m Profit from Deadly Spill," *Sunday Times* (London), May 9, 2010.

37. Mark Long and Angel Gonzalez, "Transocean Seeks Limit on Liability," *Wall Street Journal*, May 13, 2010.

38. Fortson, "Rig Firm's $270m Profit from Deadly Spill."

39. Zaid Jilani, "Transocean Dodges Paying U.S. Corporate Taxes by Locating Its Headquarters in Switzerland," Think Progress, May 14, 2010.

40. Robert Pollin and Jeannette Wicks-Lim, "Job Opportunities for the Green Economy: A State-by-State Picture of Occupations That Gain from Green Investments," Political Economy Research Institute, University of Massachusetts, Amherst, June 2008.

41. "Energy Sources, Production Costs and Performance of Technologies for Power Generation, Heating and Transport," European Commission Staff Report, November 13, 2008.

42. "Project Overview," Cape Wind Project, accessed April 20, 2010.

43. Tim Doyle, "Koch's New Fight," Forbes.com, September 21, 2006.

44. Phillip Warburg and Susan Reid, "Cape Wind Myths and Facts," *Cape Cod Times*, May 16, 2006.

45. "Green Jobs Towards Decent Work in a Sustainable, Low-Carbon World," United Nations Energy Programme, September 2008.

46. Peter Fairley, "China's Potent Wind Potential," *Technology Review*, September 14, 2009.

47. "Big Solar Power Plant Planned for Northwest China," Reuters, January 2, 2009.

48. "Green Jobs," United Nations Energy Programme.

49. Keith Bradsher, "China Is Eager to Bring High-Speed Rail Expertise to the U.S.," *New York Times*, April 7, 2010.

50. "China Plans 440-bln dlr Stimulus for Green Energy," Agence France-Presse, May 24, 2009.

51. Amanda Ruggeri, "What the Stimulus Package Does for Renewable Energy," *US News and World Report*, March 6, 2009.

A Closer Look: Why a Gallon of Gas Should Cost $10

1. "The Real Price of Gasoline," International Center for Technology Assessment, November 16, 1998.

2. Christopher Helman, "What the Top U.S. Companies Pay in Taxes," *Forbes*, April 1, 2010.

11. The Europeans Are All Right

1. Paul Ryan, "A GOP Road Map for America's Future," *Wall Street Journal*, January 26, 2010.

2. Nolan Finley, "Nanny State Will Turn U.S. into Europe," *Detroit News*, March 25, 2010.

3. Jim Manzi, "Keeping America's Edge," *National Journal*, January 3, 2010.

4. Jonathan Chait, "A Conservative Accidentally Makes the Case for Social Democracy," *New Republic*, January 5, 2010.

5. Paul Krugman, "European Decline—A Further Note," Conscience of a Liberal Blog, *New York Times* online, January 9, 2010.

6. Steven Pearlstein, "Greek Crisis Exposes Cracks in Europe's Foundation," *Washington Post*, Friday, May 7, 2010.

7. Heritage Foundation, *The 2010 Index of Economic Freedom*.

8. World Economic Forum, *The Global Competitiveness Report 2009–2010*.

9. Fraser Institute, *Economic Freedom of the World 2009 Annual Report*.

10. Chait, "A Conservative Accidentally Makes the Case for Social Democracy."

11. Paul Krugman, "Learning from Europe," *New York Times*, January 10, 2010.

12. Ibid.

13. Ibid.

14. Paul de Beer, "Why Work Is Not a Panacea: A Decomposition Analysis of EU-15 Countries," *Journal of European Social Policy* 17 (2007): 375–388.

15. Finley, "Nanny State Will Turn U.S. into Europe."

16. Jeremy Rifkin, *The European Dream: How Europe's Vision of the Future Is Quietly Eclipsing the American Dream* (New York: Penguin Books, 2004), pp. 45–46.

17. Ross Eisenbrey, "Strong Unions, Strong Productivity," Economic Policy Institute, June 20, 2007.

18. "Europe vs. America," *Wall Street Journal*, June 20, 2004.

19. George Irvin, "Europe vs. USA: Whose Economy Wins?" *New Federalist*, January 16, 2007.

20. "Questions and Answers about OVERWORK: A Sloan Work and Family Research Network Fact Sheet," Sloan Work and Family Research Network, updated May 2008.

21. Gary Becker, "Europe: A Continent out to Lunch," *Hoover Digest*, no. 2 (1999).

22. De Beer, "Why Work Is Not a Panacea."

23 Krugman, "Learning from Europe."

24. "The Hidden Costs of Healthcare: Why Americans Are Paying More but Getting Less," Healthreform.gov, 2009.

25. "2009–10 College Prices," The College Board, 2009.

26. Krugman, "Learning from Europe."

27. Editorial, *Wall Street Journal*, 2004.

28. "Key Facts and Figures about the European Union," European Commission, 2004.

29. Anup Shah, "World Military Spending," *Global Issues*, updated September 13, 2009.

30. Max Boot, "ObamaCare and American Power," *Wall Street Journal*, March 25, 2010.

31. "Global Views of United States Improve While Other Countries Decline," BBC/Project on International Political Attitudes, April 18, 2010.

32. Boot, "ObamaCare and American Power."

33. *Human Development Report, 2006: Beyond Scarcity: Power, Poverty and the Global Water Crisis*, United Nations Development Programme. 2006.

34. Mark Rank and Thomas Hirschl, "Estimating the Risk of Food Stamp Use and Impoverishment during Childhood," *Archives of Pediatrics & Adolescent Medicine* 163, no. 11 (2009): 994–999.

A Closer Look: The Incredible Shrinking Americans

1. John Komlos and Benjamin Lauderdale, "Underperformance in Affluence: The Remarkable Relative Decline in U.S. Heights in the Second Half of the 20th Century," *Social Science Quarterly* 88, no. 2 (June 2007).

2. Ibid.

3. Ibid.

4. Ibid.

5. Ibid.

6. Ibid.

7. *Human Development Report, 2006: Beyond Scarcity: Power, Poverty and the Global Water Crisis*, United Nations Development Programme, 2006.

8. Michelle Chau, "Low-Income Children in the United States: National and State Trend Data, 1998–2008," National Center for Children in Poverty, Columbia University, November 2009.

9. Mark Rank and Thomas Hirschl, "Estimating the Risk of Food Stamp Use and Impoverishment during Childhood," *Archives of Pediatrics & Adolescent Medicine* 163, no. 11 (2009): 994–999.

10. Komlos and Lauderdale, "Underperformance in Affluence."

12. "Illegal" Immigration Isn't Hurting Your Prospects

1. "GOP Presidential Primary Debate," CNN, June 5, 2008.

2. Andrea Nill, "Armey Accuses 'Destructive' Tancredo of 'Alienating' Hispanics," Think Progress, March 15, 2010.

3. U.S. Bureau of Labor Statistics, "Foreign-Born Workers. Labor Force Characteristics for 2008," March 26, 2009.
4. Wayne Drash, "Study: 4 Million 'Illegal' Immigrant Children Are Native-Born Citizens," CNN, April 14, 2009.
5. "O'Reilly Claimed to Have Exposed the 'Hidden Agenda' behind the Immigrant Rights Movement: 'The Browning of America,'" Media Matters for America, April 14, 2006.
6. David Card, "The Impact of the Mariel Boatlift on the Miami Labor Market," National Bureau of Economic Research, August 1989.
7. Rachel Friedberg and Jennifer Hunt, "The Impact of Immigrants on Host Country Wages, Employment and Growth," *Journal of Economic Perspectives* 9, no. 2 (Spring 1995).
8. Teresa Watanabe, "Migrant Studies Counter Negative Images," *Los Angeles Times*, February 28, 2007.
9. *Becoming an American: Immigration and Immigrant Policy*, Final Report of the United States Commission on Immigration Reform, 1997.
10. United States Census Bureau, "Profile of the Foreign-Born Population in the United States: 2000," December 2001.
11. Editorial, "How Immigrants Saved Social Security," *New York Times*, April 2, 2008.
12. "Rightweb Profile: Federation for American Immigration Reform," Institute for Policy Studies, July 2004.
13. Walter Ewig, "Restrictionist CIS Twists Facts on 'Marriage Fraud,'" Immigration Policy Center, December 3, 2008.
14. George J. Borjas, Richard B. Freeman, and Lawrence F. Katz, "Searching for the Effect of Immigration on the Labor Market," National Bureau of Economic Research Working Paper 5454.
15. Doug Henwood, "The Economics of Immigration," *Left Business Observer,* no. 113 (May 2006).
16. Ibid.
17. Ted Robbins, "Virtual U.S.-Mexico Border Fence at a Virtual End," NPR's *Morning Edition*, March 17, 2010.
18. Jeffrey Passel and Roberto Suro, "Rise, Peak and Decline: Trends in U.S. Immigration 1992–2004," Pew Hispanic Center, September 27, 2005.
19. Deborah Meyers, "From Horseback to High-Tech: US Border Enforcement," Migration Policy Institute, February 2006.
20. DetentionWatch Network, "About the U.S. Detention and Deportation System," updated 2010.
21. Spencer S. Hsu and N. C. Aizenman, "DHS Corrects Report That Overstated ICE Deportations under Obama," *Washington Post*, March 8, 2010.
22. Spencer S. Hsu and Sylvia Moreno, "Border Policy's Success Strains Resources," *Washington Post*, February 2, 2007.
23. "ACLU Challenges Illegal Detention of Immigrant Children Held in Prison-Like Conditions," ACLU press release, March 6, 2007.
24. Amnesty International, USA, "'Why Am I Here?' Children in Immigration Detention," June 18, 2003.
25. Anna Gorman, "Family Detention Sites in Works," *Los Angeles Times*, May 18, 2008.
26. Nina Bernstein, "Immigrants Challenge U.S. System of Detention," *New York Times*, May 1, 2008.

27. Melissa Taylor, "U.S. Citizen's Near-Deportation Not a Rarity," *Minnesota Star-Tribune*, January 26, 2008.
28. Leslie Berestein, "Detention Dollars," *San Diego Union-Tribune*, March 4, 2008.
29. Ibid.
30. Passel and Suro, "Rise, Peak and Decline."
31 "NAFTA's Promise and Reality: Lessons from Mexico for the Hemisphere," Carnegie Institute for International Peace, November 2003.
32. Ibid.
33. Annette Bernhardt and Siobhan McGrath, "Trends in Wage and Hour Enforcement by the U.S. Department of Labor, 1975–2004," Brennan Center for Justice, September 2005.
34. Ibid.
35. "Fact-Checking the State of the Union Address," *Washington Post*, January 28, 2008.
36. Tom Frederickson, "NYC Rampant with Overtime Violations: Report," *Crain's New York Business News*, June 19, 2007.
37. Ivan Light, "How Los Angeles Deflected Mexican Immigrants to the American Heartland," Migration Policy Institute, December 2007.
38. Ivan Light, "How Wage Law Enforcement Deters Hiring of Low-Wage Undocumented Immigrants and Disperses Them to Other Low-Wage States—The Los Angeles Case Study," Migration Information Source, October 2007.

A Closer Look: The Real Cost of Stupid Immigration Laws

1. "Two Arizona Cities to Sue over Immigration Law," CNN, May 5, 2010.
2. "Response to Arizona's Immigration Law," *Boston Globe*, May 5, 2010.
3. Heath Urie, "Boulder Suspends Official Travel to Arizona over Immigration Law," *Boulder Daily Camera*, May 4, 2010.
4. Jane Well, "Immigration and the Boycott of Arizona," NBC News, May 3, 2010.
5. "How Much Will Arizona's Immigration Bill (SB1070) Cost?" Immigration Policy Center, April 21, 2010.
6. Joshua Holland, "Why Harsh Immigration Crackdowns Will Never Work," AlterNet.org, May 13, 2008.
7. Ibid.
8. Miriam Jordan, "Arizona Squeeze on Immigration Angers Business," *Wall Street Journal*, December 14, 2007.
9. Ken Belson and Jill Capuzzo, "Towns Rethink Laws against Illegal Immigrants," *New York Times*, September 26, 2007.
10. Jill Whalen, "City Asks Federal Judge to Reconsider Ruling," *Hazelton Standard-Speaker*, July 21, 2009.
11. Howard Witt, "Oklahoma Asking, Where Have the Immigrants Gone?" *Chicago Tribune*, February 14, 2008.

13. Blacks Still Kept Back

1. Lloyd Marcus, "Black Republican Rebukes Steele," LloydMarcus.com, April 26, 2010.
2. Gabriel Winant, "*National Review*'s White People Summit on the Problems of Black America," Salon.com, April 2, 2010.
3. Myron Magnet, "Freedom vs. Dependency," *Wall Street Journal*, July 20, 2004.

4. Paul Gorski, "The Myth of the 'Culture of Poverty,'" *Education Leadership* 65, no. 7 (April 2008).
5. Algernon Austin and Jared Bernstein, "Why Bill Cosby Is Wrong," *Counterpunch*, November 15, 2006.
6. Gorski, "The Myth of the 'Culture of Poverty.'"
7. Ibid.
8. Ibid.
9. Ibid.
10. Jean Hardisty, "Promoting Marriage to Cure Poverty?" *Peacework*, no. 374 (April 2007).
11. Ibid.
12. Sharon Lerner, "Marriage on the Mind," *The Nation*, July 5, 2004.
13. Ibid.
14. Hardisty, "Promoting Marriage to Cure Poverty?"
15. Tannette Johnson-Elie, "Study Shows How Deeply Black Men Face Discrimination in Hiring," *Milwaukee Journal Sentinel*, October 8, 2003.
16. Bootie Cosgrove-Mather, "'Black' Names a Résumé Burden?" CBS News, September 29, 2003.
17. Ibid.
18. Diana Henriques, "Review of Nissan Car Loans Finds That Blacks Pay More," *New York Times*, July 4, 2001.
19. Manny Fernandez, "Study Finds Disparities in Mortgages by Race," *New York Times*, October 15, 2007.
20. Meizhu Lui, "The Wealth Gap Gets Wider," *Washington Post*, Monday, March 23, 2009.
21. Author interview, May 2006.
22. Stephanie McCrummen, "Ruling on Racial Isolation in Miss. Schools Reflects Troubling Broader Trend," *Washington Post* staff April 20, 2010.
23. *State of Black America 2009*, Urban Institute, March 2009.

A Closer Look: The African American Economy, Before and After the Crash

1. David Goldman, "Black Unemployment 'a Serious Problem,'" CNNMoney.com, December 4, 2009.
2. *The State of Black America, 2010*, Urban Institute, March 25, 2010.
3. "Employment Situation Summary," Bureau of Labor Statistics, April 2, 2010.
4. Algernon Austin and Jared Bernstein, "Why Bill Cosby Is Wrong," *Counterpunch*, November 15, 2006.
5. Algernon Austin, "Reversal of Fortune: Economic Gains of 1990s Overturned for African Americans from 2000–07," Economic Policy Institute, September 18, 2008.
6. Julia Isaacs, "Economic Mobility of Black and White Families," Brookings Institution, November 2007.
7. "Income Gap among Black, White Families Up," Associated Press, November 13, 2007.

14. Unions Still Matter

1. Lawrence Mishel and Matthew Walters, "How Unions Help All Workers," Economic Policy Institute, August 26, 2003.
2. Charles Noble, "How Bush Won," *Logos* (Winter 2005).

3. Ibid.

4. Steven Greenhouse, "Labor Leaders: We Did It," *New York Times*, November 5, 2008.

5. Joshua Holland, "Corporate America Prepares for Battle against Worker Campaign to Roll Back Assault on the Middle Class," AlterNet.org, August 8, 2008.

6. Lawrence Mishel and Ross Eisenbrey, "Union Declines Hurt All Workers," *Salt Lake Tribune*, December 12, 2005.

7. "National Right to Work," American Rights at Work, accessed March 16, 2010, www.americanrightsatwork.org/the-anti-union-network/national-right-to-work/.

8. Nathan Newman, "How Corporate Right Lies about Union Corruption," Labor Blog, February 14, 2006.

9. Cited in David Sirota, *Hostile Takeover* (New York: Crown, 2006).

10. Dan Roberts, "US to Step Up Scrutiny of Unions," *Financial Times*, April 4, 2005.

11. Cited in Sirota, *Hostile Takeover*.

12. "Unionbusters 101," American Rights at Work, accessed March 16, 2010, www.americanrightsatwork.org/the-anti-union-network/for-profit-union-busters/unionbusters-101.html.

13. Art Levine, "Union Busting Confidential," *In These Times*, September 24, 2007.

14. Kate Bronfenbrenner, "No Holds Barred—The Intensification of Employer Opposition to Organizing," Economic Policy Institute, May 20, 2009.

15. John Schmitt and Ben Zipperer, "Dropping the Ax: Illegal Firings during Union Election Campaigns," Center for Economic and Policy Research, January 2007.

16. Mackinac Center for Public Policy, "Checking the Premises of 'Card Check': A Nationwide Survey of Union Members and Their Views on Labor Unions," July 20, 2004.

17. Jordan Barab, "Union Organizing in the 21st Century: Card Check and Roach Motels," Firedoglake, May 30, 2006.

A Closer Look: Whither the $20-an-Hour Wage?

1. Louis Uchitelle, "The Wage That Meant Middle Class," *New York Times*, April 20, 2008.

2. Ibid.

3. Viveca Novak, "Why Workers Can't Win," *Common Cause*, July–August 1991.

4. Barry Hirsch and David Macpherson, "Union Membership, Coverage, Density, and Employment among Private Sector Workers, 1973–2009," Union Membership and Coverage Database.

5. Robert Reich, Beth Shulman, and Karla Walter, "Interactive Map: Unions Are Good for Workers and the Economy in Every State," Center for American Progress, February 15, 2009.

6. George E. Johnson, "Changes over Time in the Union-Nonunion Wage Differential in the United States," in Jean-Jacques Rosa, ed., *The Economics of Trade Unions: New Directions* (Boston: Kluwer Nijhoff, 1984).

7. Uchitelle, "The Wage That Meant Middle Class."

8. Ibid.

15. There's Nothing Free about Free Trade

1. Sarah Anderson et al., "Executive Excess 2004: CEO Pay Soars at Companies That Send Jobs Overseas," Institute for Policy Studies, August 31, 2004.

2. Author interview, May 2006.
3. Alan Blinder, "On the Measurability of Offshorability," *Vox*, October 9, 2009.
4. Todd Tucker, "New Research: Win-Win from 'Free Trade' Is a Big Lie," AlterNet, October 30, 2007.
5. Author interview. August 2005.
6. Lori Wallach and Patrick Woodall, *Whose Trade Organization?* (New York: The New Press, 2004).
7. Author interview, December 2005.
8. Mary Bottari and Lori Wallach, "NAFTA's Threat to Sovereignty and Democracy: The Record of NAFTA Chapter 11 Investor State Cases, 1994–2005," Public Citizen, February 2005.
9. Ibid.
10. Ibid.
11. Tim Tagaris, "CAFTA: A Not So Ringing Endorsement," Talking Points Memo, February 5, 2006.
12. Thomas Edall, "CAFTA in Peril on Capitol Hill: One Business Leader Gives Lawmakers an Ultimatum," *Washington Post*, June 12, 2005.
13. Tom Hamburger, "Chamber Vows to Spend Big on Campaign," *Los Angeles Times*, January 08, 2008.
14. Warren Vieth, "11th-Hour Brokering Paved Way for Bush's Trade Pact Triumph," *Los Angeles Times*, July 29, 2005.
15. Lori Wallach, "CAFTA Wins in Razor-Close Costa Rica Vote," AlterNet, October 8, 2007.
16. Naomi Klein, "Doha, the Economic Frontline," *The Guardian*, November 8, 2001.
17. Aileen Kwa, "Europe's Trade Agenda at the WTO and the Positions of ASEM Developing Countries," *Asia Europe Crosspoints*, September 13, 2002.
18. Matthew Swibel, "Crustacean Nation," *Forbes*, December 1, 2004.
19. "The Great Catfish War," *New York Times*, July 22, 2003.
20. Ibid.
21. Ibid.
22. Joshua Holland, "Seafood Fight!" AlterNet.org, December 6, 2004.
23. Ibid.

A Closer Look: Corporate America Says You Can't Have a Green Economy

1. Obama/Biden Campaign, "Fact Sheet: New Energy for America," August 25, 2008.
2. "Presidential Candidates' Key Proposals on Health Care and Climate Will Require WTO Modifications," Public Citizen, February 2008.
3. Obama/Biden Campaign, "Fact Sheet: New Energy for America."
4. "Presidential Candidates' Key Proposals on Health Care and Climate Will Require WTO Modifications."
5. Ibid.
6. Ibid.
7. Tara Lohan and Joshua Holland, "Van Jones: How We Can Lead Our Country out of Crisis," AlterNet.org, October 23, 2008.

Index